UNDERSTANDING EU POLICY MAKING

Understanding EU Policy Making

Raj S. Chari and Sylvia Kritzinger

Pluto Press
London • Ann Arbor, MI

First published 2006 by Pluto Press
345 Archway Road, London N6 5AA
and 839 Greene Street, Ann Arbor, MI 48106

www.plutobooks.com

British Library Cataloguing in Publication Data
A catalogue record for this book is available from the British Library

ISBN 0 7453 1971 8 hardback
ISBN 0 7453 1970 X paperback

Library of Congress Cataloging in Publication Data applied for

10 9 8 7 6 5 4 3 2 1

Designed and produced for Pluto Press by
Curran Publishing Services, Norwich, England
Printed and bound in the European Union by
Antony Rowe Ltd, Chippenham and Eastbourne, England

Contents

Figures

Tables

Acknowledgements

Books cannot be written in isolation: we are indebted to numerous people throughout the European Union and North America who have helped us along the way. This book was accomplished by fits and starts, and we sincerely thank Roger and the Pluto Press family, as well as Chris and all the staff in Curran Publishing Services in the UK for their encouragement, patience and constructive comments throughout the process.

Raj Chari is particularly indebted to the late Vincent Wright of Nuffield College, Oxford, a friend and mentor who helped inspire much of this book. Many of the tables and graphs presented in the Economic and Monetary Union Chapter were based on ideas he raised in one of his informal conversations in the late 1990s that (refreshingly) had little to do with 'political science' in the first place. Sylvia Kritzinger also acknowledges scholars whose ideas have influenced this book, including Bob Jessop from the UK and Susie Pernicka and Monika Feigl-Heihs in Austria.

In Ireland, we are indebted to Eddie Hyland who read over the entire manuscript and whose theoretical ideas were invaluable for the conception of a European integration theory incorporating the concept of a 'dominant economic class'. Many of these ideas served as a complement to those that have guided the book from its inception, raised by comparative politics scholars and political theorists in Canada; these included Hans Michelmann, Richard Nordhal and Duff Spafford from the University of Saskatchewan, as well as Grant Amyot and Phil Wood from Queen's University (Ontario), where Raj Chari undertook his political science training.

We are deeply indebted to Arantza Gómez, of Trinity's Institute for International Integration Studies directed by Philip Lane, who offered her expertise in gathering the data for the empirical chapters. Freya Frank, formerly an undergraduate in Trinity, also provided essential background research assistance in the early phases, while Rory Costello, a Trinity post-grad, was invaluable in the final stages. Mary Brew, Billie Crosbie, Michael Gallagher, Eithne Healy, Michael Marsh and Alan Matthews of Trinity, as well as Francesco Cavatorta of Dublin City University, proved to be wonderful colleagues during the research and writing phases, offering solid insights from which this book has benefited. The MSc students (graduating class 2006–2007) taking Raj Chari's class on public policy given at Trinity's Policy Institute offered brilliant comments on draft chapters from which this book has greatly benefited.

In Austria we thank Gerda Falkner, Oliver Treib and Caroline Wörgötter for their insights into social policy, Martin Kniepert, Gertraud Fellner and Helga Pülzl for their help with the CAP-chapter, and Irina Michalowitz for discussions on EU interest-group behaviour. Special thanks also from Sylvia Kritzinger to Franz Steinbauer, Alice Ludvig, Bettina Stadler and Tanja Schrott for their discussions and patience.

We also thank Martha Peach and José Elguero from Madrid as well as the several high-level officials in Spain who have offered their advice throughout. The various EU officials who have informally given us their interpretation of public policy dynamics in Europe over the last few years have also opened our eyes in many ways.

Finally, our families and friends, most particularly Celia Chari, Isabel Rozas, Ranga and Raji Chari, Julius and Johanna Kritzinger and Patrick Martini, stand above anyone for putting up with us while researching and writing this book. Of course – as the usual rider goes – any errors remain our own.

Acronyms

ACP	African, Caribbean and Pacific
AMUE	Association for the Monetary Union of Europe
BDI	Bundesverband der Deutschen Industrie (German employers' association)
CAP	Common Agricultural Policy
CCME	Churches' Commission for Migrants in Europe
CCP	Common Commercial Policy
CEC	Conference of European Churches
CEEP	Confédération Européenne des Employers Publics
CEOE	Confederación Española de Organizaciones Empresariales (Spanish Employers' Association)
CEPOL	European Police College
CFSP	Common Foreign and Security Policy
CNPF	Conseil National du Patronat Francais (French employers' association)
COGECA	General Committee for Agricultural Cooperation
COPA	Committee of Agricultural Organizations
COREPER	Committee of Permanent Representatives
CPE	Coordination Paysanne
DEC	Dominant Economic Class
DG	Directorate General
EAGGF	European Agriculture Guidance and Guarantee Fund
ECB	European Central Bank
ECJ	European Court of Justice
ECOFIN	Economic and Financial Affairs Council
ECOSOC	Committee on Employment and Social Affairs of the EP
ECRE	European Council of Refugees and Exiles
ECSC	European Coal and Steel Community
EEA	European Economic Association
EEB	European Environment Bureau
EEC	European Economic Community
ELDR	Liberal Democrats
EMP	Euro-Mediterranean Partnership
EMS	European Monetary System
EMU	Economic and Monetary Union
EP	European Parliament
EPC	European Political Cooperation
ERT	European Round Table of Industrialists
ETUC	European Trade Union Confederation
EU	European Union

EURODAC	EU fingerprint database
FDI	Foreign Direct Investment
FNSEA	Fédération Nationale des Syndicats d'Exploitants Agricoles
GDP	Gross Domestic Product
ICMG	International Catholic Migration Commission
ICMSA	Irish farmers' lobby
IGC	Intergovernmental Conference
ILGA	International Lesbian and Gay Association
INI	The National Industry Institute (Spanish state holding company)
JHA	Justice and Home Affairs
MCR	Merger Control Regulation
MEP	Member of the European Parliament
MS	Member State
MTF	Merger Task Force
PPE	Christian Democrats
PSE	Social Democrats
QMV	Qualified Majority Voting
SEA	Single European Act (1986)
SGP	Stability and Growth Pact
TEU	Treaty on European Union
UNICE	Union of Industrial and Employers' Confederations of Europe
VAT	Value Added Tax

1 A supranational or a decentralized EU?

Politics is policy. This statement is no surprise to speakers of European languages with Latin roots such as Spanish, where the word *política* means both politics and policy. It may be a surprise to English speakers who may associate the word "policy" with something that is detached from a world of politics that we sometimes distantly observe on our televisions. However, policy is significant precisely because it consists of political decisions that have a significant impact on all citizens' lives.

Several examples of policies that may be made by governments on a daily basis help illustrate why policy per se is significant to you as a student and a citizen. One example is seen when a government decides to raise taxes on products that come across the border and are imported into your country: this will affect the goods that you can buy as well as the prices that you pay for them. Another example is seen when a governmental regulatory agency oversees the process of two companies seeking to merge together. If the regulatory agency allows a merger that entails massive layoffs, then this may affect the unemployment levels in your city if one of the companies is based there. Or, perhaps you or your family are considering buying a house. If a central bank raises its interest rates, this will ultimately determine your decisions regarding whether or not you can afford a new dwelling. What do you plan to eat tonight? If a government decides to help farmers by way of subsidizing their operations, this may determine what products are available on the market and, inevitably, on your dinner plate. Another policy decision of importance to your life would be whether or not there is a hike in the minimum wage. This will have an impact on your spending during the next month and may even decide whether or not you will be able to make ends meet during the year. A government clamping down on immigration may also change the social fabric of your society. And if your government decides to go to war against another country, then you may be killed or injured if there is retaliatory action. This was recently seen in Spain and the UK where governmental participation in the Iraq War was directly linked to bombs later being planted in Madrid and London, killing hundreds of innocent citizens on public transport. Policy matters because decisions made by your leaders have significant impacts on your lives.

Over the last 25 years public policies that affect European citizens' lives have not only come from national governments. Rather, students of politics, economics and sociology have paid increasing attention to

European Union (EU) policies because the supranational level has gained increasing competences as European integration has deepened over recent decades. Where national governments used to have sole prerogative to legislate in a policy area, the EU is increasingly gaining power to make policies on behalf of its member states.

The European integration project started in the 1950s as an answer to the horrors of the Second World War. Integration measures were regarded by the founding fathers as guaranteeing peace across Europe, and especially between the historical enemies France and Germany. The first steps towards integration related to economic issues: the Treaty of Paris was signed by Belgium, France, West Germany, Italy, Luxembourg, and the Netherlands in 1951 to form the European Coal and Steel Community (ECSC), and the Treaties establishing the European Economic Community (EEC Treaty) and the European Atomic Energy Community (Euratom) were signed by the same six countries in 1957, leading to the creation of the European Community. Although the 1960s and 1970s witnessed a type of deadlock among the various member states of the EU, wherein it was difficult to achieve consensus on the future of the European Union, the 1970s would represent a turning point. Because international economic pressures threatened to force Europe into a recession, the EU was forced to respond in a way that would ensure its future longevity.

These external forces were no different from those facing the United States at the time: pressures from economies such as Japan that increasingly exported to the United States, coupled with the oil crises throughout the 1970s, forced a declining United States to change policies in order to re-establish itself as world economic giant. In the case of the EU, the road to recovery from a similar economic decline during the late 1970s and early 1980s lay in developing and consolidating the single European market. Such a market represented a huge free-trade area within which businesses could operate and increase their economic strength. Thereafter, a single currency was seen as a means to copper-fasten the status of Europe in the world economy.

With this in mind, one may argue that the supranational level has gained increasing responsibility precisely because of economic globalization: the independent force of national governments may, in some cases, be less effective for the future of Europe in the global economy than the force of a centralized EU voice. In order to secure a strong foundation for Europe's place in the world economy, the member states that comprise the EU may seek to exert a unified force under the banner of the EU in certain areas. The idea of developing strong, cohesive policies in the face of economic globalization can be regarded as one of the main driving forces in European integration, resulting in the Single European Act (1986), the Maastricht Treaty (or Treaty on European Union (TEU), 1992), the Amsterdam Treaty (1997), the Nice Treaty (2001) and diverse enlargement rounds.[1] The most recent step, which has been taken by the EU, but which seems close to being shelved since French and the Dutch electorates vetoed the idea in referendums, was the so-called European Constitution of 2005. The Constitution represented a further deepening of European integration by deciding where Brussels could have increasing policy competences and by setting the basis for a firm political union of the 25 states that currently comprise the EU.

In this regard, observers have alluded to the importance of several key policies, which this book denominates as 1st order policies, which have been significantly developed at the EU level over the last 25 years: single market policies, concerned with the establishment of an integrated capitalist market where economic actors can thrive; competition policies, which seek to ensure a level playing field in this free-trade area; economic and monetary policies, which serve as a basis for a common currency that facilitates trade and allows the EU to move towards becoming an economic hegemon vis-à-vis the United States and Japan; and a Common Agricultural Policy, which represents a price-support system for farmers that guarantees production of essential products for European citizens. In these 1st order policy areas one sees a centralized and strong EU that seeks to make its mark on the world in the context of other major players in the world economy such as the USA, Japan, China, India and Russia.

The main institutions of the EU (such as the European Commission) and representatives of national interests (such as the Council of Ministers) classify 1st order policies as being of "high importance", or a priority to develop: harmonization of policies on this dimension across the EU level will eventually establish a strong position for Europe in the globalized economy vis-à-vis other international players. This "deepening" of the integration process will eventually result in a diminishing, if not completely nullified, role for national governments in these policy areas. Broadly speaking, 1st order policies are those in which major efforts to reach integration have been made, and therefore where integration in terms of harmonization and transfer from the national to the supranational level has taken place smoothly. European-wide policies are promoted and guaranteed because deepening integration in these issues has been considered positive and absolutely necessary by the parties involved. National differences do not prevent common agreements. Supranational and domestic players regard themselves as winners when finding a European-wide solution, whereas they believe that adherence to independent national measures would result in a negative-sum game for all.

In contrast to such 1st order policies are what we define as 2nd order ones. Here one sees a decentralized EU, where national governments have maintained their sovereignty. In such areas, the EU level has not fully "taken away" the power of national governments: national governments have not transferred power to the EU-level and are reluctant to do so. In other words, the EU's policy competences in such areas remain weak and ill defined, and intervention by the EU is regarded with suspicion. Key examples where there is little evidence of full harmonization are seen in social policies where, despite calls for a EU-wide Social Charter in the early 1990s, member states of the EU still maintain legislative power over key aspects of labour market rules that regulate the working conditions, including minimum wages, unemployment regulations and social security. Another example is seen in immigration policies, where member states have retained a large degree of control in determining which immigrants can come into their countries. And a final example is seen in foreign policies, where member states have not acted in a unified manner under an EU flag, but rather have retained their sovereignty to pursue independent military action abroad. This was acutely seen in the recent Iraq War where Europe remained almost shamefully divided: on the one hand, states such as the UK, Spain and Italy pursued military action alongside the USA, while others such as France and Germany were against war.

With these ideas in mind, one sees that in contrast to 1st order policies, it is more difficult to achieve EU-wide consensus when 2nd order policies are negotiated. As such, significant supranational agreements that nullify, or at least diminish the importance of, national level politics would not be expected to be found in 2nd order EU policy areas. Because integration here is mistrusted, challenged, or not actively pursued, national sovereignty in these policy areas is thus broadly accepted. In these areas, member state governments and their legislatures have the final say, leaving a myriad of nationally based rules governing these policy areas.

With the above in mind, this book has two driving questions. First, can we find solid evidence of 1st and 2nd order policies at the EU-level? Second, if so, why and how do policies become of 1st and 2nd order nature? Working hypotheses that will be tested throughout this book are that there are several 1st order EU policies, largely economic in nature, that are deemed a priority for the EU by actors at both the supranational and the domestic levels, and that there are several 2nd order ones that have relatively less importance. We hypothesize that developing 1st order policies will largely benefit capital actors and allow the EU as a whole to be a significant, perhaps even hegemonic, economic power in the global economy. Such policies include single market policies, competition policies, monetary policy and agricultural policy; they have been adopted to create a competitive and efficient, but also protected EU market wherein major capital actors can thrive in the context of globalization. Below such 1st order policies, however, are those that can be considered "2nd order", which do not necessarily form a key part of the EU policy-making agenda and which domestic and EU leaders may sometimes effectively ignore. We hypothesize that such 2nd order policies are not of particular concern to capital actors. As mentioned earlier, they include social, immigration and foreign policies, which largely remain under the remit of national governments.

This book first tests the above working hypotheses about the existence of 1st and 2nd order policies in the EU by focussing on the policies' evolution over time. Second, it examines what factors lead to a policy becoming 1st or 2nd order in nature. It does so by examining which actors have been involved in the formulation of the policies and analysing their desires to see a "two-dimensional" EU public policy space develop, where some policies are deemed more of a priority than others. On the basis of this examination of the actors involved, the book characterizes the policy formulation process by referring to theories of policy making that have been considered essential in the literature on European integration and comparative politics, as discussed below. In other words, several significant, interlinked, questions will be asked in a way not hitherto addressed in existing texts[2] by fully studying competition, single market, economic and monetary, social, agricultural, immigration and foreign policies in the EU:

- What has been the historical development of each policy?
- Through analysis of its history and evolution, can one characterize the policy as indicative of either a strong centralized EU, or a weak, decentralized one where there has been a lack of harmonization? In short, does the evolution point to a 1st or 2nd order policy?
- Which actors have been involved in the formulation of aspects of the policy? Which factors, such as the potential desire to increase economic power and secure a role for Europe in the global economy, have guided these actors to act in such a way?
- Given the nature of the actors that have been involved, how can one theoretically characterize the policy's development in the light of different theories taken from the literature on EU integration and comparative politics?
- Taking all the policies together, does analysis of the answers to the latter two questions help us better understand why policies become of 1st order or 2nd order in nature?

Policy making at the European level: definition of key terms and structure of book

While we have already defined the concept of 1st and 2nd order policies, it is useful at this stage to briefly define three terms – policy formulation, actors, and theoretical characterization – that constitute key elements of the questions addressed in the book. Turning to the first key term, policy formulation, we refer to a two-stage process in policy making, drawing on concepts previously outlined by Peterson.[3] Peterson's three-stage process refers to, first, a "policy-setting" stage; second, the "policy-shaping" stage where policy is formulated by interactions among different actors; and, third, the "history-making" stage, where decisions formulated through the policy-setting and policy-shaping stages are formally agreed on, for example in the European Council or diverse intergovernmental conferences (IGCs).[4] Although the last stage of his analysis is less important for the purposes of this book, because it is often a pure formality in the policy process, the first two stages are of significance for our purposes. However, we argue that a change of terminology may help clarify what exactly occurs at these stages. We thus define Stage 1 as being representative of a *policy-initiation stage*. Whereas "policy setting", as referred to by Peterson, may be conceived as simply laying out the full blueprints of a policy, "policy initiation" in our view clearly indicates the "institutional setting" responsible for first thinking that new rules, regulations or directives need to be pursued. Similarly, the term "policy shaping", as used by Peterson, in our view does not capture the dynamics when policy is actually "negotiated". From this perspective, policy is not simply "shaped", it is "bargained" over between actors. Hence, we refer to the second stage of policy formulation as the *negotiation stage*.

Turning to the next key term in the research objective, namely the concept of "actors" which is discussed in more detail in Chapter 2, we refer to both public officials and specific private actors – also referred to as lobby groups – that may partake in the different stages of the policy formulation process. Among public officials we identify "EU Institutional" players that include several key agents. The most prominent are: the Council of Ministers, comprised of ministers of national-level governments; the European Commission, which is headed by Commissioners who theoretically represent the interests of the EU as a whole; the European Parliament (EP), which consists of members elected from each country every five years; and the European Court of Justice (ECJ), which is the highest court within the EU judicial system. The second set of actors, which we refer to as the "EU lobby groups", include economic groups, professional groups and public interest groups which aim to influence EU institutional actors, especially at the policy negotiation stage. Building on the pre-existing literature on EU lobby groups, Chapter 2 argues that the economic lobby group is comprised primarily of capital actors. Professional groups include both trade unions and the farm lobbies, while public interest groups consist of organizations such as, for example, those concerned about gender issues. While this chapter is essential reading for those students new to the study of the EU, students and practitioners with a working knowledge of EU institutions and interest groups who are more eager to learn about theoretical issues involved in policy making may skip straight to Chapter 3.

The term "theoretical characterization", which is discussed more fully in Chapter 3, refers to the different decision-making models found in both EU integration studies and the literature on the comparative politics of industrialized states that may add insight into the interaction of actors who participate at the different stages of policy formulation. Five main theoretical perspectives are used in this book: supranational governance, intergovernmentalism, pluralism, corporatism and dominant economic class theory. The first two perspectives are the supranational governance and intergovernmentalist perspectives, which we will argue in a similar vein to Peterson are of value in order to understand policy initiation at the EU level; they are representative of the two major theories recently focussed on by scholars of EU politics. Supranational governance[5] broadly suggests that EU institutions, with a particular focus on the Commission, play a determinant policy role by unilaterally initiating policies.

The second theoretical strand, intergovernmentalism,[6] is distinguishable from the supranational governance approach because it focusses more closely on the actions of one of the EU institutions, namely the Council of Ministers. It argues that EU policy-formulation is driven solely by national interests as represented in the Council and that the other EU institutions, such as the Commission and Parliament, are of secondary importance, given that they have a limited role or simply decide on those matters that the Council of Ministers have delegated.

The third, fourth and fifth perspectives, which represent theoretical approaches rooted in the literature of comparative politics, are the pluralist, corporatist and dominant economic class perspectives. We argue, contrary to Peterson and most other scholars theorizing on EU politics, that these perspectives may be particularly useful in understanding developments at the stage when policy is being negotiated. Pluralism argues that all interest groups have roughly equal access to the policy-making process, and hence have a virtually equal ability to influence policy making.[7] Corporatism contends that specific interest groups, namely those representing capital and labour, enjoy semi-institutionalized fixed positions in the policy-making process.[8] The dominant economic class (DEC) perspective, which is a new theoretical perspective to the study of European integration developed in this book on the basis of writings by neo-Marxist scholars, suggests that corporate capital can exert disproportionate influence on policy making to the exclusion of other interest groups.[9]

By incorporating these different theoretical perspectives in order to better understand policy formulation in the EU, this book suggests that a plurality of theories are needed in order to understand key aspects of European integration. Using the empirical evidence uncovered in the policy chapters, as discussed below, the theoretical characterization of the policy initiation and negotiation stage may take on different forms, depending on the policy being studied. For example, if the evidence suggests that the Commission played a main role, this suggests the importance of supranational governance; if the Council played a key role, then intergovernmentalism is of value; if several interest groups were allowed to help negotiate, this suggests pluralism; if only labour and business developed policies along with the EU executive, this points to corporatism; and if capitalist economic actors acted alone to the exclusion of other social interests, this points to the significance of the DEC perspective. As elaborated in Chapter 3, there are different possible theoretical combinations of perspectives which may be exemplified in each of the policy areas, particularly given that the analysis offered here distinguishes clearly between the initiation and negotiation phases of policy.

We encourage even those readers who are familiar with the different theoretical perspectives used in this book to read over Chapter 3, because it underlines an essential argument not hitherto fully developed in the literature: a plurality of theories from different sets of literature is essential in order to understand how EU policy is formulated across different policy areas. We are of the view that having a plurality of theories helps bridge a debate currently seen in two different disciplines that have attempted to understand the EU. On one side of the debate, students of EU politics have analysed the merits of "EU specific" theories, such as supranational governance and intergovernmentalism, in explaining European integration.[10] However, absent from this debate is the desire to fully transpose other theoretical models from the comparative politics literature, in order to help better characterize EU integration. On the other side of the debate, there are several studies of interest group behaviour in the EU.[11] Yet there is no firm or tight analysis of how these developments may be tied together with key theoretical debates from the comparative politics literature, while being linked to those theories utilized by students of EU integration.

With these points in mind, incorporating several theoretical perspectives in order to better grasp EU public policy formulation transcends the existing literature in two main ways. First, it adds further theoretical insights on the role of interest groups in European integration, moving beyond the traditional debate regarding whether or not the supranational governance and intergovernmentalism perspectives are important in understanding EU integration. Second, it attempts to more fully integrate analysis of all potential actors involved in policy making, including EU interest groups, across different policy areas with analysis of EU institutions, while simultaneously being guided by theoretical debates from the comparative politics literature.

Having considered Chapter 2 which is concerned with EU institutions and actors and Chapter 3 which deals the different theoretical perspectives to be used in the study, readers can then turn to Chapters 4 through 10 which constitute the empirical heart of the book. These chapters offer an examination of the evolution and formulation of seven main EU public policies: single market policies (concerned with creating a single, integrated European free-trade area), competition policies (which include initiatives to create a level playing field in this market by way of regulating mergers, promoting liberalization, and controlling state aid), economic and monetary policies (the creation of the single currency, or euro), agricultural policies (whose objective is to subsidize farming activity in the single market), social policies (which have the theoretical objective of guaranteeing workers' rights in the European market), freedom, security and justice policies (dealing with issues such as immigration, asylum and citizenship rights in the EU), and external policies (including political relations with countries outside the EU as well as economic accords with other non-EU states.)

Before we outline the structures of the empirical chapters wherein specific policies are examined, readers should note that analysis of these issues is based on the idea that they offer a representative sample of the types of policies that fall within the two main traditional classification schemes: the Three-Pillar classification and Hix's[12] five-fold classification. In more detail, the first scheme is based on what are traditionally referred to as the "Three Pillars" of the EU. Of the pillars, the first (and largest) refers to areas of traditional cooperation in the Community. These include, as discussed in this book, single market, competition, economic and monetary union, agricultural and social policies, as well as others not analysed here such as environmental, trade, transport and regional policy. The second pillar, introduced in the Maastricht Treaty, relates to issues of common foreign and security policy. Specific policies within this pillar include external security (as reflected in the examination in this book of the EU's position towards the Iraq crisis), conflict prevention and dealing with economic crises. The third pillar, also established in Maastricht, relates to cooperation in justice and home affairs. EU policies with regard to immigration, asylum, internal security and international crime are examples of policies found within this pillar. Taken together, the key policies studied in this book represent a sample across a wide range, reflecting the main issues within each of the three Community pillars.

A second classification system of EU policies is seen in the work of Hix, who refers to five broad types of policy areas: regulatory, redistributive, economic and monetary, citizen freedom and security and foreign policies. The policies studied here are also representative of each type of area as analysed by Hix. More concretely, single market, competition and social policies are examples of regulatory policies; agricultural policy is an example of redistribution; EMU fits within economic and monetary policies; immigration is an example of citizen freedom and security policies; and the analysis of external relations fits within the rubric of foreign policies. The book does not include analysis of all potential policies under the three pillars or Hix's classification, since it was felt that more could be learned about the policy process by focussing more deeply on a representative sample of a limited number of policies rather than attempting a comprehensive list at an inevitably more superficial level. From this perspective, the objective is to analyse specific policies more deeply and then seek to draw generalizations based on this account, an accepted method of analysis for studies having a small-N sample.

The empirical chapters examining a specific policy are organized similarly in order to ensure comparability of findings and a cohesive structure. There is no reason, however, why students or practitioners interested in a specific policy area should not turn directly to the chapter relevant to their interest. Each empirical chapter has two main sections:

- The first section considers the main objectives of the policy and its historical evolution. This section concludes by highlighting whether or not the policy has demonstrated characteristics of being either a 1st order or 2nd order policy in terms of its impact and its evolution. For example, if evidence is found that harmonization and transfer from national to supranational law has taken place in the policy area, this would suggest that the policy is 1st order. If, however, national legislation is still of prime importance, resulting in the EU having a weak or limited role in the policy area, this would suggest that it is a 2nd order policy.
- The second section turns to a more detailed analysis of the formulation phase of a recent reform, regulation, directive, or agreement within the policy area in order to better understand which actors have driven (or not) the policy process and for what reasons. Based on this evidence, particular attention will be paid to the idea of whether or not elements of supranational governance, intergovernmentalism, pluralism, corporatism or the dominant economic class perspective are manifest during policy initiation and negotiation. A theoretical characterization of the formulation process of each policy will then be made.

Turning to specific findings uncovered in the empirical chapters, Chapter 4 examines and explains the development of the EU's single (or internal) market policy, which is primarily concerned with the free movement of goods, services and capital between EU member states. In order to better gauge the evolution of the policy, the first section of the chapter examines the main phases of the policy's development since the 1950s, highlighting the fact that in the wake of economic decline in the 1970s a single integrated capitalist market was deemed necessary in order to ensure Europe's competitive position in a global economy. The chapter then considers in more detail the evolution of internal market policy in terms of its economic impact over the last 15 years. Using the most recent Eurostat data available for 2004, particular attention is paid to the evolution of the percentage of EU-led single market directives that have been adopted at the national level, the increased levels of intra-EU 15 trade over the last decade, the rise in investment flows both from and to the EU, and the integration of the European economy as a whole into the world economy. The first section of the chapter concludes that internal market policy constitutes a 1st order policy, given that one sees a strong, centralized EU in this policy area: competences in this area have been fully transferred to the supranational level.

The chapter's second section then offers a focussed examination of the Single European Act's "1992 Programme", which represents the cornerstone of internal market policy. Adopted in 1986, the 1992 Programme introduced close to 300 measures aimed at ensuring the free movement of goods, services and capital by removing physical, fiscal and technical barriers between member states' borders. This was done with an overall aim of promoting the economic growth of the European market in the world economy while creating economic conditions that would allow businesses to operate effectively and efficiently. The second section thus starts with an analysis of developments that began in 1979, highlighting the way that the European Court of Justice (ECJ) served as a catalyst in the drive towards the completion of the single market in the policy initiation stage with its ruling in the well-known Cassis de Dijon case. The ECJ's decision in Cassis determined that goods produced in one member state (in this case, the French liqueur Cassis de Dijon) must be allowed to be sold in another EU member state (which is this case was Germany). This decision by the ECJ was seized by an entrepreneurial European Commission under Jacques Delors in the mid 1980s, who saw an integrated single market wherein capital could thrive as the key means to buttress the European economy and make it more competitive against other global players. The Commission then negotiated the details of the 1992 Programme with economic actors who secured representation through the European Round Table of Industrialists (ERT), which is one of the most significant corporate lobby groups in the EU, as discussed by authors such as Balanyá et al.[13] It will be demonstrated that such capital actors were concerned with the creation of the single market in order to reduce transaction costs while increasing profits for European business. The ERT also desired to make the single market a competitive zone for the development of a strong Europe within the global economy. Given this evidence, it will be argued that it is useful to take account of the perspectives of both the supranational governance and the dominant economic class when theoretically characterizing the formulation of single market policy.

Chapter 5 examines and explains developments in competition policy, which is concerned with setting regulations in order to ensure the development of a competitive, neo-liberal single market. The chapter examines the evolution of the four main aspects of competition policy: state aid control, where the EU is empowered to ensure that unfair, market-distorting subsidies are not given by states; liberalization, which deals with ending the monopoly positions of some firms in the EU; anti-trust policies, which seek to prevent companies from engaging in restrictive practices; and merger control, where the Commission must approve mergers that have a Community dimension in order to ensure that a competitive European market is maintained. Given the evolution of competition policy, the first section concludes that this constitutes a 1st order policy because responsibilities in this area have been fully transferred to the supranational level. For example, member states have agreed that Brussels regulations with regard to liberalization and state aid must be adhered to.

The second section gives a more detailed analysis of one of the major policies developed in the last 15 years: the Merger Control Regulation (MCR), a policy whose negotiation has received little academic attention to date but whose importance is evident, given the hundreds of firms that merge every year in order to cut costs and generate higher profits. The merger phenomenon particularly took off after the late 1980s as firms sought to amalgamate resources in order to increase their competitiveness in the global economy. The evidence uncovered points to the significance of the Commission in the initiation stage of the policy, given its goal to create a European-wide "one-stop shop" for merger control. Hence, it will be argued that the policy initiation phase can be best characterized by ideas raised in the supranational governance perspective.

When turning to negotiation of the MCR, however, one sees (in a similar vein to the 1992 Programme discussed in Chapter 4) that the Commission did not act alone in formulating the details of the MCR. Rather, the direct participation of capital actors, specifically those acting under the banner of the ERT, was once again manifest. The ERT, which was aware of the Commission's aim to regulate the merger process, rationally concluded that, by participating in the process, it could prevent the Commission from pursuing regulations that would be unfavourable to the interests of capital. The ERT also believed that influencing the nature of the regulations could help capital consolidate the position of capital actors in the global economy. This points to the additional importance of the DEC perspective in understanding policy negotiation in competition policy.

Chapter 6 focusses on Economic and Monetary Union (EMU), highlighting its principle objective of imposing centralized monetary and fiscal discipline with a view to achieving low inflationary economic growth in a single currency area. The first section pays specific attention to the evolution of the policy by highlighting how several member states pursued policies at the domestic level in order to attain the so-called convergence criteria enshrined in the Maastricht Treaty: low inflation rates, low long-term interest rates, and lower deficits and debts. It underlines the national reforms that were made, including spending cuts in social welfare programmes and increased labour market deregulation, in order to meet the criteria for participating in a single currency. Using time-series data between 1994 and 2004, the first section also details the evolution of the European currency[14] in world markets, including the increasing currency shares of the euro vis-à-vis the US dollar and Japanese yen over the last five years and the increasing value of the euro exchange rate versus international currencies, in order to highlight the "success" of the single currency, which reflects national governments' desires to create a leading world currency in order to underpin the European economy. Because EMU is reflective of a policy area witnessing a large transference of power from the member state to the supranational level, the first section argues that it is representative of a 1st order policy.

The second section examines the formulation of EMU, contending that a leading role in the policy initiation stage was played by Commission President Jacques Delors, who drafted the blueprint for EMU in the Delors Report of 1989. Nevertheless, when the specific details of the policy were negotiated, the evidence highlights how the Council of Ministers played a leading role in terms of defining the convergence criteria, setting up the institutional structure of monetary union and prescribing a timetable with regard to completion of the various "stages" of EMU. As in Chapters 4 and 5, the evidence suggests that capital actors, acting again through the ERT, who believed that a single currency zone would be highly beneficial for business operating in the single integrated market and competing against other firms on the world stage, also participated in the policy process by suggesting dates for completion of EMU that were accepted by the Council of Ministers. Given the actions of the various actors throughout the policy process, it is argued that supranational governance theory helps inform our understanding of EMU policy initiation, while the intergovernmental and DEC perspectives help explain developments when the policy was negotiated.

Chapter 7 turns to evaluation of the Common Agricultural Policy (CAP), which represents the main redistributive policy of the EU. The first section of the chapter emphasizes that the main objective of CAP is to redistribute EU budgetary funds to farmers in order to subsidize production of certain products deemed essential or beneficial to the Community. The CAP also theoretically seeks to maintain some level of a traditional farming community in Europe. Based on analysis of the evolution of the policy, this chapter argues that CAP is a 1st order policy because it represents a long-standing centralized policy at the EU level and, moreover, that it is one of the most important redistributive policies, given that it receives the largest percentage of the EU budget.

The second section examines the policy formulation process manifest during three initiatives aimed at CAP reform over the last 15 years: the MacSharry Reform of 1992, the Agenda 2000 reform process and the Fischler Reforms of 2003. It is argued that in all three processes, policy initiation was started by the Commission. The policy negotiation processes were later spearheaded by national actors who actively participated alongside larger, business-like, farming-interest representatives of what can be defined as "corporate farmer" players with sizeable amounts of land. Such large landowners sought to ensure that reforms to the CAP would not decrease their subsidies as they benefited most from them. Hence, reforms to the CAP were difficult to achieve and resulted in only minor changes. With this evidence in mind, this account of the policy process suggests again the importance of the supranational governance approach in explaining how the policy was initiated, coupled with the intergovernmentalist and the DEC perspectives in understanding how it was negotiated.

Chapter 8 examines social policy in the EU. Analysing social policy, one sees a generally weak and decentralized EU. This has resulted in fewer EU-wide norms in this issue than in others. Moreover, one observes that social policy still remains within the realm of national sovereignty, while EU-wide measures are regarded with suspicion. Hence, in contrast to the policies analysed in the previous four empirical chapters, social policy is representative of a 2nd order policy. The first section of the chapter offers evidence to support this argument by analysing the evolution of the policy area over the last 50 years since its inception. It suggests that while a legal basis for EU social policy was provided for in the early stages of the European Community, member states were not particularly interested in promoting EU-wide norms on issues such as improving working conditions, guaranteeing equal wages, or promoting gender equality. Rather, they were more concerned about the "economic" goals of the EU – namely, to develop the single market, competition policy and monetary union as ways to make Europe more competitive in the world economy. As analyses of the evolution of Brussels' social policy initiatives show, states are more willing to agree to non-binding proposals from Brussels on issues surrounding social policies than to directives which have a greater legal force.

The second section then examines and explains the formulation of the Social Charter in the late 1980s and the Social Protocol of the early 1990s. It argues that while both initiatives had the potential to safeguard the rights of workers in the EU, national administrations – particularly in the UK – sought to adopt only minimalist standards, watering down the proposals put forward by the Commission. This eventually resulted in both initiatives having rather limited impact in terms of benefiting European workers. Evidence shows that labour and employers' lobby groups were also represented in the negotiation process and put their different views on the issues. It is concluded that while the Commission was important in initiating both of these policies, negotiation outcomes can be understood by focussing on the roles of the Council, corporate actors and trade unions, where the Council played a predominant role in minimizing the impact of the policies. This suggests the importance of supranational governance, intergovernmentalism and corporatist perspectives in explaining policy developments.

Chapter 9 examines what are referred to as "freedom, security and justice" policies of the EU, which relate to issues such as immigration, asylum, citizenship and crime control. Some of the main data presented in the first section describe the evolution of EU immigration between 1990 and 2002, the percentage of non-nationals that live in EU member states, and the evolution of the phenomenon of asylum seekers seeking refuge in the EU between 1998 and 2003. Despite the importance of issues such as immigration and asylum, however, evaluation of the policy shows that freedom, security and justice policies remain of 2nd order status. It will be demonstrated that there are three reasons for this: there is a lack of deep integration in several issue areas; there is a lack of full harmonization of policies at the EU level as member states seek to maintain their autonomy in defining key policies such as who should be allowed to enter and stay within their borders; and there is a lack of centralization in the coordination of policies concerning such things as immigration and asylum.

In order to better understand policy formulation in the area of freedom, security and justice policies, the second section pays detailed attention to the policy process during the formulation of the Family Reunification Directive of 2003. This was a significant achievement because it represented the first Community-wide attempt at regulation in the area of legal immigration. Analysis of the policy process indicates that the Commission provided the overall blueprint for the regulation and was therefore critical in the policy initiation stage. However, the Council was more significant in terms of setting the specific details of the regulation during the negotiation phase. This included, for example, tighter restrictions on who was eligible for reunification than the Commission proposed, ensuring that there were tight application procedures, adding specific clauses to the directive to ensure that public security in member states be maintained, and ensuring that member states could unilaterally revoke any residency permits should they feel this necessary. These issues were emphasized by the Council with the view of reinforcing member state sovereignty in immigration policy.

The second section also argues that despite the strength of the Council in the negotiation phase, there is some limited evidence to suggest that a number of interest groups, such as the European Council on Refugees and Exiles (ECRE), which called for less rigid rules to be applied to asylum seekers seeking family reunification, did exercise some influence in the negotiation process. Other interest groups, however, such as the European Region of the International Lesbian and Gay Association (ILGA Europe) that pressed for the EU-wide reunification regulations to be applicable to partners and children of same-sex couples, had relatively less success against the Council, which dismissed any such notions on the basis of its belief in the concept of the "traditional" family. Given this evidence, the section concludes that the supranational governance perspective is of value in explaining the policy initiation aspects of the policy. The intergovernmentalist and, to a more limited extent, pluralist perspectives are of greater value in explaining policy negotiation in immigration policy.

Chapter 10 closes the empirical analysis of the book by examining the EU's external policies, of which there are two main aspects. The first relates to the EU's external political relations, as embodied in the Common Foreign and Security Policy (CFSP). The second aspect concerns the EU's external economic policies, which include trading agreements made between the EU and other states. The first section thus considers the evolution of foreign political relations through an examination of the EU's CFSP. It contends that the divergent security interests of the different member-states has resulted in the CFSP being rather toothless: some European states, such as the UK and Spain, have blindly sought to follow the interests of the United States when it comes to "making war" on the world stage; others, such as France, are completely opposed to this; while others, such as Ireland, have preferred to maintain their neutrality.

The first section then concentrates on the second aspect of external policies by considering the main objectives of different bilateral and multilateral agreements. Attention is specifically given to the Euro-Mediterranean Partnership (EMP) over a ten-year period since its inception in 1995. The EMP is significant because it seeks to promote trade between the EU and countries of the southern coast of the Mediterranean, while it also theoretically makes this trade conditional on the fulfilment of democratic rule and an end to human rights abuses in some of these states. Based on in-depth analysis of the situation in Morocco, particularly since 9/11, the section argues that the EMP can be considered a failure in terms of reaching its overall objectives: even though there is increased trade between different EU member states and the Mediterranean region, human rights abuses have escalated in Morocco, a state led by an increasingly authoritarian regime. It concludes that the EU has failed to promote its values of human rights and democratization because of the interests of member states such as France and Spain who wish to have authoritarian regimes in power in some of these countries in order to promote "regional stability" and continued economic benefits. This highlights the fact that external policies are not driven by European institutions and EU norms per se, but are guided by the interests of specific member states. Supranational agreements that are deemed more significant than national preferences are not found in the overall evolution of the policy area: because decisions based on domestic concerns remain paramount, the overall issue area is representative of a 2nd order issue.

The second section analyses the European dynamics surrounding the American invasion of Iraq in 2003. We emphasize that the formulation process here is different to other policies studied in this book because no EU policy towards the Iraq War was made per se. Nevertheless, we particularly question why the EU was unable to formulate a unified policy position in order to deal with the most significant international conflict of the decade to date. The section highlights how different member states had different interests based on their historical relationships with the United States. It is also argued that although there was a weak institutional structure at the supranational level that prevented the emergence of a centralized EU voice in this area, this is of limited importance as the Council of Ministers had the final say with regard to an EU decision in any case. Given the evidence, it is thus argued that the intergovernmentalist perspective is the most relevant in explaining policy initiation and negotiation in external relations.

Chapter 11 summarizes the main findings of the book. The first conclusion is that, considering all of the policies studied in this book, there is evidence suggesting a discernable hierarchy of EU policies. Single market, competition, economic and monetary, and agricultural policies constitute 1st order policies that reflect a strong and centralized EU seeking to exert itself as a unified actor on the world stage. Social policy, freedom, security and justice as well as external policies constitute 2nd order policies, where the EU is limited in speaking with a unified voice and where member states still retain sovereignty. We then attempt to link these findings of the existence of a hierarchy of policies to our examination of the actors involved in the formulation of the policies. The main argument that is drawn out in this regard is that what unites 1st order policies is that major economic actors, such as the European Round Table of Industrialists, have played key roles in their formulation. Such capital actors have actively worked alongside the Commission or the Council to create these policies, with the main goals of creating and consolidating a single, efficient, neo-liberal, common-currency market wherein capital can thrive. Such a market will serve as the basis for a competitive European economy on the world stage, something which is equally desired by EU institutional players at both the domestic and supranational levels. In other words, the formulation of 1st order policies has seen the active participation of the dominant economic class seeking to pursue policies that serve their own interest, and has gained the enthusiastic support of both supranational and domestic policy makers seeking to place the EU in a competitive position in the world economy.

It will also be argued that what unites 2nd order policies is either the lack of desire, or actual antipathy, by capital to formulate social policies or its general indifference towards a policy area in which member states seek to retain full sovereignty (freedom, security and justice as well as external relations). This lack of desire to pursue EU-wide regulations in some policy areas, such as social policy, is due to the costs they would impose on business: social policy does not represent a policy that will allow for concomitant increase in profits or accumulation for capital actors operating in the global economy. Further, business has no interest in shaping developments that member states wish to maintain exclusive control over, such as immigration and common or foreign security policies. Second order policies also reflect the firm determination by member states to hold on to traditional dimensions of sovereignty. Given these ideas, we argue that it does not really matter whether or not policy formulation is initiated at the supranational or the national level. Rather, the inclusion or the exclusion of capital actors in the negotiation stage of a policy helps determine whether or not it will become a priority for Europe. From this perspective, we argue that theories of European integration, such as supranational governance or intergovernmentalism, are not as significant in explaining European integration and the development of policy as some scholars have argued. Rather, the DEC perspective is of more value in explaining why deeper integration has been achieved in some policy areas than in others.

Beyond these main findings, to borrow a phrase from George Orwell, perhaps our biggest goal is to demonstrate to the reader that all policies in Europe are equal, but that some policies are more equal than others. The politics of the EU is pushed and pulled by a combination of 1st and 2nd order policies whose classification can be understood in the context of developments in the world economy and the desires of the dominant economic class to create a "profitable" Europe within which they can thrive. With this in mind, in order to understand the policies that affect every citizen of the EU one has to examine not only the role of European leaders at the national and supranational levels, but also the desires of unelected and unaccountable economic élites who act in their own self-interest and seek political participation in order to promote the development of some policies over others in order to benefit themselves. Politics is policy: indeed, policy is politics.

2 Who's coming to play?
Policy-making actors in the EU

The concept of "actors" is a crucial one in the broad political science literature that examines policy making, even though one may argue that different studies focus on different actors at different times. This ultimately results in much debate, if not confusion, with regard to which actors can be considered the most important when different public policies are formulated. Taking from the ideas raised in the political science literature focussing on domestic level politics, several types of actors have been analysed. For example, some authors who focus on the role of executives suggest that the main – if not the only – actors in the policy process are core executives, such as the Cabinet.[1] Others, who focus on the role of bureaucracies, argue that specific civil servants – in some cases from powerful ministries – may exercise a disproportionate influence in determining how a policy's objectives are defined.[2] Others, who focus on the role of representative assemblies that are elected by mass publics, may see as the main actor the elected body that debates bills and drafts before policy output is achieved.[3] Those whose work stems from a formal legal tradition consider that the courts are the ultimate arbiters of the "legality" of a policy according to constitutional or legal norms.[4] Theorists whose analysis is based on examination of political parties uphold the argument that it is these actors in government that transform electoral mandates into policies and should thus be seen as the driving force behind legislation.[5] Others, whose work focusses on the role of interest groups, contend that a main set of actors in public policy development are representatives of those who share common interests and collectively organize in order to exert influence.[6] And yet others, who focus on the action of specific economic interest groups, ultimately conclude that the most important actors in policy making are those who represent the interests of capital, specifically firms and multinationals.[7]

This chapter will apply these concepts from the broad political science literature, while adding some simplicity to the matter by classifying the different actors. It will develop the argument that there are two broad "types" of potential actors when EU public policy is made. Drawing on ideas raised by those writing on core executives, bureaucracies, legislative assemblies and the role of courts, the first set of actors can be broadly defined as what many would refer to as the "EU institutional" players. These include the Council of Ministers, the Commission (in its dual role as both core executive and bureaucracy), the European Parliament and the ECJ. The second set of actors, which we refer to as the "interest groups" and which the literature often also refers to as lobby groups, seek to influence EU institutional actors. Such groups can be categorized along three main dimensions: economic groups, professional groups and public interest groups. We will analyse the various organizations that fit within these categories: economic interest groups consist of capital actors, professional groups include trade unions and the farm lobbies, and public interest groups are those organizations usually devoted to a single cause.

Each actor will be briefly discussed in the following subsections. It is important to note at this stage that there are other texts more appropriate for those seeking either a historical analysis of the evolution of each of the actors or a more detailed analysis of the structure and composition of the EU institutions in particular.[8] With this in mind, the main objective of each of the subsections will be to highlight two main points in an integrated fashion. First, what are the basic characteristics of these actors and, particularly in the case of the institutions, what are their theoretically defined powers? Second, what have been the more general, observations in the recent literature regarding the role of these actors in the EU policy-making process? These two main objectives, which will highlight the main characteristics of each of these players in the light of recent developments, will ultimately prepare the reader for the next chapter, whose goal is to place such actors within different theoretical explanations of public policy formulation.

The EU institutions

The Council of Ministers

The Council of Ministers, or Council of the European Union, is the institution that represents the interests of each of the member states. Before May 2004 there were 15 member states, but enlargement and the inclusion of ten central and eastern European states saw this number increase to 25. As several introductory texts on the theme suggest, there is no one Council per se, but rather there are many: each council consists of the national ministers in the corresponding policy areas. As result, there are several councils, with two of the most significant being General Affairs (comprising foreign ministers) and ECOFIN (finance ministers). The Council presidency rotates on a six-month basis, and meetings are held in the member state holding the presidency. Of these meetings, among the more significant that attract widespread media and academic attention are those of the "European Council", held at least once every six months and consisting of the heads of state or government of each member state, as discussed by authors such as Drake, Ortega, Maachi and Edwards and Wessala.[9] However, the meetings of prime importance in terms of policy development in each issue area are council meetings that take place at various times throughout the whole year.

The Council has two main formal policy-making powers. The first is to reject or amend proposals that emanate from the Commission, the institution that has the exclusive right to initiate EU legislation. Prima facie, this role may seem insignificant vis-à-vis the power of the Commission (as discussed in more detail below). However, the fact that the Council must approve any Commission proposal has led commentators such as Moravcsik[10] to suggest that it effectively exercises power over the Commission. Moreover, there is an element of "informal governance" that allows the Council theoretically much room to manoeuvre and perhaps even set the agenda for, the Commission: informally, there is nothing to stop the Council from persuading the Commission to initiate a piece of legislation in a specific policy area that is in the former's interest.[11] This idea is related to a second main power: the Council is empowered to define the long-term goals of the EU. To this end, the idea of "delegation" is key: the Council is effectively empowered to "delegate" its power to the Commission. In other words, the latter pursues the long-term goals defined by the former. One may argue that the Maastricht Treaty institutionalized this idea by empowering the European Council with the central role of defining, or at the very least supporting, major initiatives.[12] Nevertheless, given the nature of the "dual executive" of the EU, even though the Council's support is a precondition of major initiatives, it does not necessarily follow that it has the most impact in defining the nature of specific policies when they are formulated. To this end, it is necessary to turn to analysis of the Commission.

The European Commission

Historically there were 20 members of the European Commission, with that number rising to 25 on enlargement, with each government appointing one commissioner. Commissioners are charged to represent the interests of the EU as a whole, not the member state from which they are appointed. They are usually former politicians and may vary in ability and seniority. This helps determine which "portfolio" or directorate general (DG) they will head as decided upon by the President of the Commission (who is chosen by the heads of the member states). In many respects, a DG can be considered a Brussels-level equivalent to a ministry found in domestic-level politics. Examples of DGs of specific relevance to the policies studied in this book include the Internal Market, Competition, Economic and Financial Affairs, Agriculture, Employment, Environment, Freedom, Security and Justice, and External Relations DGs. Table 2.1 outlines all of the present DGs and other services, the specific policies which fall under their jurisdiction, the commissioner presently in charge, and his/her nationality.

The Commission has two main powers, which relate to both the formulation and implementation of policy. The first power, which

Table 2.1 The European Commissions' directorates-general and services, 2004–2009

Concept	Directorate General/Services	Issue areas/duties	Commissioner responsible	Nationality
Policies	Agriculture	Agriculture and rural development.	Mariann Fischer Boel	Denmark
	Competition	Mergers, state aid and anti-trust.	Neelie Kroes	Holland
	Economic and Financial Affairs	Economic and monetary policies.	Joaquín Almunia	Spain
	Education, and Culture,	Education and training; youth; sport; civil society; culture.	Ján Figel	Slovakia
	Employment, Social Affairs and Equal Opportunities	Employment, labour market regulation and social protection.	Vladimír Špidla	Czech Republic
	Transport	Transport policies.	Jacques Barrot*	France
	Energy	Securing energy supplies for Europe.	Andris Piebalgs	Latvia
	Enterprise and Industry	Enhance competitiveness of European enterprises.	Günter Verheugen*	Germany
	Environment	Promotion of environmental protection and efficiency.	Stavros Dimas	Greece
	Fisheries	Fishing activity; farm fishing; fish processing and marketing.	Joe Borg	Malta
	Health and Consumer Protection	Food safety, public health, animal welfare.	Markos Kyprianou	Cyprus
	Information Society and Media	IT research; citizen participation in Information Society.	Viviane Reding	Luxemburg
	Internal Market and Services	Promotion of free movement; monitors implementation of single market regulation.	Charlie McCreevy	Ireland

	Joint Research Centre	Reference centre of EU's science and technological development.	Janez Potocnik	Slovenia
	Justice, Freedom and Security	Citizenship; rights; fight against crime and terrorism.	Franco Frattini*	Italy
	Regional Policy	Economic and social development of less-favoured regions.	Danuta Hübner	Poland
	Research	Coordinate research activities; develop EU research and technology.	Janez Potocnik	Slovenia
	Taxation and Customs Union	Administers and controls the application of the Union's customs code.	László Kovács	Hungary
	Development	Combat poverty and promote development in developing countries.	Louis Michel	Belgium
	Enlargement	Oversee enlargement process and policies towards new neighbors.	Olli Rehn	Finland
	EuropeAid Cooperation Office	Implement the Commission's external aid instruments.	Benita Ferrero-Waldner	Austria
	External Relations	Coordination of Commission's external relations activities.	Benita Ferrero-Waldner	Austria
	Humanitarian Aid Office - ECHO	Provide emergency assistance for natural disasters and armed conflict outside EU.	Louis Michel	Belgium
	Trade	Implements EU external trade policy.	Peter Mandelson	UK
General services	European Anti-Fraud Office	Fights fraud, corruption, and misconduct in European institutions.	Siim Kallas*	Estonia
	Eurostat	Provide EU with statistical information service	Joaquín Almunia	Spain

(Continued on next page)

Table 2.1 continued

		Margot Wallström	Sweden
	Communication	Inform media and citizens of Commission's goals, and policies.	
	Publication Office	The publishing house of EU institutions.	Ján Figel	Slovakia
	Secretariat General	Organises and coordinates work of all DGs, ensuring collective responsibility.	José Manuel Barroso**	Portugal
Internal Services	Budget	Managing and implementing the EU budget	Dalia Grybauskaite	Lithuania
	Translation Service	Provides translations services for Commission (in the 11 official languages).	Ján Figel	Slovakia
	Group of Policy Advisors	Provide advice to the Commission on all aspects of future EU policy.	José Manuel Barroso**	Portugal
	Internal Audit Service	Audits the internal control systems in the Commission.	Siim Kallas*	Estonia
	Interpretation	Provides interpretive services.	Ján Figel	Slovakia
	Legal Service	Legal advice to Commission.	José M'l Barroso**	Portugal
	Personnel and Administration	Handles human resources, IT systems and security.	Siim Kallas*	Estonia
	Informatics	Defines the IT strategy of the Commission; provides information technology and telecommunications infrastructure.	Siim Kallas*	Estonia
	Infrastructure and logistics	Manages social infrastructure/logistics.	Siim Kallas*	Estonia

Source: Authors' elaboration of data found on http://europa.eu.int/comm.

* Vice president of the Commission. ** President of the Commission.

relates to its role in policy formulation, is that the Commission has the sole right among all EU institutions to initiate legislation in most policy areas, as discussed above. As reflected in the works of those such as Nugent and Saurugger[13] and Lamy,[14] even in areas of Justice and home affairs and external relations where the Council theoretically enjoys virtually full power without significant Commission input, the Commission has become increasingly involved, as seen in the issue of immigration policy and development aid. The second power, which relates to its role in the implementation phase and closely mirrors a bureaucratic function, is that the Commission ensures that EU legislation is complied with. However, it is a difficult task for a staff of slightly over 28,000 to attempt to ensure that all EU legislation is being adhered to, as seen in a major aspect of competition policy: the monitoring of state aid.[15]

A main issue in the recent literature highlights not so much the Commission's "powers" per se, but rather, as MacMullen[16] as well as Stevens[17] have argued, its abuse of power under the Santer Commission and the ramifications of this. After allegations of presumed fraud, mismanagement and nepotism by the French and Spanish Commissioners, Cresson and Marin, 1999 witnessed the collective resignation of all 20 members of the College of Commissioners. In the wake of this, the Commission was faced with what Vos refers to as a double challenge: not only to deal with the "growing increase in its workload through reform of its working practices" but also to "institute control mechanisms to increase the transparency of its activities".[18] Although the Commission has considered embarking upon major reforms relating to management and accountability since the fall of the Santer Commission,[19] such reforms may not necessarily increase effective governance on part of the Commission. Debates on this topic culminated in the publication of the Commission's White Paper on Governance, which highlighted the need for reforms throughout the 2000s that would increase legitimacy and transparency as well as efficiency, even though writers such as Horeth claim that this document "reveals a lack of understanding of the preconditions for successful governance in the multi-layered system of the EU".[20]

Taking both the Council and Commission together and comparing their powers, some commentators have concluded that the both institutions form a "dual -executive" at the supranational level.[21] On the one hand, the Commission has a leading role in developing regulations in key policy areas (such as the Budget and international trade) while ensuring that policies are implemented. On the other hand, the Council can amend or reject Commission proposals, while defining the long-term goals of the EU. The main strength of this dual character is that it "facilitates extensive deliberation and compromise in the adoption and implementation of policies", while its main weaknesses is that it "lacks overall leadership".[22] This last point particularly emphasizes that, even if we accept the idea that there is some sort of "executive" power, policy making in the EU is not necessarily centred exclusively in these two main institutions. This is because the lack of leadership allows other potential policy participants to influence the process. The way power oscillates between the two members of the executive has also been likened by some authors to a "Swinging Pendulum".[23] This implies that at some points one of the institutions will take a lead, and that after a period of time the other will regain dominance.

Regardless of how one classifies the relationship between the Council and the Commission, it is necessary to turn to developments in other EU institutions in order to understand the workings of the EU. These include the EP, which is the only elected body in the EU, as well as the ECJ.

The European Parliament

The European Parliament (EP) is the representative assembly consisting of the 732 Members of the European Parliament (MEPs) that are elected by EU citizens. From this perspective alone, this institution lies in stark contrast to the Commission (which is appointed) and the Council of Ministers (who, although being elected representatives in the member states, are not directly elected to the Council). Compiling the data from latest EP elections in 2004, Table 2.2 (page 28) highlights two main points.

First, as seen in the final column, the number of representatives is directly related to the population of the member state. Second, as seen in the bottom row, MEPs sit in the EP not on a national basis, but rather as members of party groups. As Pennings[24] argues, on the basis of an analysis of 1999 European election manifestos, there are significant ideological differences between the groups that offer voters choices during EP elections. Hix[25] further suggests that "transnational party group affiliation is more important than national affiliation for determining how MEPs eventually vote" in the EP. The main parties, along the right–left axis across the ideological spectrum, are the Christian Democrats (PPE), the Liberal Democrats (ELDR), and the Social Democrats (PSE). The representation of the other smaller groups is related to the idea of "2nd order elections" raised in the literature. This thesis argues that smaller groups do not gain representation in the EP because they are voters' first choice. Rather, voters have voted for these smaller, largely unknown parties in order to demonstrate their discontent with national administrations.[26]

Although the literature generally agrees that the axis of executive power lies between the Council and the Commission, the exact role of the EP in the formal policy-making process has been the centre of some debate. On the one hand, the more pessimistic observers argue that the

EP is simply a symbolic institution (popularly referred to as a "talking shop") that has virtually no substantive power and offers just the façade of a representative assembly. On the other, optimists contend that formal EP power is increasing, particularly since the early 1990s and the 1997 Treaty of Amsterdam.[27] To support this contention, the optimists point to four main powers that have recently developed and taken shape. First, there are several aspects of developments in the EU that cannot be decided on without the EP's approval. These can be specified as: the admission of new member states into the Union; major international agreements between the EU and other countries (but certainly not including foreign policy initiatives); the method of election to be used in EP elections; and the role of the European Central Bank (ECB).

A second significant power, since 1993, includes the EP's active role in the appointment of new commissioners; even after the member states have nominated commissioners, each must appear before the EP that eventually approves or disapproves the make-up of the next Commission.[28] The third major power is in the approval of the EU budget. Although the Commission and Council clearly have strength in determining budgetary details, the EP can in theory amend the budget and eventually reject it on its final reading, although this has not occurred since the 1990s. And the fourth main power, clearly seen in the legislative process, is the EP's gain in what is referred to as the "co-decision" procedure. Here, the EP has the power to amend and/or reject legislation in specific policy areas, including the internal market, public health, consumer protection, and culture and education. Critical observers suggest, however, that even tough application of co-decision has notably increased the powers of the EP, it remains limited because several important policy areas either have no EP involvement (as in competition policy, EMU monitoring, the CAP and CFSP) or a limited one (as in structural funds and environmental policy).

The European Court of Justice

The composition of the Court of Justice includes 25 judges and 8 advocates general (who help draft the Opinions of the judges), serving renewable terms of six years. The ECJ's main responsibility is to ensure the law is observed in the interpretation and applications of the various treaties. There are four main types of actions that can be taken by the ECJ.[29] First, the ECJ can decide whether or not an member state has complied with Community law; such cases are usually referred from the Commission. If a member state is found guilty and refuses to comply even after an ECJ judgment, the court may impose a penalty. Second, a member state, the Commission, the Council or even the Parliament may ask the ECJ to review the legality of legislation emanating from Community institutions. Third, the ECJ can penalize an EU

Table 2.2 Sixth parliamentary term, 2004–2009

	PPE-DE	PSE	ELDR	VERTS/ALE	GUE/NGL	IND/DEM	UEN	NI	Total
Belgium	6	7	6	2				3	24
Czech Rep.	14	2			6	1		1	24
Denmark	1	5	4	1	1	1	1		14
Germany	49	23	7	13	7				99
Estonia	1	3	2						6
Greece	11	8			4	1			24
Spain	24	24	2	3	1				54
France	17	31	11	6	3	3		7	78
Ireland	5	1	1		1	1	4		13
Italy	24	16	12	2	7	4	9	4	78
Cyprus	3		1		2				6
Latvia	3		1	1			4		9
Lithuania	2	2	7				2		13
Luxemburg	3	1	1	1					6
Hungary	13	9	2						24
Malta	2	3							5
Netherlands	7	7	5	4	2	2			27
Austria	6	7		2				3	18
Poland	19	10	4			10	7	4	54
Portugal	9	12			3				24
Slovenia	4	1	2						7
Slovakia	8	3						3	14
Finland	4	3	5	1	1				14
Sweden	5	5	3	1	2	3			19
UK	28	19	12	5	1	10		3	78
Total	268	202	88	42	41	36	27	28	732

Source: Data found on: http://wwwdb.europarl.eu.int/ep5/owa/p_meps2.repartition?ipid=1103391&ilg=EN&iorig=home&imsg
and http://www.europarl.eu.int/presentation/default_en.htm

institution for inaction over a case that it should have monitored. Finally, by way of what is called the preliminary ruling system, the ECJ can be asked by national courts to render opinions on the European dimensions of a case, ultimately allowing for harmonized application of Community law.

The literature has offered two main views of the policy-making power of the ECJ.[30] On the one hand, throughout the 1960s, 1970s and 1980s, it was seen as being one of the driving forces behind European integration, with landmark cases such as Dassonville and Cassis de Dijon which abolished quantitative restrictions on imports and all measures of equivalent effect, and embedded the principle of "mutual recognition" of products made and sold across the single market (as discussed in Chapter 4). Regardless of its formal powers, however, its effective power can be limited for two reasons. First, enforcement mechanisms are weak. For example, even though the Court may impose fines on member states or firms for non-compliance with Community decisions, the ECJ has little power to do anything if the penalized party still refuses to comply. This is because there is no fully established European "police force" to implement decisions of the Court. Second, the ECJ has no policy jurisdiction over important areas such as foreign policy As a result, regardless of how "activist" the Court may be, its impact in certain issue areas can never be more than limited. Despite these arguments on the Court's lack of effective powers, recent work by Stone Sweet[31] nevertheless highlights the point that member states do eventually comply with court decisions, even though it may take time. This is because member states do not want to undermine the legal character of European integration, and because the ECJ is slowly expanding its influence through decisions in issue areas such as gender equality and pensions.

One may argue that such issue areas have come to light in the first place because of the action of various interest groups that have helped redefine the agenda. With this in mind, we turn to a more detailed examination of interest groups in the EU.

Key to Table 2.2

PPE-DE: Group of the European People's Party (Christian Democrats) and European Democrats
PSE: Socialist Group in the European Parliament
ELDR: Group of the Alliance of Liberals and Democrats for Europe
VERTS/ALE: Group of the Greens/European Free Alliance
GUE/NGL: Confederal Group of the European United Left-Nordic Green Left
IND / DEM: Independence / Democracy Group
UEN: Union for Europe of the Nations Group
NI: Non-attached members

EU interest groups

A major argument often found in the literature on this subject is that beyond formal EU institutions such as the Commission, Council, the EP and the ECJ, interest groups have strongly influenced the formulation of EU public policy. Pioneering examples of this work (which took up the themes of earlier American-based literature on interest representation by those such as Dahl[32]) include the work of Mazey and Richardson,[33] Pedlar and Vanschenden[34] and Greenwood.[35] An interest group can be defined as any group, or set of actors, that has common interests and seeks to influence the policy-making process in such a way that their interests are reflected in public policy outcomes. Different studies have pointed to the influence of different groups, ranging from individual corporate groups, to larger umbrella associations. Different studies have also categorized the various types of interest groups in different ways. For example, building on ideas raised by the European Commission that suggested there were two types of organized interests (profit-making and non-profit making), Watson and Shackleton[36] have recently offered a useful typology to classify different types of lobby actors in the EU. Particularly noteworthy is their distinction between private interests that pursue specific economic goals and public-interest bodies that pursue non-economic aims.

Guided by ideas raised in the literature, we argue that, given the policies studied in this book, it is useful to consider a three-fold characterization of organized interests: namely, economic groups, professional groups and public groups.[37] This classification suggests that it is necessary to differentiate between some actors that Watson and Shackleton classify as "private interests". For example, Watson and Shackleton consider that trade union and farm interest groups are representative of "private economic interests" similar to capital actors. However, there is a clear difference between capital interest groups and those of labour and farmers: Chapter 3 will demonstrate how neo-Marxists argue that capital actors are the owners of the forces of production and generally seek to influence policy making in order to ultimately gain financial benefits for themselves. Labour and farmers' groups, which generally have fewer resources at their disposal than capital, are not necessarily motivated to achieve the same final objective. Rather, one may argue that they are also motivated by other "professional" concerns which transcend simply economic ones. For example, the main concerns for labour have been related not only to wages, but also to health and safety standards in the workplace for all workers. Similarly, many farmers have been preoccupied not only with receiving subsidies, but also with the environmental standards of farming practices. With this categorization in mind, we turn to the first of the main groups, comprised exclusively of capital.

Group 1, The economic interests: economic élites seeking dominance in Brussels.

Authors such as Coen,[38] Cowles,[39] Bennett,[40] and Schmidt[41] suggest that economic élites have begun to demand a more privileged EU policy-making role, given the increased transfer of regulatory competences from the state level to Brussels over the last 25 years. In turn, these demands have been "met with concomitant supply of access to the policy-process by political actors in EU institutions" seeking policy expertise.[42] There has subsequently been a "gradual development of the firm into a sophisticated political actor, capable of establishing alliances and ... direct links with the [European] Commission".[43] The literature on the political activity of economic actors has pointed out the way they use multi-level or dual lobbying strategies at both member state and EU levels. While earlier works by Mazey and Richardson and Greenwood recognized that "issues make politics and determine focus", Coen's analysis of developments in trade, social, fiscal, technical and environmental issues was one of the first to hypothesize that "firms play a complex multi-level game when seeking to influence the [European] policy process".[44] The argument here is that where the EU has direct competency, capitalist interests will seek to lobby Brussels directly.[45] "Directly" lobby in this context refers to the idea that firms are increasingly bypassing European and national-level umbrella organizations such as the Union of Industrial and Employers' Confederations of Europe (UNICE) that previously represented such firms. This may be because firms seek to cut costs, while also maximizing their own ability to raise their own concerns without using an intermediary.

Other works making similar arguments to Coen, but focussing more on the roles played by specific business organizations, include Cowles, who highlights the role of the European Round Table of Industrialists (ERT) in the 1992 Programme[46] and of American firms in influencing Brussels policy making through the EU Committee of AmCham.[47] Balanyá *et al's* work on the ERT, in particular, is path-breaking in the sense that it offers rare insights into the organization and goals of that organization. Founded by 45 leading companies in 1983, the ERT has "been one of the main political forces on the European scene for well over a decade".[48] Balanyá *et al's* study highlights how the ERT was founded with the "express intention of revising the unification process and shaping it to the preferences of European corporations".[49] Similar works that have followed this analysis include Van Apeldorn's study, which pays attention to the political activities of the European Round Table throughout the 1980s and 1990s.[50]

Even though the rate of business activity has varied across member states, as examined in the works of those such as Coen, Bennett and Schmidt,[51] and despite differences in business activity across sectors, as seen in the recent work of Bartle,[52] the general argument suggests

that business is being drawn to this new centre of European governance and enjoys a privileged position based on its expertise and
techno-cratic knowledge in certain issues. In order to explain this
overall "Europeanization" of the political activity of economic actors
in particular, and interest groups in general, one may argue that Hix's
supply–demand model offers valuable insights, highlighting both
institutional context and private actors' desires to influence EU
policy.[53] Because EU institutions, in particular the Commission,
increasingly gained regulatory competences and became the drivers
of initiatives previously taken in the domestic domain, this impelled
business interests to seek to influence policies that directly affected
them.[54] Large firms enjoyed both greater resources and more technical
expertise than other social interests, which subsequently found it
difficult to either compete or achieve a strong bargaining position. In
turn, their demands were well received by EU officials who were
especially interested in seeking policy expertise from those most
affected by the policies, and whose participation enhanced the legitimacy of supranational institutions.[55] Implicitly, the supply–demand
model calls into question arguments for the autonomy of EU institutions such as the Commission, Council, the EP and ECJ (as explicitly
discussed by Schneider and Cederman,[56] Golub[57] and Alter,[58] and
implicitly argued by the authors cited above who point to the
primacy of EU institutions). The argument focussing on firms
suggests that there are "constraints" on EU institutions precisely
because of the new role of private actors, particularly business.[59]

Although the overall argument that economic élites play an important role in policy making is suggested in the literature, one may argue
that more convincing and detailed evidence across several policy areas
is required in order to fully demonstrate whether or not capitalists actually do influence the formulation of specific policies and, if so, which
ones. Indeed, Wessels' data does demonstrate that of over 1,600 interest
groups in Brussels during the mid 1990s, the largest number (over 500)
were individual companies.[60] Greenwood's data from 2001 shows that
in a little more than five years, among rather more than 2,300 interest
groups the number representing business had skyrocketed to over
950.[61] Coen convincingly argues that businesses have allocated more of
their resources to activities in Brussels. When firms are questioned in
opinion polls, a large percentage are found to believe that they have
access to the Commission.[62] Yet, even though firms represent the largest
set of interest groups, have allocated resources and perceive themselves
as being influential at the EU level, the literature has failed to offer a
systematic analysis across all major policies to demonstrate that
economic interests do play key roles in affecting Brussels' policy in
different issues. For example, how much influence did business have in
the recent formulation of merger control regulations, a question we will

turn to in Chapter 5, and how does this compare to its power during the formulation of EU initiatives on immigration, as discussed in Chapter 9? Notwithstanding the many analyses devoted to the actions of economic interests, it is necessary to turn to other interest groups active in Brussels' policy making, as commented on by the literature.

Group 2. The professional interests

While the previous discussion highlighted how capital actors, which represent private economic interests, have attempted to influence Brussels' decisions making, here we consider those groups which may seek to represent the professional interests of those working in a specific area. Examples of such groups include farmers and trade unions. We will first consider whom these groups represent. We will then reflect on their main objectives. And, third, we will evaluate these groups' policy-making impact as captured in the literature to date.

THE WORKERS' LOBBY: ETUC

The European Trade Union Confederation (ETUC) is an interest group of significant size whose broad objective is to voice the concerns of workers in the EU. Like UNICE, ETUC is a large umbrella organization which represents 79 National Trade Union confederations in 35 different European countries as well as 11 European based industry federations. Founded in 1973 to provide a counterweight to neo-liberal forces of European economic integration , it claims to represent 60 million members.[63]

In its own words, ETUC has as one of it main objectives to:

> influence European legislation and policies by making direct representations to the various institutions (Commission, Council and Parliament) and by ensuring trade union participation in extensive multi-faced consultation processes with European authorities ... in areas such as employment, social affairs and macro-economic policy.[64]

However, in terms of its influence in EU policy making, writers present a somewhat mixed picture. Some[65] have highlighted how ETUC was able to gain some influence by way of the 1992 Maastricht Treaty when there was, in principle, an institutionalization of its role as a social partner alongside business in the area of social policy. This led some authors to consider that a type of "corporatism" was appearing in the area of social policy.[66] However, Britain's refusal to sign the "Social Agreement" seems to have vitiated the force that ETUC could theoretically exercise, especially in terms of labour market regulations on hiring, firing, wages and indemnity, which remained exclusively under national jurisdictions, as was seen especially in "lower-wage, highly precarious" states such as Spain.[67] However, there has been no extensive analysis of ETUC's role in other social policy initiatives since the Social Charter. One of the objectives of Chapter 8, on Social Policy, is therefore to analyse the role of labour when the Social Protocol was formulated.

THE FARMERS' LOBBY: COPA

The Committee of Agricultural Organizations (COPA) was founded in 1958 to represent the interests of farmers from the different member states. In 1962, it merged with the General Committee for Agricultural Cooperation (COGECA), which represented the agricultural cooperatives in the EU. Today, COPA represents over 14.5 million people working full or part time on EU agricultural holdings, as well as 30,000 agricultural cooperatives. In terms of structure, the organization has an assembly of representatives delegated by the member organizations, which draws up the general policy guidelines of COPA. The guidelines laid down by the assembly are then represented and articulated by a Praesidium, chaired by the COPA president and comprising various senior officials of COPA-COGECA, which then seeks to influence the various EU institutions, most particularly the Commission, given its role in the formulation of the Common Agricultural Policy (CAP).

COPA has four main objectives, guided by its overall goal of defending and developing a European model of agriculture.[68] The first is to examine any matters related to the CAP; the second is to represent the interests of the agriculture sector in Europe; the third is to seek solutions of interest to all farmers; and the fourth is to develop further relations with all relevant Community officials and representatives.

In terms of influence, there is little doubt that COPA has been effective in expressing its view of the vital importance of the EU's CAP from the time when it was first developed throughout the late 1950s and 1960s. The organization led calls for the preservation of the European farming way of life and highlighted the need for subsidies not only to preserve the profession, but also to sustain the environment. However, some also acknowledge that farming interests have generally failed to see the problems associated with the CAP. For example, as Dobson and Weale argue, over time the CAP became "inefficient, wasteful and environmentally damaging".[69] In such a scenario, measures were taken by the Commission to make it more efficient and competitive, first with the MacSharry reform in the early 1990s, then the Agenda 2000 Programme of the late 1990s, and finally the recent Fischler reform of the early 2000s. Although it is generally assumed that COPA's involvement, especially in the reform process has been substantial, little analysis has been made of the potential policy-making role of COPA in the last 15 years, an examination which will be undertaken in Chapter 7.

Group 3. Public interests

A third type of group can be identified as representing public interests. These groups are non-governmental organizations that represent the concerns of members interested in developments in a particular issue area without necessarily seeking any economic or professional advantage per se. They include groups concerned with issues such as human rights, the environment, animal rights, and health and safety.

One of the most significant groups in the last few years in the EU has been the European Council of Refugees and Exiles (ECRE). This represents a network of NGOs that seek to ameliorate the conditions of refugees seeking asylum in the EU. The ECRE seeks "to promote the protection and integration of refugees in Europe based on the values of human dignity, human rights, and an ethic of solidarity" by pursuing three main objectives:

- advocating a humane and generous European asylum policy and promoting the development of a comprehensive and coherent response by the international community to refugee movements
- strengthening networking between refugee-assisting non-governmental organizations in Europe
- developing the institutional capacity of refugee-assisting non-governmental organizations in Europe.[70]

Another example of a public interest group is seen in the International Lesbian and Gay Association (ILGA), which is represented in the EU by ILGA-Europe. ILGA's goals are to "work for the equality of lesbians, gay men, bisexual and trans-gendered people and their liberation from all forms of discrimination".[71] These objectives of equality and liberation are pursued through lobbying the EU and member state governments, undertaking forms of protest if necessary, and informing the public. There are two main examples of how ILGA-Europe has lobbied the EU. First, it contributed to EP reports in the 1980s and 1990s to ensure that the concerns of ILGA were reflected[72] and has taken part in various Commission-funded projects in order to better highlight how homosexuality and lesbian visibility was a European issue. Second, the organization "played a significant role in ensuring that the EU Treaty of Amsterdam (i.e. the Amsterdam Treaty) empowers the Union to take appropriate action to combat discrimination based on sexual orientation."[73]

The European Environment Bureau (EEB) is another non-governmental organization that represents 143 members based in 31 countries. Its main purpose is to improve the EU's impact on the environment. As with COPA, annual general meetings provide a mandate for the Executive Committee, which then establishes contact with the EU's main policy makers. Examples of such contacts include an annual meeting with the President of the Commission as well as six-monthly meetings with the country that holds the presidency of the Council. Article 3 of the EEB's Articles of Association, agreed in October 2001, identifies the organization's main objectives as including the protection and conservation of the environment, promotion of environmental research, increasing public awareness of the environment, and making policy recommendations to the EU.[74] With regard to the last point, and in terms of policy-making influence, the literature has emphasized two main points (although specific analysis of EEB's activity in environmental policy making remains weak as much of the literature assumes that environmental policy is led by specific member states who take the lead in pursing environmental reform).[75] First, the main EU-level environment association has been successful in gaining funding through DG Environment, having received over 40,000 EUR in 1995 alone.[76] Second, given this funding, the EEB in particular has carved itself a niche as one of the main lobby groups involved in developing EU-wide environmental regulations. This is reflected in the almost privileged access it has to both the Commission president once a year and to the country holding the presidency of the Council.

Conclusions

This chapter has examined the two broad types of actors potentially involved in EU public policy making. The first set, referred to as the "EU institutional" players, consists of the Council, the Commission, the European Parliament, and the Court of Justice. The second set, referred to as the "EU interest groups", has been categorized along three main dimensions: the economic group (specifically, capital actors), professional groups (such as trade unions and the farm lobby) and public interest groups (such as environmentalists). Before turning to analysis of the different roles each of these actors may have played in the formulation of different EU policies, the next chapter offers different theoretical explanations of public policy formulation and considers how the actors discussed in this chapter fit into them.

3 Understanding EU policy making: major theories and new insights

The aim of this chapter is to illustrate the main theoretical perspectives used in this book in order to explain policy formulation at both the initiation stage and the negotiation stage. These perspectives are rooted in theoretical frameworks established in the literature of comparative politics of industrialized states, as seen in works of those such as Alford and Friedland,[1] and in the literature on EU politics. The five main perspectives that are considered are: supranational governance, intergovernmentalism, pluralism, corporatism and the dominant economic class perspective.

In order to set up our analysis of the first two perspectives, which we argue are of particular value in understanding policy initiation, we start the chapter with a reflection on the concept of *institutionalism* as seen in the works of those such as Evans, Rueshemeyer and Skocpol.[2] We highlight how supranational governance and intergovernmentalism can be placed within the institutionalist tradition. *Supranational governance* theory broadly argues that EU institutions – particularly the Commission – play a determining role in autonomously initiating and making policies on the basis of their own interests. One may contend that the second theoretical strand, *intergovernmentalism*, shares some ideas with supranational governance, but is distinguishable because it focusses more closely on the actions of one of the EU institutions – the Council – and the actions of national actors per se. Based on works of those such as Moravcsik,[3] this perspective suggests that policy making is specifically driven solely by the interests and actions of European Union member states as represented in the Council of Ministers. We argue that understanding these concepts provides us with the theoretical tools needed to comprehend, first, why actors from either the supranational or national institutional level may initiate the policy-making processes and, second, which policies are more like to be taken up by which institutions and why.

Following analysis of both supranational governance and inter-governmentalism, the reader can turn to our examination of the three other major theoretical perspectives: pluralism, corporatism and DEC theory. We argue that these perspective that outline different methods of interest intermediation may be of further value when considering developments after policy initiation has taken place, or during the policy negotiation stage. The *pluralist* perspective, which is based on the work of Dahl,[4] argues that specific interest groups having roughly equal access to the policy-making process all have the ability to influence policy making. The *corporatist* perspective, as seen in Schmitter and Lembruch's work,[5] argues that specific interests – namely capital and labour – enjoy a monopoly of representation and together with the state formulate public policy. The *dominant economic class* (DEC) view, which represents a new perspective developed in this book for the study of European integration and which is based on writings by neo-Marxist scholars, suggests that economic élites can directly or indirectly exert disproportionate influence on policy making to the exclusion of other social interests such as organized labour. The chapter concludes by examining how all five of the perspectives will inform the analysis of the subsequent empirical chapters that follow.

Institutionalism: an overview

The core argument of institutionalism is that political institutions matter in determining political behaviour.[6] They influence the structure of political discourses and processes, set the agenda, provide information, and influence their actors' preferences and identities. In short, they set the rules of the game.[7] As Stone Sweet *et al* put it, "an institution is a complex of rules and procedures that governs a given set of human interactions."[8] Further, organizations arising from particular institutions develop their own interests and try to establish rules that favour an expansion of their power and interests. Thus, institutions are not static actors as oftentimes assumed by the behaviouralists: at times, they may shape political processes. As Peterson and Shackleton state "they determine political, economic, and legal outcomes in ways that are often crucial."[9]

Although institutionalism has developed several different variants in the comparative politics literature – almost to the extent that one may be left with the impression that almost everything in politics constitutes an institution – one may argue that there are three important strands found within the tradition of "new institutionalism"[10]: historical institutionalism,[11] sociological institutionalism[12] and rational choice institutionalism.[13] The first type assumes that individuals have historically used institutions in a rational and a cultural way. On the one hand, individuals are utility-maximizers, and on the other, individuals see institutions as being representative of symbols and of stability. Interestingly, historical institutionalism regards institutions as being "unjust" in terms of giving differentiated access to different groups seeking to participate in decision making. Yet, the strand does recognize that institutions are not the only important factor within the political process by pointing to the salience of both societal developments and beliefs.[14]

Sociological institutionalism focusses more precisely on the impact of culture on the characteristics of institutions in terms of treaties, procedures and bureaucratic practices.[15] Future political developments and outcomes are in some senses already predictable because they are placed in a type of "cultural context" even before they are conceived. Moreover, sociological institutionalism assumes that institutions help create images and identities of individuals engaged within the institutions.[16]

Collective action dilemmas are what characterize rational choice institutionalism. Although actors are considered to be rational, instrumental and utility-maximizing, their interactions are structured by institutions which govern appropriate and alternative interactions between actors.[17] They also provide the information needed to minimize uncertainty, thereby allowing policy outcomes to be reflective of each actor's preferences. Furthermore, rational choice institutionalists assume that institutions are created in order to increase benefits for all involved in the policy-making process.[18]

For students of EU politics, the approaches within institutionalism are valuable on two grounds. First, they can help us better understand the importance of supranational institutions and how one can characterize those that have their basis in domestic level politics. Second, ideas from institutionalism can help us better explain how political actors use both supranational and national institutions in order to initiate policy processes. We thus turn to a more complete discussion of supranational governance, which highlights the importance of EU institutions in policy making, and the intergovernmentalist perspective, which underlines the importance of domestic ones. Analysis of institutional developments at both levels of governance can be used to understand the policy formulation process in general, and policy initiation in particular.

Supranational governance: the non-state-centric perspective

What does supranational governance mean? Initial insight into this question can be found by highlighting the development of EU-institutions using the theory of neo-functionalism. Neo-functionalism as discussed by authors such as Haas[19] first argues that nation states are forced to enter into relationships with others in order to gain economic benefits, which are presumably no longer confined within state borders. This leads to the development of supranational institutions. Once these larger, regional-level institutions are established by national governments, they start to act independently. Such institutions are then able to become influential as "the emergence of governance beyond the state has been a response to the inability of traditional formal state institutions to manage the size and complexity of the regulatory tasks facing them."[20] The hypothesis of neo-functionalists is that supranational institutions will expand authority and competence through what is referred to as a "spillover" process, whereas national governments will inevitably lose power. Through the so-called "spillover" effect, supranational actors will try to expand their power to fields other than economic. Neo-functionalists argue that the advantages of a supranational institution gaining more power are both efficiency and political autonomy. Thus, the main idea here is that once European institutions have been given a significant role in the policy process in economic matters, power may be extended in other policy areas: gaining an important role and expanding it will shape the direction in which the future European integration process will be conducted.

Guided by these ideas, authors such as Sandholtz and Stone Sweet[21] have developed what is commonly referred to as the "supranational governance" perspective (often also referred to as supranationalism) in order to understand EU decision making. In order to explain EU policy making, we should also focus on developments in some of the EU institutions discussed in Chapter 2, particularly the European Commission, as well as the European Parliament and the ECJ. In their view, supranational institutions have played decisive roles in constructing the EU and are the central forces for further integration, exerting a major influence on future integration steps. As discussed by Stone Sweet and Sandholtz, supranational institutions influence "state thinking and preference formation".[22] From this perspective, one may argue that policies at the European level are not the products of member states' interests and bargaining, as argued by intergovernmentalists (as discussed below). Rather, they are a consequence of dynamics within supranational institutions such as the European Commission. According to the literature, there are two major reasons why supranational institutions are becoming increasingly emancipated.[23] First, they are becoming the central source of information, resulting in an advantage over national actors. Second, they possess advanced technical expertise in the policy fields transferred from the national level, thus allowing them to shape a policy's development as desired.

Given these dynamics, EU-institutions can thus pursue "a political process of collective problem solving"[24] and establish themselves as the centre of supranational governance, where the term "governance" includes the initiation and negotiation of policy processes.[25] From this vantage, supranational governance suggests that problems can be identified, formulated and solved only within EU-institutions, thereby relegating the role of national authorities in the policy process. In a similar vein to arguments found in neo-functionalism, Armstrong and Bulmer[26] also argue that as policy responsibilities increase over time, supranational institutions will attempt to deepen European integration. Hence, we can find the same principles as seen in the description of "spillover" effects: after the first steps of integration are taken, the newly created institutions at the supranational level will seek to advance their power position and further deepen the integration process.

In sum: supranational governance (or supranationalism) views EU decision making as embedded in the processes that are provoked, sustained and directed by the pro-integration activities of supranational organizations and the growing density of supranational rules; the actions of national governments are of secondary importance. In other words, policy processes are mainly initiated by supranational institutions that, convinced that they have better problem-solving capacities than national institutions with regard to transnational problems and concerns, are also interested in expanding their regulatory power. In this view, nation states have lost their power in terms of being able to shape regional integration policies that affect citizens: as Puchala puts it "transformations in intra-European international relations primarily are driven by the influences of supranational agents responding to demands from transnational society."[27]

Intergovernmental governance: the state-centric perspective

One may argue that by focussing on the importance of a specific EU institution, namely the Council of Ministers, the intergovernmentalist perspective falls within the institutionalist perspective: one can legitimately situate intergovernmentalism as a part of the broader institutionalist framework because the term has been applied in the literature to explain the creation and the functioning of institutions within the European integration process.[28] Furthermore, liberal intergovernmentalism, which serves as a foundation for the concept of intergovernmentalism used in this book, extends an earlier approach termed "intergovernmental institutionalism".[29]

What is meant by the term intergovernmentalism? Based on works of those such as Moravcsik[30], this perspective suggests that policy making is driven solely by the interests and actions of the Members of the Council of Ministers, who represent the goals of each of the EU's member states, as discussed in Chapter 2. The result is that other supranational institutions, such as the European Commission, ECJ, and the EP, have little influence when EU policy is made. Intergovernmentalism assumes that national institutions dominate and structure political debates in general, and policy processes in particular, resulting in national interests shaping all goals pursued at the supranational level. National institutions aggregate the diverse interests found at the national level and any deepening of the integration process is based on agreements among nation states. An example of diverse interests may include those of economic actors at the domestic level. However, such actors do not unilaterally attempt to influence policy per se. Rather, their participation is of secondary importance to the policy process when compared with the interests of national political actors. Moreover, as Verdun argues in a critique of Moravcsik's work in particular:

in his analysis [economic interests] can only affect national government interests and preference formation, but do not affect preference formation at the EU level. Also, he does not see any independent influence on the process from any other societal actor other than national governments.[31]

From this perspective, the process of integration is itself a function of the actions and desires of political actors at the member state level and the European Union simply constitutes an institution where state interests are coordinated.[32] Member states have to be assured that further cooperation benefits them; they must have similar or identical interests, particularly economic ones; and they must be convinced that acting together results in more efficient policy-making processes.

Intergovernmentalists argue that the European integration process will evolve only if national preferences converge and only if compromises are made between member states. National institutions first define their preferences or set of interests at the domestic level: national political and economic interests are the first factors to be evaluated before considering further integration steps. Only after deliberation at the domestic level will domestic actors engage in a bargaining process with other national governments. Given this dynamic, authors such as Hoffmann[33] have viewed integration as being only possible in technical functional sectors (or what can be referred to as "low politics"), leaving significant areas such as security and defence (issue areas that can be considered "high politics") outside the scope of meaningful integration.

Hence, in contrast to the supranational governance perspective, intergovernmentalism argues that nation states only cooperate on the basis of self-interest, without giving up sovereignty, and with the goal of increasing "policy making" efficiency: they do not aim to establish a supranational level of governance per se. From this perspective, supranational institutions are only agencies responding to national institutions and executing national interests. Supranational institutions themselves possess only marginal influence as the main power resides in national institutions, so that the European integration process remains solely a "national affair". Also EU policy processes themselves are reminiscent of a type of interplay between national institutions that meet at the supranational level in the form of the Council of Ministers. The Council of Ministers was thus established to enhance bargaining efficiency and helps to improve cooperation, including establishing decision-making procedures that accelerate policy agreement between states while reducing the cost of monitoring compliance with such policies.

Authors such as Hoffmann do recognize that other political institutions, such as supranational ones, may exercise some influence in the political process. However, nation states may either turn hostile towards such institutions, or factor them out of decision-making processes if that is good for their political future. An example may be seen when it is in a government's interest to give the impression that national governments alone brokered a compromise, without the participation of EU institutions such as the Commission, in order to maximize its vote in an upcoming election. Member states' ability to exercise such autonomy ensures that the political focus will never shift away from the domestic venue. Moreover, in contrast to supranational institutions, national ones have legal sovereignty and political legitimacy and, when important decisions are made, may seek to turn to the electorate for approval. As such, any decision for or against the deepening of the European integration process has to be made to appear as "democratic" as possible.

In sum: intergovernmentalism argues that developments at the EU level can be explained as stemming from the effort, the work and the interaction of member states on an intergovernmental basis. Intergovernmentalists reject the supranational governance assumption that European integration is being driven and constructed by supranational institutions. Rather, European integration has been on the agenda because of the actions of member states and their national demands. As such, member states hold the main bargaining power to formulate EU policies and decide on the nature of European integration.

Taken together, both the supranationalist and intergovernmentalist perspectives suggest that in order to comprehend the European policy processes, one "must understand the institutional environment in which power operates".[34] In other words, it is crucial to capture whether policy processes are mainly initiated by either national or supranational institutions, because the institutional level structures the policy processes while assigning importance, influence and power to actors who may potentially gain a privileged position over others in the policy-making processes. Considering these two theoretical perspectives, and keeping in mind our previous discussion of the "initiation" phase of policy formulation, our empirical chapters following this chapter will seek to better understand the kinds of institutions that actively initiate and govern this stage of the policy process. The main question to be considered is: do supranational institutions, in particular the European Commission, or intergovernmentalist ones, in particular the Council of Ministers, initiate policy? In the supranational governance view, institutions such as the Commission will try to initiate and govern the policy-making process at the European level while minimizing the potential influence of national institutions. According to the intergovernmental governance theory, national institutions will seek to play a dominant role in this stage of the policy process, using supranational institutions as tools to achieve desired ends: the Council of Ministers will delegate power to the Commission in the policy-making process only after the process has been initiated by the Council.

Regardless of the dynamics involved during policy initiation, the dynamics surrounding policy negotiation may witness other, non-institutional, actors playing a dominant role. Such actors may be reflective of specific interest groups that seek to influence policy to achieve their own goals. Thus, we turn to discussion of different theoretical perspectives that capture the influence of these types of actors in the policy process.

Theories of interest intermediation: an overview

Whether supranational or domestic in their nature, EU institutions may be amenable to various forms of policy negotiation. As mentioned by different authors, such as March and Olsen as well as Bulmer,[35] institutions are not necessarily neutral and may offer greater access to policy making to some political, economic and social actors with particular interests than to others. Thus, depending on the openness of the institutions, an interest group may or may not be allowed to influence policy either exclusively or alongside a plurality of other interests. In other words, supranational or national actors within governing institutions may decide whether or not to engage in consultation, and which interest groups may be consulted in the policy process.

There are many theories in the comparative politics literature that seek to capture the role of interest groups in EU politics (as discussed in Chapter 2) when policy negotiation takes place. Authors writing on the EU, such as Hix[36], identify three main theories of interest intermediation at play in the European integration process: pluralism, corporatism and consociationalism. Pluralism, as discussed in more detail below, argues that freely emerging interest groups have open and equal access to influence the EU policy-making process. In the classical pluralists' view, there are no constraints that might prevent actors from participating. Corporatism, as seen in the work of Greenwood *et al*[37] and Falkner[38], argues that specific interests – particularly capital and labour – enjoy a monopoly of representation, having fixed positions in EU policy making. Consociationalism is similar to corporatism, but argues that the representation of groups participating in the policy-making process is based on differences of religion, languages and culture.

One may argue that there are two main shortcomings in applying any of these models in order to better understand policy negotiation in the EU. First, although pluralism and corporatism may be useful in helping understand the formation of different policies (as discussed in more detail below), one can almost dismiss the consociationalist perspective from the beginning. In more detail, the plethora of different religious and linguistic groups in the EU makes it unlikely that this method of interest intermediation is of serious importance. While the consociationalist perspective has been of value in examining policy making at the domestic level of EU states such as Belgium,[39] the dynamics found within the model have not been observed in any policy area at the EU-level. Given this conclusion, the consociationalist model will not be dealt with here, though this chapter will further illustrate the significance of ideas raised in the pluralist and corporatist schools that will then be tested throughout the book in the analysis of the policy negotiation phase of each of the policies examined.

A second shortcoming is the implicit assumption in these models that opposing or diametrically conflicting interests are regularly admitted into the EU policy process. For example, the classical model of pluralism assumes that all potentially opposed groups can participate in the process, while corporatism divides society into two opposing groups that are guaranteed representation, and consociationalism suggests that no specific cultural group can gain a monopoly of representation. However, there are other theoretical models that better capture those policy processes where one private interest seems to have a privileged position in the policy process while other opposing groups with equally vested interests are systematically denied a policy role. As such, it is necessary to consider ideas raised by neo-Marxist scholars that lead to what we denominate as the "dominant economic class" (DEC) perspective in understanding how public policy is made. The ideas in this perspective point to the specific, unhindered policy influence of certain economic interests (or capital actors). Before elaborating on the ideas put forward by neo-Marxists, it is first necessary to offer a more detailed analysis of how pluralist and corporatist theories explain the negotiation of public policy.

The pluralist perspective

The pluralist perspective, as seen first in the work of Dahl,[40] argues that all groups with a vested interest in a policy area will be able to gain access to the policy-making process and therefore will have an equal opportunity to influence the policy's development. Schmitter defines pluralism as:

> a system of interest representation in which the constituent units are organized into an unspecified number of multiple, voluntary, competitive, non-hierarchically ordered and self-determined categories which are not specially licensed, recognized, subsidized, created or otherwise controlled in leadership selection or interest articulation by the state, and which do not exercise a monopoly of representational activity within their respective categories.[41]

The idea here is that lobby/interest groups represent a type of "counterbalance" to the state and, perhaps more importantly, to other interest groups seeking to influence policy negotiation. All different interests within society will be represented in an ideal pluralist world, thereby preventing any single interest from dominating the political process. Examples of different interest groups, as seen in Chapter 2, may include economic, professional and public interest groups. Pluralists argue that as the state and its functions become more complex, the number of interest groups that seek to influence policy makers will also concomitantly increase.[42] In a pluralist society, the state's role is ideally to evaluate the various arguments put forward by different, oftentimes competing, interest groups. Authors have suggested that this method of organizing opposing interests leads to a type of "social equilibrium" in the sense that all interest groups have roughly equal power in the process and no group is systematically excluded from important decisions. The model of "countervailing power" that subsequently ensues, as discussed by Galbraith,[43] leads automatically to a system of "checks and balances", ensuring fair procedure in policy processes. Galbraith argues that the emergence of interest groups helps create others: whenever a group representing a particular set of interests arises, this automatically leads to the creation of a group representing the opposite set of interests. Countervailing powers will prevent one set of interest groups from growing too big, thereby ensuring that weaker groups will be involved in the policy-making process. Such dynamics will lead to an approximately equal access to the policy-making process.

Key to the concept of pluralism is that of polyarchy, which literally stands for "many powers". As visualized in Figure 3.1, the negotiation of public policy "X" can see the political participation of several interest groups that have a specific interest in the policy in question, in this case, groups A, B, C, and D.

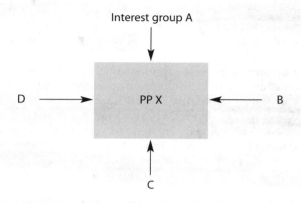

Figure 3.1 Conceptualizing polyarchy

Figure 3.2 offers a more detailed, hypothetical example of a policy related to the environment: here one may see, for example, the policy participation of industrialists, trade unions, environmental groups and perhaps even farmers, all of whom have vested interests in influencing the policy so that its final outcome is reflective of their desires.

Although there may be numerous lobby groups with potential access to and voice in the overall policy-making process, Figure 3.2 suggests that it is reasonable to expect that only groups which have a vested interest in a specific policy area will participate in the specific policy process. In turn, no one single interest will ever dominate. In other words, interest groups will focus their resources and expertise on issues that they are familiar with and that are of major importance to them.

Pluralism also argues that interest groups may seek to participate in the formulation of more than one public policy, though not all will necessarily do so. These two ideas can be seen when one compares Figure 3.2 with Figure 3.3 (overleaf) which identifies the potential actors involved when another public policy, in this case immigration, is negotiated.

Comparing Figures 3.2 and 3.3, one can see that two main interest groups in both examples – capital actors and trade unionists – may have vested reasons for seeking participation in both environmental and immigration policy. Capital actors may seek to influence, for example, the amounts of emissions allowed under environmental standards while also seeking to influence the types of regulations surrounding immigration since the supply of immigrant workers may have an important economic impact on business. Similarly, trade unionists may

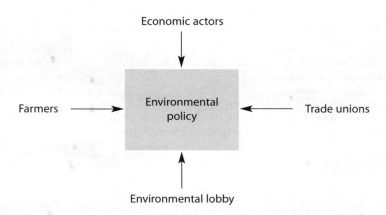

Figure 3.2 Hypothetical example of interest groups involved in environmental policy making

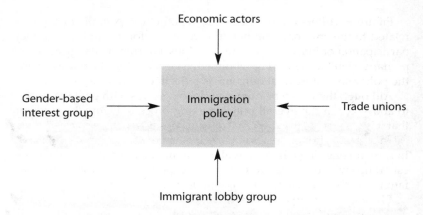

Figure 3.3 Hypothetical example of interest groups involved in immigration policy making

seek to influence both the environmental conditions within which workers work and regulations surrounding immigration that may have a long-term impact on the labour market. Comparison of Figures 3.2 and 3.3 also shows that some groups with specific interests in one policy area may not necessarily seek to influence developments in another area. This is seen in the case of environmental and farming pressure groups, who are not likely to try to influence immigration policy development but will seek to influence environmental policy, an issue about which they are more concerned. And in the case of interest groups related to immigration and gender, they may seek to participate in the negotiation of immigration policies, but seek no role when environmental policy is on the agenda. One may argue that one of the main rationales behind this type of behaviour is based not only on interests per se, but also on maximizing resource allocations: it may be too costly for gender-based interest groups to lobby for or against environmental issues even if they have some concerns in the area.

The institutional setting within which policy negotiation occurs affects the influence and impact of interest groups during policy negotiation. Pluralists' claim that there are essentially three types of institutional settings. First, institutions can be ideally neutral, attempting to reach a compromise between divergent interests and act fairly, or as intermediaries, between different groups. Second, institutions may be "ciphers" which only respond to the pressure of interest groups and can be easily biased by the strongest player. And third, there are agent-driven institutions with their own autonomous interests, simply using interest groups for their own purposes. Different theoretical views within pluralism argue that the outcome of any policy process may be partially a consequence of past lobby group influence which may have occurred in the context of different institutional settings. Thus, where particular specific interest groups have been able to dominate one policy process, it may be easier for them to influence future processes.

It is important to note that pluralist theorists saw shortcomings in their original model over time. As a consequence, "neo-pluralism" developed as a modified theory. The observation made by neo-pluralists was that in the non-ideal world, there is no such thing as perfect pluralism which would lead to a neutral role of the state. Rather, economically more powerful private interests will turn out to be dominant, further preventing equal access to the policy-making process. As such, neo-pluralism finds its basis in a different approach in economics which Dunleavy and O'Leary call "unorthodox economics".[44] Instead of acting in completely free market operations, economic actors nowadays are confronted by hierarchies which have their own rules and internalized decision procedures. Hence, they operate in a "non-free-market" environment, mainly because of factors such as market uncertainty, restriction of opportunities to only a few actors, and monopoly of information. Thus, modifying the "ideal" pluralist model by taking into account the actual dynamics of real-world economic conditions led neo-pluralists to argue that some big businesses and corporations have secured disproportionately advantageous policy-making positions. Neo-pluralists also accept that in electoral terms governments are to a certain extent dependent on the economic activity of big businesses. Governments have thus learnt to deal with the so-called "superiority" and power of corporations over political actors by adapting policies to the needs of economic actors.

However, neo-pluralists such as Lindblom[45] argue that this "power" advantage held by corporations in the policy process, should be seen as an anomaly, or something that can be reversed. In other words, if big businesses does exercise a greater influence in policy making, then the state should adopt strategies that would allow all interest groups to attain equal access once again in order to rectify what can be defined as a type of "deformed" or "corrupted" pluralism which has its foundations in the increasing abuse of power by corporations. One initiative, for example, would be to have a proactive state that determines which interests can participate in specific policy areas. Another initiative is to assign the government not only greater effective monitoring powers, but also more dynamic powers in shaping the policy agenda.

From this perspective, the main elements of the pluralist model are still assumed to be valid by neo-pluralist scholars: every private interest has the potential to participate in the policy process. If such an opportunity does not exist at the moment, as highlighted by neo-pluralists, it is the consequence of an anomaly which can be reversed. As we will see later in the chapter, ideas raised by neo-pluralists do, to some extent, overlap with those raised by instrumental Marxists that are important in understanding the dominant economic class perspective. The main difference, however, is that instrumental Marxists suggest that inequality of power between interest groups in society – something which in their view is clearly derived from the economic system within which the political one operates – is hardly something which can be seen as either an anomaly or reversible. Before analysing in more detail the ideas put forward by neo-Marxist scholars, we will turn our attention to the second main model of interest intermediation, namely, corporatism.

Corporatism

Schmitter has defined corporatism as "a mode of policy formation in which formally designated interest associations are incorporated within the process of authoritative decision-making and implementation".[46] In the original work done on corporatism, the "formally designated interest associations" referred to both employer associations and labour organizations which, along with the state, had semi-institutionalized policy-making roles and formulated policy together. The justification for these two groups, in particular, enjoying this privileged position was the idea that policy-making representation should be grounded in the economic relations in society. Given that society can be seen as divided between those who work and those who own the means of production, both sets of actors should be represented equally when decisions are made. From this perspective, the number of organizations involved in policy making is limited when compared with pluralism since certain interest groups enjoy fixed positions. Crouch and Menon[47] argue that not only do these specific interests enjoy a monopoly of representation in corporatist systems, but also the organizations themselves have a hierarchical structure and impose discipline: "if members are to be disciplined by their representative organizations, it is important that they do not have alternative organizations to choose from."

The comparative literature focussing on developments in Austria, Scandinavia and Germany has argued that the corporatist model has been historically characteristic of developments in these states since the 1940s and 1950s, while other authors have pointed to the model's relevance when analysing developments in countries going through democratic transition such as Spain in the 1970s. With regard to Germany and Austria, Crouch and Menon argue that "the growth of the modern state (originally) took the form of an association between the state and certain producer interests"[48] where the period after the Second World War saw the incorporation of employee interests. Scandinavian corporatism arose somewhat differently, from the "the pressure of very strong employer and employee interests that during the interwar years had been locked in bitter conflict".[49] Scharpf's[50] work shows how both groups sought to cooperate and formulate a coordinated economic policy in order to prevent the small Scandinavian economies from deterioration after the war. With regard to Spain, authors such as Perez Diaz[51] have pointed to the importance of the negotiated pacts between the state, business and labour during the transition to democracy after Franco.

A more recent example of corporatism has been seen in Ireland in the 1980s and 1990s. Hardiman argues that the Irish "national agreements" arrived at by the social partners during the 1980s served as the foundations for economic growth, expansion of employment, and higher living standards throughout the 1990s and into the 2000s.[52] Developing ideas raised in the original work on corporatism, Hardiman argues that social partnership since the late 1980s has been more inclusive in its membership. In her words, it "refers to a process of consultation between government and the principal organizations representing employers, trade unions and the farmers."[53] Hardiman contends that "the construction of the new institutions and practices of social partnership may ... be attributed primarily to the intense economic crisis faced by the country in the mid-1980s"[54] as well as the will of the political leadership at this conjuncture. Taylor similarly suggests that this macro-political bargaining structure proved an effective channel for change and the resolution of potential trade union conflict.[55] Although he later suggests that the nature of such agreements was increasingly influenced by neo-liberal ideology, he underlines the pacts' importance by stating that "national agreements have framed [Irish] public policy over the last decade."[56]

With these and other countries' experiences in mind, different authors have theoretically characterized different types of corporatism, although there has been some debate in the literature regarding the usefulness of the concept, given the potentially different meanings assigned to it.[57] For example, authors such as Schmitter have distinguished between two main forms of corporatism. The first is "state corporatism", where the state is in control of negotiations and is generally deemed to be authoritarian and anti-liberal. A second type is referred to as "societal corporatism". This is found in states with a history of pluralism. Societal corporatism is a process that emerges because changes in the economic system lead the government to pursue semi-institutionalized bargaining with political associations. Another variant on the theme, based on the work of Hardimann,[58] is that of the "competitive corporatist" model, which is "premised on acceptance of employer concerns about competitiveness and flexibility".

In summary, in contrast to the pluralist model, corporatism argues that a fixed number of interest groups who enjoy a monopoly of representation are involved in policy making. Yet, in contrast to neo-Marxist scholars, as will be discussed in the next section, there is an assumption that labour organizations will be "on a par" with business élites in the policy-making process. That is, there is an assumption that business cannot gain the upper hand over labour. With this idea in mind, we turn to the debate raised by élitist and then Marxist scholars.

The dominant economic class perspective

Perhaps the ideas raised in the pluralist and corporatist perspectives do not tell the whole story. Different theorists, including classical élitists, contemporary élitists and neo-Marxists, who have all analysed developments in national politics in Western states, implicitly or explicitly argue that pluralist ideals in particular are unrealistic because different types of "élites" will play dominant roles when public policies are made. As Lasswell states, "the study of politics is the study of influence and the influential. ... The influential are those who get the most of what there is to get. ... Those who get the most are élite, the rest are mass."[59] From this perspective, the policy process can hardly be seen as either open or transparent, given that certain élites always exercise unconstrained influence over mass publics. Depending on the author within the élitist tradition, these élites may be either political, social or economic. In justifying this book's examination of what is referred to as the dominant economic class (DEC) perspective, we will first consider ideas raised by the classical and contemporary élitist theorists.

Classical and contemporary élitist scholars

Mosca and Michels are considered classical élitist scholars, and writing in the early 1900s both had similar arguments regarding the role of élites in society. Overall, there are three essential points on which they both agree. First, they deny that genuine democracy is possible. Second, even if it were possible, democracy is not desirable. And third, "élites" will always rule. The first two points highlight the "normative" element within the élitist school, as will be most evident when we turn to the work of Schumpeter: there is nothing wrong with élite rule and, in fact, it may be necessary given that mass publics cannot be trusted in making important political decisions.

Turning to the specific arguments outlined by Mosca, he first suggests that there will always be a "ruling class" that dominates and attains benefits.[60] This ruling class consists of a plurality of what he refers to as "social forces" that control land, money, education and religion, and therefore have strong power positions in society. He argues that every ruling class expresses its role and position through a "political formula" that rationalizes or legitimates its rule over the state. A contemporary example may be seen in countries which claim there is a "rule by the people" that holds officials accountable: in Mosca's view, this could be considered a myth used by élites in order to justify their control given that people actually have a psychological need to be ruled.

Writing also in the early 1900s, Michels sought to understand why socialist parties compromise their principles over time.[61] He argued that the abandonment of principles is based on a type of oligarchy that will inevitably emerge in political parties, thereby distancing leaders from party members. Oligarchy is inevitable because leaders become more technocratic given that leading an organization requires knowledge and specialization: in Michels' well-known phrase, "whoever says organization, says oligarchy." As politics in the modern world becomes more and more professionally organized, the technical indispensability of leadership results. This sees the emergence of leaders as autonomous élites who are subsequently not accountable to party members. As leaders distance themselves, grassroots party members therefore become disillusioned. These dynamics result in a situation where political élites guided by technocratic skills rule.

As Mosca and Michels are considered classical élitist theorists, the work of Schumpeter is seen as representative of a more contemporary élitist thesis, given the specific focus on the role of political élites in modern capitalist democracies. Schumpeter argues that a "good democratic system" has political élites who rule: the citizens' role in the political system should be minimal, limited to a simple vote every four or five years.[62] Although one may argue that in a classical democratic system the whole people should make the main determining decisions, in Schumpeter's democratic élitist view it is government officials, not the people, who are responsible for making all decisions. The minimalist role for citizens, complemented by an omnipotent one for governments, is based on Schumpeter's view that people are ignorant, irrational, ill-informed, uninterested, easy to manipulate, and unable to arrive at an informed political will that would identify a common good. As such, political élites should be given autonomy to rule without interference.

C. Wright Mills is another contemporary élitist theorist. Unlike Schumpeter, however, Mills does not hold such negative assumptions about the abilities of citizens to participate in politics and is critical of élite dominance.[63] Examining developments in the United States, he argues that there is a power élite in control of most policy decisions and that the people themselves have little influence. The latter is due to people's isolation in society, which is not of their own doing. Mills argues that the power élite is made up of three main actors, who participate together when the major decisions are made: the high political élite (such as the president), corporations (which include leading businesses) and members of the military. These élites form a cohesive group, given that they interact with each other, come from the same social class, are educated in the same schools, move in the same social circles, and exchange roles with each other (for example, members of the corporate élite can join the political élite over time and vice versa). He contends that the middle level of power, such as legislators who are elected by the people, deals with matters of little importance. Mills further argues that the lowest level of power consists of mass societies which are manipulated by the power élite during elections. Over time, this mass public does not turns to participation in politics, but rather seeks solace in low forms of popular culture, such as television shows. In contrast to other élitist scholars, Mills gives a central concern to this type of "atomization" of society.

Thoughts of neo-Marxists: developing the DEC perspective in explaining integration[64]

Taken together, both classical and contemporary élitist scholars argue that a plurality of élites (as seen in the works of Mosca, Michels and Mills), or high-level political élites alone (as seen in the work of Schumpeter), make the crucial decisions. In contrast to classical and contemporary élitists, however, neo-Marxists argue that neither a plurality of social, economic and political élites, nor solely political élites, make major policies. Rather, economic élites, or capital actors, are the dominant voice in policy making. While there is indeed some overlap with the ideas of the élitists, one may argue that neo-Marxism as seen in the works of Miliband and Poulantzas (discussed in more detail below) can be distinguished from élitist thinking on several grounds.[65] For example, even though neo-Marxists share the same broad ideas as classical élitists about the way specific élites enjoy a predominant role in policy making, neo-Marxists are critical of the idea of élite rule. Moreover, they argue that economic actors have more significant roles than other potential actors. This is because the political system functions within and is constrained by the economic system whose defining social relations it seeks to maintain and reproduce. In other words, one must first recognize that the economic system has a determining influence on how the political system functions. In order to better understand the DEC perspective as denominated in this book, a general theoretical discussion of Marxist ideas on dominance is necessary.

The theoretical background of the Marxist "dominant economic class theory', which serves as the basis for what we refer to in this book as the DEC perspective in policy making, consists of the following claims. All societies throughout history (except for some simple hunter-gatherer societies whose economic resources consist of communally owned tribal lands) have been characterized by a major class divide. This divide is constituted by the existence of a privileged minority who own and control most of the strategic economic resources of the society, while the majority of citizens have no economic resources except their labour power. This majority is compelled by the force of circumstances (and sometimes by literal force, as with slaves) to work for the minority that controls the means of production. The nature of the strategic economic resources, as well as the social structures through which control of such resources are articulated, have varied throughout history. What has not changed, according to Marxists, is the existence of some major class divide in all societies. Marxists do not claim that actual societies are divided into only two classes. In fact, it is often the case that the class structure of a society is complicated by the existence of "intermediary" classes. This intermediary class consists of people who gain their livelihood in a way different from members of the two main classes. Examples in contemporary capitalist societies would be civil servants who work for the state as opposed to a capitalist owner; self-employed workers who usually own their own means of production but do not employ the labour of others; or someone who works for a capitalist personally, such as a chauffer or a cook, but not as someone producing goods that the capitalist may sell at a profit. Marxists claim, however, that the intermediary classes are of secondary importance: the main production and distribution of goods will be characterized by those relations constituting the major class divide.

The minority controlling the strategic economic resources are dominant in at least two senses. On the one hand, in the economic sphere, the economic élite have dominant control over production and distribution: they can and do use their control to ensure that, by and large, they live off the labour of those who produce without themselves having to engage in any significant amount of labour. Marxists refer to this as "exploitation".

On the other hand, and fundamental to our perspective of dominant class, the economic élite are dominant in the political sphere. The definition of the dominant economic class perspective used in this book therefore refers to the following idea: by whatever means, either directly or indirectly, the interests of the dominant economic class shape the nature of public policies. In other words, actual policy outcomes will always reflect the desires of and promote the interests of this dominant class, namely, capital actors. Neo-Marxists accept that other actors can exert a certain amount of power in the shaping of policy, but claim that this power is always of secondary importance, effective only when what gets decided is consistent with capitalist interests.

Some Neo-Marxists, following Ralph Miliband, suggest that economic interests are dominant because they can directly influence policy making, inevitably forcing the exclusion of other social interest groups from the policy-making process.[66] In Miliband's view, the state is an instrument that is used by capitalist actors (hence, he is often referred to as an "instrumental Marxist"). Capitalists not only control economic production, but also have links with powerful institutions, including political parties and the media. Thus, of all the potential private interests that may seek to influence the policy process, economic actors enjoy disproportionate influence in policy making and have decisive political advantages over other social actors such as trade unions. Two main factors ensure that the political system functions in the interest of capital: political interventions by the capitalist class and the fact that policies are largely formulated by an enlightened corporate vanguard. Miliband does not assume that social actors will always be silent, however. Indeed, there may be instances when labour is allowed some (limited) access to policy formulation. However, his main argument is that capitalist economic actors will attain a decisive role in public policy formulation and that policy outcomes will necessarily be biased in capital's favour.

Other neo-Marxist theorists, such as Poulantzas,[67] argue the political dominance of the capitalist class can be best seen as indirect. While Poulantzas agrees with the Miliband's assumption about the "role" of the economic system in terms of its having a determining impact on the functioning of the political system, he contends that direct participation of capital actors is not necessary. In a capitalist system, the state will inevitably act in the interests of capital even without the latter's participation. This is because the state and the political élites who wield state power are structurally dependent on a well-functioning (by definition capitalist) economy. State actors are constrained in the policies they can realistically pursue by this structural dependence: only those policies that are largely compatible with capitalist interests are feasible. In other words, the state realizes class interests without having a class affiliation per se. The "relatively autonomous state" may also make policy against the short-term interests of capital, with the view of ensuring that capital's long-term interests are served.[68]

Leaving the neo-Marxist debates between Miliband and Poulantzas to the side, the significant point of this discussion for the purposes of this book is that the DEC perspective of policy making suggests that economic élites are dominant in the political sphere and public policies are formulated in accordance with their interests. The nature of the capitalist economy and the dominant actors therein has a determining influence on the political system when public policy is made. Quite clearly, when trying to understand how policy is made, it is very difficult to find evidence of the "indirect" influence of the dominant economic class as discussed by authors such as Poulantzas. Nevertheless, and as will be the approach taken in this book, one may argue that the DEC perspective may be manifest if there is evidence of the "direct" influence of capital actors in the formulation of policy. This may include, for example, if representatives of capitalist interests are able to lobby political élites successfully through direct, intentional, political action. In order to gain a better theoretical understanding of where the dominant economic class perspective may be found in the analysis of policies in the following empirical chapters, we turn to the next section.

The explanatory power of theories

This chapter has outlined the five theoretical perspectives that will be used in this book in order to understand EU policy formulation. The first perspective, supranational governance, highlighted the key role played by supranational institutions, in particular the Commission. A second perspective, intergovernmentalism, then outlined the importance of the Council of Ministers in influencing a policy. A third perspective, pluralism, contended that various private interests could equally compete in shaping the policy. The fourth perspective, corporatism, emphasized the essential policy participation of both capital and labour organizations on a semi-formal basis. Finally, the DEC perspective suggested that among all private interests, capitalist economic actors were of paramount importance when policy is negotiated.

As indicated in Chapter 1, the objective of the empirical chapters is to test which of the five perspectives (or combinations thereof) are of value in explaining the formulation of different EU public policies. It is essential to recall at this stage what is meant by policy formulation. We claimed in Chapter 1 that there are two main stages to formulation: the policy initiation stage and the policy negotiation one. It is therefore important to consider how each of these theoretical perspectives can be used in order to understand developments during both stages. We consider two hypotheses in turn.

First, we hypothesize that in order to understand policy initiation, only the two main "institutionalist" perspectives can be of value. This is because policies to be included in the EU agenda can effectively be set only by institutional actors, in particular the Commission and the Council. Private interests have no codified, institutional power to initiate any set of EU directives, rules, regulations or reforms. As such, either supranational governance or intergovernmentalism will be of most relevance in understanding how policy was initiated in each of the policy areas to be examined. For example, if there is evidence that the policy originated in the Council of Ministers, this would suggest that the intergovernmentalist perspective is of value. Alternatively, if the evidence shows that the initiative is based on developments in the Commission, this would point to the importance of supranational governance in explaining policy initiation.

Second, we hypothesize that all five perspectives may be of value in explaining policy negotiation. This is because several different actors may have been involved in this stage. This includes potentially not only the main EU institutional actors, but also a multiplicity of private interest groups involved in interest intermediation. From this point of view, characterization of developments during the second policy stage differs from the first stage because there is the possibility that either the pluralist, the corporatist, or the DEC perspectives are of complementary value in explaining the formulation of a policy.

Given the above, and as argued by Puchala,[69] the view taken in this book is that one theory alone cannot explain how policies develop in the EU. Rather, each policy has to be analysed in detail in order to understand which of the different theories offers the most cogent explanation. A close examination of the policy processes and the actors involved in them provides the basis for establishing which theory best explains each stage of the policy process. As indicated in Chapter 1, the inclusion of a plurality of theoretical perspectives in order to better understand EU public policy formulation transcends the existing literature in two ways. First, it adds further theoretical insights into the role of private interests in the integration process, moving beyond the debate about whether or not the supranational governance and intergovernmentalism perspectives are more important when theorizing about EU integration. Second, it attempts to more fully integrate interest group behaviour with analysis of institutions, while simultaneously being guided by theoretical perspectives from the comparative politics literature. With this in mind, this book does not aim to contribute to the discussion of whether or not the European integration process can best be seen as intergovernmentalist or as a supranational-led enterprise. Rather, we are interested in examining which institutions and actors are involved in the different stages of the policy-making process, analysing how this can be theorized using a plurality of approaches, and showing how this examination may offer insights regarding whether or not such dynamics help explain the existence of "1st and 2nd order policies" in the EU.

With these ideas in mind, the different (theoretical) combinations that may exist are as follows as illustrated in Figure 3.4. The figure indicates that with regard to the first stage of the formulation process – policy initiation – we will seek to answer whether policies have been initiated by national institutions or by supranational ones. If the evidence suggests that the Council of Ministers played a key role in policy initiation, then this would point to the importance of the intergovernmentalist perspective; conversely, if the Commission plays a key role at this stage, then the supranational governance perspective will be deemed of more value. With regard to the second stage, policy negotiation, we will examine which of the potential actors are involved and, depending on which actors are seen as main participants, the stage will be characterized by one of the five main perspectives, or a combination thereof. For example, if the evidence suggests that policy negotiation was led by capitalist actors, such as the ERT, that have actively participated in the negotiation of policy (either at the supranational or domestic levels) this would point to the importance of the DEC perspective; if negotiation occurred between capital, labour and the EU executive, this would suggest the relevance of corporatism; if the policy was negotiated among several competing interest groups that bargained alongside political actors, this would indicate the significance of the pluralist perspective; if the Council alone was the main player in determining the details of the policy, this would suggest that ideas from intergovernmentalism are paramount at the negotiation phase; or, if the Commission alone outlined the policy, the supranational governance perspective will be of value.

Because different actors and institutions may be involved in both policy stages, depending on the policy in question, it is more than likely that we will find different combinations of theoretical perspectives of value in explaining different policies. After analysing developments in the different policy areas over the seven empirical chapters that follow – focussing on single market, competition, EMU, agricultural, social, freedom security and justice and, finally, foreign policies – the concluding chapter will consider whether or not the various combinations of the theoretical perspectives found may help us better understand the development of 1st and 2nd order policies in the EU. For example, does a combination of theoretical perspectives that includes the DEC perspective lead to the development of 1st order policies, whereas one including a pluralist perspective produces 2nd order policies? And, does it matter which theoretical perspective is used to understand policy initiation when assessing whether or not a policy is ultimately 1st or 2nd order in nature? Before we deal with these questions in the concluding chapter, we start the journey to a better understanding of EU policy making by focussing in the next chapter on the development of the European single market.

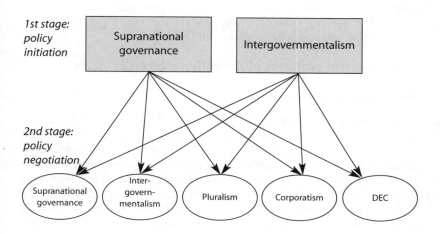

Figure 3.4 Policy formulation processes from different theoretical angles

4 Single market policy: creating a strong neo-liberal market in the global economy

This chapter examines and explains developments in EU single (or internal) market policy. In the first section it examines what are referred to as the four phases of the policy's development since the 1950s and evaluates the evolution of internal market policy in terms of its economic impact over the last 15 years. Through analysis of the different phases of the policy (particularly since the 1992 Programme) as well as the impact of internal market policy on European economic space, this section concludes that internal market policy can be seen as a 1st order policy, consistent with Patricia Hewitt's contention that the policy represents "the major economic success of the EU".[1] In the second section, the chapter offers a more detailed analysis of the formulation of the 1992 Programme, one of the most significant aspects of internal market policy in the EU's history. Dealing with developments starting in 1979, it focusses on the actions of the European Court of Justice, the Commission, economic actors, and the Council. The section concludes that the primary roles of the ECJ, Commission and economic actors are witnessed in the initiation and negotiation of the policy. Notwithstanding arguments raised by intergovernmentalists focussing on single market policy, it is argued that both the supranational governance and dominant economic class (DEC) perspectives are of more value when seeking to theoretically characterize developments in both the initiation and negotiation phases of the policy.

Objectives and evolution of the policy: a 1st order status

Four phases of single market policy

In the words of the European Commission, "The Internal Market is one of the Union's most important and continuing priorities."[2] Through Articles 9 and 49–69 of the EEC Treaty, the four "freedoms" enshrined in the European internal market are the free movement of goods, services, capital and persons. In particular, DG Internal Market is entrusted with keeping the EU's single, integrated market a high priority on the EU's agenda through development, coordination and information: it helps develop and establish legal instruments to ensure free movement in the single market, it helps coordinate internal market policy so as to ensure that there are no obstacles that would debilitate the so-called four freedoms, and it informs businesses and citizens of their rights in the single market area.

While DG Internal Market today holds these responsibilities, it is important to reflect on the differing conjunctures that the internal market has witnessed since the 1950s. One may argue that there have been four main phases in its historical evolution: the establishment of the single market in the 1950s, progress in the 1960s, floundering in the 1970s and early 1980s, and a rejuvenation with the Single Market Programme in the mid 1980s. We will consider each of these stages in turn.

The first phase, beginning in the late 1950s, corresponds to the original decision that established the principles of the single market. In this phase, the original articles of the EEC Treaty (the treaty establishing the European Economic Community) were laid down with the support of the six original member states: Belgium, the Netherlands, Luxembourg, France, West Germany and Italy. Despite the agreement of all member states to establish a single market area in which the four freedoms would be respected, it is important to note George and Bache's observation that "there is little evidence of supranational actors playing a key role in the original decision."[3] Rather, "the initiative was taken ... by the political and administrative élites in small states (such as Benelux) in pursuit of what they perceived as their national interests in being part of a larger economic grouping."[4] The idea here is that smaller states had more to gain than to lose from unrestricted borders. Or, conversely, economic protectionism would inevitably hurt small states which sought to compete economically against the larger ones. This is not to say, however, that larger states such as Germany and France would lose by the establishment in the single market, even though concerns were raised at the time by French industrialists who did not favour an internal market as much as their German counterparts. Rather, exporters from the larger states in particular would not only also have freer access to smaller markets that might have otherwise restricted the entry of a variety of goods and services, but also access to each others' large markets. From this perspective, the establishment of a single market, though spearheaded by smaller states, represented a positive-sum game for all potential actors in the Community, as opposed to a zero-sum (where some would win while others would lose) or a negative-sum game (where all would lose).

The second phase, characteristic of the internal market integration process in the 1960s, witnessed attempts to deepen internal market policy. In 1960, for example, on the insistence of the Commission, the Council of Ministers agreed "to accelerate the original timetable for removing internal tariffs and quotas and erecting a common external tariff".[5] On the one hand, full removal of internal tariffs would allow for the free flow of capital and goods that would benefit economic actors trading within the free-trade area, while on the other, a common external tariff would prevent one member state from setting individual regulations with regard to imports from countries outside the Community.

Yet despite calls for speeding up the integration process in the 1960s, the third phase of the 1970s and early 1980s witnessed a type of "reversal" of the first two phases as nationalist protectionist measures were pursued above single market goals. Both Europe and North America witnessed an economic downturn at this time as a consequence of the OPEC crises in the 1970s.[6] State officials and various economic actors responded to this decline in various sectors by pursuing protectionist measures that had a twofold purpose. On the one hand, political and economic actors sought to preserve the strength of "national champions" – domestic companies with a dominant market position which were usually but not necessarily state-owned – by restricting movement of goods across borders in order to avoid dealing with external competitive forces from other EU states. On the other hand, states sought to consolidate the strength of native capital by giving large amounts of state aid (public subsidies) to favoured companies. This would have the effect of inflating the share capital of some companies and allowing them to maintain their dominant position by making it all but impossible for any competitors to seek entry into domestic markets.

The final phase, reflecting developments since the mid 1980s, saw a significant move to "reverse the reversal" of the third phase with the development of what is referred to as the "1992 Programme". Led by Commissioner Jacques Delors, as discussed in more detail in the next section, new strategies were taken towards freeing the single market, which was suffering in several dimensions, in order to make the European economy globally competitive. For example, customs-related costs of trading products between member states were spiralling and taking a significant portion of companies' profits on intra-EU trade; some estimates placed this cost at close to 25 per cent. Another example was that value added tax (VAT) rates were not harmonized throughout the Community, so that it was less profitable to do business in some states than in others. Yet another example was seen when a number of industries, including automobile production and telecoms, lost heavily because different countries imposed different product standards. Strategies were therefore adopted to minimize these and other costs to businesses, culminating in the "1992 Programme"[7] which has subsequently shaped single market developments over the last 20 years. This programme introduced 279 measures that were aimed at ensuring the free movement of goods, services, capital and labour by removing three main types of barriers – physical, fiscal and technical – related the examples mentioned earlier. Although drafted and approved in the mid 1980s, it was called the "1992" Programme because the end of 1992 was the deadline for the introduction of the 279 measures that were deemed necessary for the completion of the single market.

Physical barriers would be reduced by pursuing directives in the 1992 Programme aimed at ending cross-border checks on goods going between one member state and another. Fiscal barriers were to be eradicated through directives to harmonize VAT rates. And technical barriers would be reduced in four ways. The first, a reaction to the Cassis de Dijon ruling by the ECJ, discussed in more detail below, was to pursue a minimalist approach to harmonization and mutual recognition of goods produced throughout the Community. Second, barriers to the free movement of capital would be dealt with though "three directives covering cross border security transactions, commercial loans and access to stock exchanges".[8] Third, in order to encourage a competitive environment when states award contracts to companies, EU public procurement policy was developed in the 1992 Programme in order to ensure such an environment prevailed in different EU member states.[9] Fourth, free movement of labour was to be encouraged through new directives guaranteeing residence rights for all EU citizens in all member states.[10]

In December 1985, the 1992 Programme and new decision-making procedures for the Council[11] were accepted by the Council in the Single European Act, which took effect the next year. By 1992, over 95 per cent of the single market directives had been accepted by the member states, helping to create a competitive environment in which capital could thrive.[12] As one observer has noted:

> The internal market is one of the EU's most important achievements: an economic area in which [there are] ... greater opportunities for producers and consumers. ... [It] fostered economic integration between European regions and ensured higher levels of growth and cohesion.[13]

Measuring the success of the single market

This "success" of the single market programme is reflected in time-series data which track the evolution of the internal market in terms of member states compliance with EU initiatives, increased trade between member states, increased cross-border investment by EU states, increased trade with global giants and increased integration of the European economy into the global market.

Turning to the first of these indicators, one of the main issues concerning implementation of the 1992 Programme related to transposition of legislation. In the words of the Commission in the ten-year report on the functioning of the internal market, "Sometimes, member states do not implement on time the EU [Internal Market] Directives which they themselves have agreed."[14] However, analysis of the data in Figure 4.1 shows

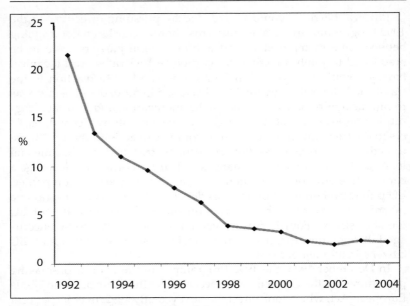

Figure 4.1 Average EU transposition deficit

Source: Eurostat.
Note: Yearly data represent the average of the transposition deficit data recorded in both May and November by the European Commission, except for 2004 where only June data is used.

that, while there was a large transposition deficit in the early years after the 1992 deadline for completion of the internal market, this problem has decreased substantially over the 15-year period.

Figure 4.1 indicates that even though in November 1992 as many as 20 per cent of all EU internal market laws were not being implemented, the rate fell to approximately a tenth of this by November 2002. Part of this reduction is due to the fact that in 1997 DG Internal Market established what were referred to as "scoreboards". These highlighted which member states were (or were not) complying with EU regulations, an intended consequence being to "shame" member states who were not compliant.

Turning to increased trade within the Community, Figure 4.2 shows that as states have increasingly applied single market directives, intra-EU trade has increased substantially, almost doubling in value between 1993 and 2003.[15] This suggests that as the single market has become more integrated and competitive, a process enhanced by the 1999 adoption of the single currency discussed in Chapter 6, the volume of its trade has increased dramatically and has resulted in a stronger European economy.

The growth of this single market has made Europe a leading world power in the global economy. Although the single market comprising the

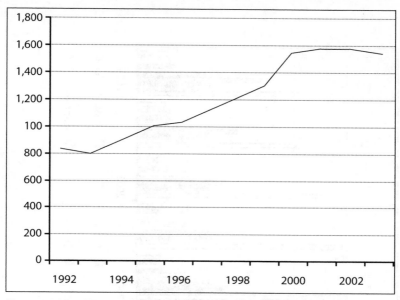

Figure 4.2 Intra EU-15 trade total product (€1,000 million)

Source: Eurostat.

EU-25 represents only about 7 per cent of the world's population, the EU economies accounted for almost 20 per cent of world trade in 2005 (18.4 per cent of world trade in goods and 27 per cent of services). As such, by 2005 the EU was the world's biggest exporter and second-biggest importer.[16]

In order to discern recent trading trends and identify the main trading partners of this unified Europe, Figure 4.3 (next page) identifies the top ten countries from which the EU imports goods and services. From an analysis of the data over a ten-year period between 1994 and 2004, several observations can be made. First, the highest amount of imports came consistently from the United States. However, it is interesting to note that imports started to fall slightly after 2000 and reached their lowest point in 2003. This may have been a consequence of the strained relations between the EU and the United States during the Iraq War, but also reflects the increasing strength of the China and Russia in the world economy, strengths into which the EU market seeks to tap. For several years, Japan was the second-largest exporter to the EU, but from 2002 it was relegated to third place as imports from China surged ahead. By 2004, Chinese imports had increased five times from their value in 1994, reflecting a steady positive growth throughout the period.[17] Other major exporters to the EU are the Russian Federation and Switzerland. Switzerland, which had been the third largest in 1994,

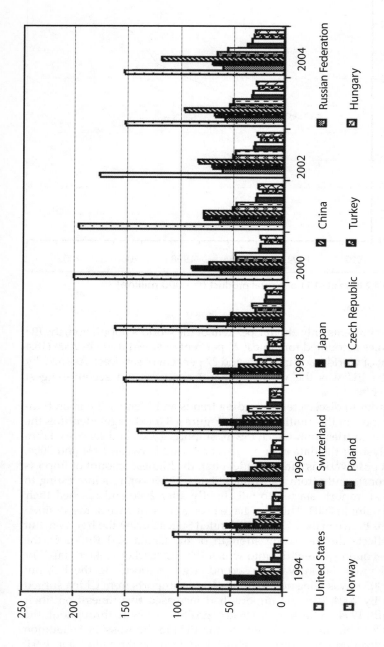

Figure 4.3 Imports to EU-15, 1994–2004 (€1000 million)
Source: Eurostat.

Legend:
- United States
- Switzerland
- Japan
- China
- Russian Federation
- Norway
- Poland
- Czech Republic
- Turkey
- Hungary

had fallen to fifth position by 2004 due to the increasing strength of the Russian Federation. This demonstrates Russia's ability to continue to integrate its economy with the EU as more central and eastern European states joined the enlarging Union.

Figure 4.4 shows EU exports from the EU-15; an overlap in terms of the main trading partners previously seen in Figure 4.3 can be clearly observed. As in Figure 4.3, one sees in Figure 4.4 that the largest export market within the world economy is the United States throughout the time series, even though 2003 and 2004 see a slight slowing down compared with the levels between 2000 and 2002. In contrast to Figure 4.3, which showed that Switzerland's position as an exporter had declined, this country maintains the rank of second-largest trading partner in terms of imports from the EU throughout the period. Between 1994 and 2002, Japan was ranked third, but from 2003 onwards the third place was taken by China, reflecting the trend seen in Figure 4.3. In terms of trading figures, however, one notices that a comparison of data from Figures 4.3 and 4.4 shows that the Chinese sell more to the EU than the EU exports to China, and this negative external balance of goods and services has been most acute since 2000. Turkey has become an export market of increasing importance, moving from ninth place in 1994 to seventh place in 2004.

In terms of the goods that are traded in the global economy, the most significant imports into the EU since 1997 have been machinery and transport equipment (which constituted 40.66 per cent of imports in 2004[18]), followed by other manufactured goods (25.66 per cent in 2004). Mineral fuels, lubricants and related materials have been the third-largest imports (18.1 per cent), followed by chemicals and related products (9.23 per cent) and food and drink products (6.32 per cent). Similar trends are seen for exports: the largest exports are machinery (44.67 per cent of all exports in 2004), followed by other manufactured good (32.2 per cent), chemicals (15.32 per cent), food, drink and tobacco (4.75 per cent), and mineral fuels (3.02 per cent).

Given the increased trade within and volume of the single market, coupled with the ability of the European single market to place itself in a strong position within the world economy by continuing to deal with major international players, it is no great surprise that the actual investment flows of the EU-15 have also generally increased. This is captured in Figure 4.5, where direct investment flows are measured as a percentage of the GDP. The top line shows EU outward flows to non-EU countries, and the lower line inward flows from non-EU countries. The former suggests that, over time, EU countries have increased their levels of investment in non-EU countries; this indicates that, as the internal market has developed, EU capital has gained increasing strength that allows it to adopt investment strategies beyond the Community. The lower line suggests that the internal market has seen

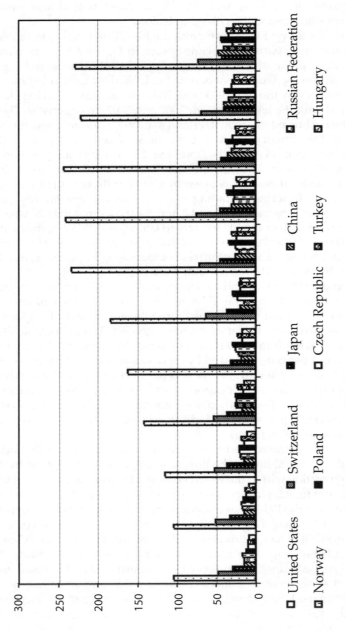

Figure 4.4 Exports from EU-15, 1994–2004 (€1000 million)
Source: Eurostat.

- United States
- Norway
- Switzerland
- Poland
- Japan
- Czech Republic
- China
- Turkey
- Russian Federation
- Hungary

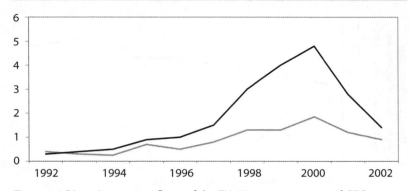

Figure 4.5 Direct investment flows of the EU-15 as a percentage of GDP

Source: Eurostat.
Note: top line shows EU outward flows to non-EU countries; lower line shows inward flows from non-EU countries.

a steady increase of investment from third-country competitors, high-lighting the fact that the internal market has to some degree created an open area that is amenable to international investment and trade. Foreign direct investment (FDI) from non-EU countries reached its peak in 2000, when it was approximately five times higher than in 1990. With these observations in mind, one may argue that while single market policy has resulted in EU capital increasing its ability and strength to invest in international markets, foreign capital is also more likely to invest in a free-trade area in which profits can be easily made, given the effects of functioning in a free-trade area.

All these dynamics have therefore resulted in a single market area that is more integrated into the global economy, as seen in Figure 4.6. The "trade integration" index developed by Eurostat measures how the single market area is becoming increasingly integrated within the inter-national economy. Figure 4.6 depicts the trade integration of goods (top line) and of services (lower line); the higher the value of the y-axis, the higher the level of trade integration within the global economy.[19] Although service integration reached a peak in 2000 and has since declined slightly, the top line demonstrates an overall positive slope over the eleven-year period, suggesting an increasing integration within the global economy with regard to goods. Like the top line (although not having attained a local maximum value in the time series), the bottom line similarly indicates an overall positive slope, albeit to a lesser degree. This suggests that services of the EU are increasingly becoming integrated within the global economy, reflecting the success of 1992 Programme which sought to develop a strong, single, integrated market which was internationally competitive.

Beyond the transposition and economic data that reflect the success

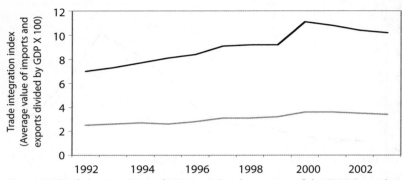

Figure 4.6 Trade integration in the international economy of the EU-15: goods and services

Source: Eurostat.
Note: top line shows trade integration of goods; lower line shows integration of services.

of the internal market since the 1990s, the EU has also set up an innovative mechanism, SOLVIT, to help ensure that supranational single market policies are enforced effectively. Based on a Commission proposal for effective problem solving in the internal market first outlined in November 2001 and approved by the Council in March 2002, SOLVIT represents a non-judicial dispute mechanism that seeks to find effective solutions to problems businesses and citizens may encounter in the internal market. Of course, citizens and businesses may seek to remedy such problems – particularly the non-transposition of EU directives by member states – by raising a formal complaint that may eventually involve the EU's legal system, a process which may be lengthy. SOLVIT was proposed by the Commission as an alternative mechanism offering rapid solutions to internal market problems. Such problems may include those encountered both by businesses, such as administrative obstacles in the internal market, and citizens, such as residency rights, recognition of professional qualifications, and social security benefits. In terms of "problem solving" when there is a perceived misapplication of internal market rules, SOLVIT allows citizens and businesses to make complaints to their nationally based SOLVIT centres, which in turn seek to find a solution working in conjunction with both the state where the problem has occurred and the main Brussels SOLVIT centre. Usually solving problems within its self-imposed ten-week deadline, SOLVIT has found remedies to dozens of cases since 2002; examples of issues that have been dealt with include market access for products and services (22 per cent of cases), recognition of professional qualifications (21 per cent), social security benefits (14 per cent) and taxation issues (11 per cent).[20]

Single market policy and its 1st order status

To sum up, the evidence assembled here helps demonstrate that single market policy can be best considered as a 1st order policy. In terms of its evolution, the first part of this section highlighted the different phases of the policy's development. It was argued that while internal market policy developed favourably in the 1950s and 1960s, the 1970s saw a retreat from free trade as member states pursued protectionist policies in the face of economic downturn. This protectionism was reversed with the development of the 1992 Programme in the mid 1980s, which introduced various directives and measures to remove physical, fiscal and technical barriers previously raised by member states in the single market. At that time, it was considered a priority to deepen the integration process at the EU level in trade policies, with a concomitant diminution in the role of national governments in legislating in this area, in order to promote the free movement of capital, goods, services and people in the single market. The chapter went on to discuss the impact of single market policies. Member states have increasingly transposed single market directives from Brussels, thereby demonstrating that the transfer from national to supranational law has taken place and that major efforts towards integration in this area have been made. High levels of transposition by member states also demonstrate that not only has the domestic level abrogated much of its authority to legislate in this area, but also that all parties involved agree that deeper integration of the internal market was necessary. It was also argued that the success of internal market policy can be measured by analysis of data showing increased trade and investment in the single market area. The has allowed the single market to become a strong one vis-à-vis other major international players with which it trades and to become increasingly integrated into the world economy.

We now turn to a detailed analysis of developments surrounding the initiation and negotiation of the 1992 Programme in order to better understand which actors were involved, and how this can be theoretically characterized on the basis of the various models presented in Chapter 3.

Formulation of the 1992 Programme

It should be noted from the beginning that the formulation of the 1992 Programme and the Single European Act has resulted in heated academic debate. As Anderson's work points out, "the debate revolve[d] around the point at which the political consensus underpinning the SEA emerged and around those [actors] most central to the outcome."[21] Given this, one may see the debate as revolving around the two main schools of EU integration theory,[22] both of which were discussed in Chapter 3. On the one hand, authors such as Sand-holtz and Zysman argue that, "the renewed drive for market unifica-tion can be explained only if theory takes into account the policy leadership of the Commission,"[23] pointing to the importance of the supranational governance perspective in explaining the formulation of the single market initiative of 1986. On the other hand, authors such as Moravcsik[24] contend that the Single European Act is best understood by focussing the analysis on the actions of, desires of and negotiations within the Council of Ministers, suggesting the impor-tance of the intergovernmentalist model. While considering the ideas raised in the academic debate over the reasons for the 1992 Programme, this section has two main objectives. First, we seek to answer the question: which actors were involved in both the policy initiation and negotiation stages? Second, given these actors' partici-pation in these two conjunctures of policy formulation, how can one best theoretically characterize these developments? In order to answer these questions, while doing justice to the wide range of academic articles on the theme that point to the importance of differ-ent theoretical perspectives, we start with a chronological examina-tion of developments first during the policy initiation stage (1979 to early 1985) and then the policy negotiation one (1985–86).

Policy initiation: the ECJ and the European Commission ... and a glass of Cassis

As discussed in Chapter 2, few political science analyses have exam-ined the policy-making role of the European Court of Justice. However, in their analysis of judicial politics, Alter and Meunier[25] provide a useful analysis of the effects of the 1979 Cassis de Dijon decision by the ECJ on the development of the Single European Act. In this case:

> the Court was asked to rule indirectly on the legality of a German law that required spirits to have a minimum alcohol content of at least 25 per cent. The effect of this law was that the French liqueur Cassis de Dijon, which had an alcohol content of 15 per cent to 20 per cent, could not be marketed in Germany. ... [T]he Cassis cases was selected as a test case by the plaintiff's lawyer to ... provoke harmonization in the alcohol industry. ... [T]he German govern-ment defended the validity of its regulation primarily on health grounds ... claiming that alcoholic beverages with low alcohol content might more easily induce a tolerance toward alcohol than more highly alcoholic beverages.[26]

In its decision, the ECJ ruled against the German government and, by extrapolating from the case, stated that there is:

No valid reason why, provided that they have been lawfully
produced and marketed in one Member State, alcoholic bever-
ages should not be introduced into any other Member State.[27]

In Alter and Meunier's view, the Cassis verdict "acted as a catalyst,
provoking a political response by the Commission, which attempted to
capitalize on the verdict to create a 'new approach to harmonization'",[28]
eventually resulting in the Single European Act. At the time of the
Cassis judgment, the Commission was seeking to remove technical
barriers in order to increase the efficiency of trade within the Community. Given that the Cassis ruling offered provocative language in order
to advance mutual recognition of goods to be traded within the
Community, the Commission seized upon it to justify eradication of
barriers found in the internal market.

In the wake of the Cassis ruling the Commission, acting as a "policy-
entrepreneur",[29] initiated discussion of further integration of the internal market with a communication in 1980 that outlined the need for
member states to consider other states' viewpoints when commercial or
technical rules for the movement of goods were being considered with
the goal of ending internal protectionism. In the words of Alter and
Meunier, "the Commission used the verdict as a justification to redirect
its harmonization policy in a way that promoted freer trade and further
integration,"[30] despite some opposition from member states such as
France, Germany and Italy which, in contrast to intergovernmentalist
arguments discussed later, originally opposed the Commission's
proposals as they feared that mutual recognition of goods would
decrease quality and safety standards. From this perspective, while the
ECJ did not make policy per se, the Cassis decision reflects how the
court can act as a "provocateur": the decision precipitated a political
process whereby the Commission, acting as an entrepreneur, effectively
used the ruling as a means to open the discussion on ways of making
trade more efficient, an objective to which the Commission had for
some time been committed.[31]

After expressing its desires for increased liberalization of the internal market in 1980, the Commission went further in 1984, calling for a
decrease in not only technical, but also physical and fiscal barriers.
Internal Market Commissioner Karl-Heinz Narjes "produced a
comprehensive package of proposals to complete a European Common
Market in late 1984 [even though there was] no outpouring of support
from government leaders".[32] The point to note here is that even in the
early 1980s the Council of Ministers did not itself spearhead proposals
for internal market liberalization. Rather, believing that barriers to
trade within the Common Market did more harm than good, the
Commission elaborated on its own provocative suggestions in the
wake of the Cassis case to continue to push for greater freedom of trade

in Europe. The 1984 document from the Commission[33] "listed hundreds of pre-existing pieces of legislation – ranging from standardization to social actions to environmental issues – deemed necessary for the creation of an internal market".[34]

In sum, this analysis of ECJ's Cassis de Dijon ruling of 1979, paving the way for the calls by the Commission between 1981 and 1984 for internal market reform, highlights how the initiation for the 1992 Programme stemmed from two main EU institutions: the ECJ and the Commission. On the one hand, the actions of the ECJ served as a catalyst for internal market reform. On the other, the Commission adopted a two-pronged strategy. It used the Cassis decision as a means to open up debate and take the first steps towards reform of the internal market. Second, the Commission persistently articulated the need for reform, despite reservations raised by some member states. Clearly, the Commission was tenacious throughout this five-year span; even though its ideas and proposals in the early 1980s were not altogether well received by member states, it continued to insist that reform of the internal market was necessary. Full negotiation of this proposal would take place shortly after Delors took over in 1985, as discussed below.

Given these dynamics, one may reasonably argue that ideas raised in the supranational governance theoretical perspective help explain developments in the initiation phase of the policy: EU institutions were largely responsible for putting the internal market reform package on the agenda in the late 1970s and early 1980s, despite some concerns being raised by some member states. Interestingly, in contrast to the lessons of other policies discussed in this book where supranational governance appears crucially important in light of the key role of the Commission (as seen, for example, in the next chapter on Competition policy), the ECJ also plays a key role in the initiation phase of the 1992 Programme. Although direct policy output per se did not flow from the ECJ, the fact that it provoked the Commission to take initial steps towards developing a policy, while at the same time providing a justification for that policy, demonstrates how the Courts can have an indirect policy-making role.

Policy negotiation: Jacques Delors meets the ERT (for the first time)

Turning to the negotiation phase of the 1992 Programme, one may argue that this starts with the new Commission President Jacques Delors' comments in early 1985 when taking over his post. Following the 1984 package presented by the Commission, in January 1985 the Delors-led Commission would clearly signal its intention to embark upon unprecedented single market reform. Gillingham interestingly characterizes Delors as a:

high strung, overbearing, rude, thin-skinned, dynamic, inex-
haustible, creative, independent, deeply mystical, outwardly
conventional, elusive and maddening though irreplaceable
loner ... [who] put the collective body of Euro-guardians in the
front ranks of the drive to integrate Europe ... [and] intended to
construct a powerful new, united "Europe" that was immune
to globalization and strong enough to contest the international
leadership of the United States.[35]

Within days of becoming Commission President, Delors told the EP of
"the new Commission's intention to ask the European Council to pledge
itself to completion of a fully unified market by 1992, to be achieved with
the help of a programme comprising a realistic and binding timetable."[36]
    There are three main, related, reasons why Delors was so in favour
of deepening the single market, beyond the fact that he believed that if
monetary union was to be achieved a single, integrated market had
first to be established. First, as alluded to by Gillingham above, Delors
sought to "revive" Europe after the European economic downturn of
the 1970s and amid fears that Europe would not be competitive with
the USA and Japan, which had been gaining increasing economic
strength in the world economy since the early 1980s. The importance of
the "economic factors" described by Cameron[37] is echoed by George
and Bache who argue that:

    by the mid 1980s there was a net flow of investment funds from
    Western Europe to the United States. This augured badly both
    for the employment situation in Europe in the future, and for
    the ability of European industry to keep abreast of the techno-
    logical developments that were revolutionizing production
    processes. ... When European industrialists were asked what
    would be most likely to encourage them to invest in Europe,
    they replied that the most important factor for them would be
    the creation of a genuine continental market such as they expe-
    rienced in the United States. It was therefore ... [in] an attempt
    to revive investment and economic growth that governments
    embraced the free-market programme.[38]

Second, Delors knew that of the various options available that could
be taken to revive Europe, internal market reform would meet with
the most agreement among all member states because of their increasing dependence on intra-community trade. As Cameron states, "as
the member states became more dependent on trade in general in
decades before the development of the 1992 initiative, they also
became more dependent on trade with other members of the
Community."[39] Cameron's data specifically demonstrates that while

in 1960 countries such as Germany, France and Italy saw 30 per cent of their exports going to other EU states, by 1985 this figure had increased to 50 per cent. Delors therefore knew that completion of the internal market would be something that many states would be in favour of, given that a "deregulated, free market Europe appealed to the new governments of the right in Britain and West Germany while the failure of the French socialist experiment ... removed any opposition from Mitterrand."[40]

A third reason, which builds on the arguments raised in the second point, for Delors to pursue internal market reform was not just that many member states would be in favour of it, but that the UK in particular would support the initiative. In other words, many observers consider that the UK (oftentimes referred to as the "awkward partner") represents in mathematical terms the "lowest common denominator" of all member states: because the UK often opposes major EU reforms, if that country's support can be guaranteed right from the beginning then the chances are greater that the package will be approved by the rest of the Council. Delors knew that under Thatcher, the UK would be in favour of the strong liberalization measures that the 1992 Programme would prescribe. From this perspective, Delors was to strategically pursue this specific reform in the full confidence that one of the main potential obstacles – the UK – would back the Commission. This interpretation suggests that the Commission did not pursue this policy in response to the dictates of some members of the Council, as intergovernmentalists would argue. Rather, the Commission choose policy options strategically, knowing full well that certain key members of the Council would not offer resistance; this interpretation adds strength to arguments put forward by supranational governance scholars who point to the primary role of supranational EU institutions in policy shaping. Echoing these ideas, Wallace also argues that Delors chose single market policy precisely because he knew it would gain the acceptance of the UK, not that the UK dictated to the Commission what needed to be done:

> The internal market is important not only for its own sake, but because it is the first core Community issue for over a decade ... which has caught the imagination of British policy makers. ... The pursuit of a thoroughly liberalized domestic European market has several great advantages: it fits Community philosophy, it suits the doctrinal preferences of the current British Conservative government.[41]

Following Delor's comments in early 1985, at the end of March that year the European Council expressed agreement with his plans for the creation of the single market. As such, the Council sanctioned the Commissioner for Trade and Industry, Lord Cockfield, to pursue a report on freeing the internal market. By June 1985 Lord Cockfield, a man close to Delors and highly trusted by him, presented the White Paper on Completing the Internal Market.[42] His main remit was to consider the measures necessary in order to better enshrine the four freedoms. Outlined in the paper were approximately 300 directives that were aimed at ensuring the free movement of goods, services, capital and labour by removing physical, fiscal and technical barriers. Most of these proposals would eventually be reflected in the final version of the 1992 Programme that was later approved by the Council.

The evidence suggests that these reforms outlined in the White Paper shared strong similarities to ideas raised by capital actors. The work of Cowles[43] specifically shows that the reforms borne in the Cockfield report have strong similarities with the themes outlined by the capital actors in the European Round Table. In other words, during the time that Delors was expressing the need for internal market reform in 1985, it can be seen that capital actors in the form of the ERT were putting forward similar ideas and proposals about the reforms that ought to be pursued. The ERT itself was formed in the early 1980s in a time of low economic growth, high levels of inflation and low profit margins, and one of its main objectives was to reform the internal market. Recognizing the poor organization structures of UNICE in the 1980s, the CEO of Volvo, Pehr Gyllenhammar, along with other top industrialists such as Phillip's CEO Wisse Dekker and Fiat's Umberto Agnelli, sought to develop the ERT as a means to "to spur growth, and to build industry and infrastructure in Europe".[44] The work of authors such as Balanya *et al* highlights how, even from the beginning, the ERT's access to European Commissioners was unchallenged, while it also maintained privileged connections with members of the increasingly powerful European Parliament.[45]

In terms of themes of interest shared by the ERT and the Commission with regard to single market reform, Cowles' work demonstrates how, while Delors was emphasizing in speeches the need for specific reforms in the internal market, members of ERT were simultaneously formulating similar blueprints for change in order to consolidate the profitability of European businesses operating in the continent. For example in January 1985:

> Wisse Dekker, CEO of Philips, unveiled a plan, "Europe 1990" before an audience of 500 people including the newly appointed EC Commissioners. The plan laid out in precise terms the steps needed in four key areas: trade facilitation (elimination of border formalities), opening up of public procurement markets, harmonization of technical standards, and fiscal harmonization (eliminating the fiscal Value Added Tax frontiers) – to open up a European Market in five years.[46]

As seen in Table 4.1, among business groups surveyed who would later express their concerns to the Commission,[47] the most important issues related to physical and technical barriers, while fiscal constraints were the least important. Of these, the highest ranking were administrative delays, national standards and border delays.

Upon closer examination, one sees that the comments initially made by Dekker of the ERT, as well as the areas of concern raised by other capital interests, are reflected in the main themes addressed in the Commission's White Paper, demonstrating how both sets of actors worked together during the negotiation of the policy. This "Commission–capital" coalition, as the literature has referred to it, first clearly manifested itself in the formulation of the 1992 Programme, even though it appeared again in the development of other policies as seen later in the book (namely Merger Control Regulation and Economic and Monetary Union). In the negotiation of the 1992 Programme, the two actors differed on only one count: whereas capital optimistically sought a 1990 deadline for the completion of the internal market, the Commission more realistically planned it for 1992.

There are three possible explanations that may help us better understand why capital actors and the Commission worked together in the development of the 1992 Programme. One explanation relates to "resource dependencies". The argument here is that EC institutions, increasingly responsible for shaping the regulatory environment, were understaffed and in need of the expertise offered by private interests.[48] Similarly, capital relied on the EU institutions for specific information when considering its attitudes towards internal market reform, including standards of services, employment practices and price traditions. Access to this type of information was clearly crucial for rational capital actors seeking to minimize the uncertainty of their operating environment in the world economy. And in order to secure access to reliable sources of information,

Table 4.1 The major market barriers in the EU as ranked by business

Administrative barriers (technical barrier)	1
National standards and regulations (technical barrier)	2
Physical frontier delays (physical barrier)	3
Community law (technical barrier)	4
Restrictions in the capital market (physical barriers)	5
Differences in VAT (fiscal barrier)	6/7
Regulation of freight transport (physical barrier)	6/7
Government procurement (technical barrier)	8

Source: Ceccini Report, 1998.
The numbers on the right represent the rank-ordering of each of the concepts, based on responses by business leaders.

European businesses had to establish networks with European institutions if they were to be successful players in an increasingly globalized world. As a result of these resource dependencies, the Commission and capital forged a close relationship

A second, related explanation relates to the overlap of medium to long-term interests held by both the Commission and capital. Delors and the Commission might have had more general, Europeanist interests in cementing a place for Europe in the global economy. But the Commission's achievement was crucially dependent, as they knew, on revitalizing the European economy. This revitalization, which was also in the interests of major capitalist businesses, needed the input and explicit support of capital actors: capital's negotiation with the Commission of the details of the 1992 Programme was therefore vital. Similarly, from capital's perspective, the support of the Commission was necessary to fulfil the medium and long-term economic goals of capital, which sought to create single market conditions (such as the free movement of goods, service and capital throughout the EU) which would allow big businesses to make more money.

A third explanation relates to the desire of both participants to "cement" their present and future role in EU regulatory policy. Moreover, economic actors needed to have strong relationships with the Commission in order to help shape the Community's policy agenda so that it would reflect their economic interests.[49] Rose argues with reference to the Single Market that economic actors, such as manufacturers, pressured Brussels "to adopt policies defined in terms of economic interests instead of national interests"[50] and to base policy on rationally based economic concerns. In this specific policy area, capital realized that centralization of market regulation would significantly reduce business transaction costs, thereby allowing businesses to increase profits and seek further market expansion. Thus organizations such as the ERT, as well as individual businesses in general, supported the 1992 Programme and demanded privileged policy-making access.[51] On the other hand, if the Commission had isolated itself from the principal actor operating in the internal market, namely capital, its recommendations for internal market reform would have lost serious legitimacy. This could have left the impression that the Commission was a "non-credible" policy-maker, not only in the eyes of capital actors, but also, potentially in the eyes of the Council. This is something which the Delors Commission would have wanted to avoid – especially in its first year of functioning – given not only the potential embarrassment at the time, but also the damage it would inflict on their ability to pursue other future reforms, including those to competition policy and the creation of the Economic and Monetary Union as discussed in Chapters 5 and 6 respectively.

Irrespective of analysing the role of the Commission–capital coalition in the negotiation of the 1992 Programme, it is necessary to attempt to evaluate the relative importance of the actions of the Council in this process. As discussed earlier, in March 1985 the Council sanctioned Cockfield to produce a White Paper. Thereafter, in June 1985, with few changes to the ideas outlined in the Cockfield Report, the Milan Council accepted the objectives of the White Paper and the completion date of the end of 1992.[52] And in December 1985, the Council finally agreed on the Single European Act, the main parts of which consisted of the 1992 programme and the acceptance of qualified majority voting (QMV) for certain issue areas. Given these actions, there is little doubt that there was a formal role for the Council in the process, most significantly that of giving the final approval. However, what remains less clear is the significance of its role during the formulation process. Those pointing to a major role for the Council in the policy formulation, such as Moravcsik who argues from the intergovernmentalist perspective, contend that the Council delegated the Commission to pursue the Cockfield White paper, that capital actors were not engaged until late in the process, and that other EU institutions (such as the EP and ECJ) had insignificant roles in policy formulation.[53] The intergovernmentalists argue that specific member states were of importance in producing the Single European Act.[54] These included the UK, which sought increased liberalization, as well as Germany and France, both of which desired internal market reforms because they were export economies. Germany and France also supported integration in general and believed that the 1992 Programme could be used to work towards their desired goals of liberalization.

However, one may contend that the intergovernmentalist arguments are relatively weak on at least three grounds. First, although the Council formally authorized Lord Cockfield to produce the White Paper, this can be seen as a natural, if not necessary, reaction to developments that had already taken place. These developments included: the 1979 Cassis decision of the ECJ that had signalled the need for reform; calls by the Commission in the early 1980s for internal market reform in the wake of Cassis, which were largely ignored by the Council at the time; the proposals outlined in early January 1985 when Delors had clearly indicated the Commission's desire for internal market reform; and capital's open support for the Commission and its call that the internal market ought to be pursued. In other words, if the Council sanctioned the White Paper, it was only because it could no longer afford to ignore the issue, given the dynamics of the previous six years.

Second, the actions of the ERT clearly demonstrate that business was involved in the process well before both the Milan and Luxembourg Council meetings. It is therefore somewhat debateable to argue that its participation came after the fact as claimed by intergovernmentalists. Even Moravcsik in his later work recognized the importance of the Commission and business by stating that, "the decisive impulse stemmed from far-sighted Commission officials like Etienne Davignon, Jacques Delors and Arthur Cockfield ... backed by a coalition of visionary multinational businessmen who, strongly supportive of market liberalization, convinced or circumvented reluctant national leaders."[55]

A third point has already been discussed in examining the reasons why Delors placed completion of the internal market at the top of the agenda when he came to power. One may contend that the Commission chose internal market reform knowing that member states, especially the UK, would agree with it, not because such states had demanded or instigated the calls for such a reform beforehand. Besides, it was not just the UK, Germany and France that would be in favour of the Commission's reforms. Other EU states, such as Spain led by Felipe González, sought supranational neo-liberal reforms, urged on by neo-liberal elements within his Cabinet and aware of the need to justify pursuit of such policies at the domestic level.[56] In Socialist Spain's view, as in that of Socialist France, Brussels was seen as useful scapegoat for pursuing reforms that would have otherwise been difficult to achieve at the domestic level, given potential opposition from various social actors such as trade unions.

In summary, analysis of developments in the negotiation phase of the 1992 Programme highlights the importance of the actions of both the Commission and capital actors. This was particularly evident in the way the Commission was led by Jacques Delors who, when taking over the Presidency in 1985, clearly intended to pursue the reforms and was willing to work alongside actors from European business in the form of the ERT to achieve internal market reforms, forming a Commission–capital coalition in the process. Although the Council itself did have a formal role in approving the 1992 Programme, it was argued that its bargaining power in negotiating the policy was relatively weak compared to the other main actors. It was the Commission–capital coalition that shaped the policy which major member states had different reasons for accepting. In light of this, one may reasonably argue that both the supranational governance and DEC perspectives help explain the negotiation of the 1992 Programme. Or, from a different vantage point, ideas from the intergovernmentalist, pluralist and corporatist perspectives are less relevant in explaining the shaping of the 1992 Programme.

Conclusions

The first section of this chapter analysed the broad objectives and evolution of EU single market policy. It argued that while the overall objectives of internal market policy are to promote the free movement of goods, services, persons and capital, the evolution of the policy area reveals different conjunctures or phases of its development. The first phase, seen in the late 1950s, was when the principles of the single market were established; in the second phase (of the 1960s), there were some attempts to deepen the integration process; in the 1970s there was a phase when member states reverted to protectionist measures; and in the final phase, seen in developments since the mid 1980s and the passage of the 1992 Programme, numerous measures to eradicate physical, fiscal and technical barriers were implemented, resulting in a deepened integration of the European market intended to secure a competitive position for the EU within the global economy. After analysis of the evolution of the internal market in terms of the percentage of EU-led directives that have been transposed at the national level, the increased levels of intra-EU 15 trade over the last decade, the increased investment flows both from and to the EU, and increased integration of the European economy in the world economy, it was concluded that internal market policy constitutes a "1st order" policy, given that competences in this area have been fully transferred to the supranational level.

The second section offered a more detailed analysis of the formulation of a specific aspect of internal market policy, the 1992 Programme. The first part of the section highlighted the importance of two main actors in the initiation phase. The first was the ECJ which, in its Cassis de Dijon decision, served as what was referred to as a "policy provocateur". The second major actor was the Commission, which used the Cassis case to justify its own goals for single market reform and stressed the need for reform to a sceptical Council throughout the 1980s. Given this, and keeping in mind the five theoretical perspectives outlined in Chapter 3, the evidence suggests that the policy initiation phase can be best characterized by ideas developed in the supranational governance perspective, because of the importance of the ECJ and the Commission in initiating the 1992 Programme through its actions between 1979 and 1984. Turning to policy negotiation, the evidence suggests that the Commission, led by Delors who took over its Presidency in 1985, and capital in for the form of the ERT were both instrumental in the negotiation of the 1992 Programme. It was argued that this Commission–capital coalition can be explained when one considers both "resource-dependencies" between the actors and their desires to cement their present and future policy-making role. It was argued that, even though the Council had a formal role when the 1992 Programme had to be approved, this institution nevertheless played a relatively limited role in terms of initiation and negotiation of the details of the policy when compared to other actors. As such, it was argued that both the supranational governance and DEC perspectives are of most relevance when seeking to theoretically characterize developments during the negotiation of the policy.

5 Competition policy: ensuring a competitive European market

In the first section of the chapter, we will consider the broad objectives of EU competition policy. While offering a brief analysis of the evolution of the overall policy area and aspects of its implementation process, we will examine whether or not the policy has the characteristics of being either a 1st order or 2nd order policy in terms of its impact and its evolution. The second section offers a more detailed analysis of a specific reform pursued in the policy area, focussing on the Merger Control Regulation of 1990. We will specifically consider which actors were involved in the initiation and negotiation process and, based on this analysis, how one should theoretically characterize these developments. The chapter argues first that EU competition policy can be considered a 1st order policy. The second main argument is that the major actors involved in the policy formulation process include both the Commission and representatives of capital, suggesting that both the supranational governance and the dominant economic class (DEC) perspectives are of value in explaining the policy.

Objectives and evolution of competition policy and its "1st order status" in the integration process

Competition policy seeks to ensure a level playing field for business in the single, integrated European market. This broadly means that member state governments should seek to improve economic competitiveness and that neither public nor private enterprises should be given a privileged market position vis-à-vis their competitors. As laid down in Article 3.g of the EC Treaty, regulations have been established in order to ensure that "competition in the internal market has not been distorted". Such regulations are seen in four main areas: state aid, liberalization, anti-trust measures and merger control. This section considers the broad objectives and evolution of each in turn and then concludes that the policy has attained a 1st order status. The reader will note that the discussion of the objectives and evolution of the four areas is together comparatively larger than that of many other policy areas considered in this book. While this discussion reflects the complexity and depth of the subject, it also offers significant examples of developments in competition policy over the last decade. This will enable the reader to see the full dynamics acting in this policy area, which many observers of EU politics contend remains one of the most exciting.

State aid control: hand it over

State aid control seeks to prevent market-distorting subsidies that prevent fair competition in the single competitive market. Through Articles 87 and 88 of the TEU, as well as the Transparency Directives of 1980/1993, the European Commission is legally empowered to investigate and prohibit market-distorting aid.[1] In its most common form, state aid comprises subsidies given by member states to public or private firms; in some cases, aid may also be given to promote regional development, research and training. While it is generally acknowledged that regulation of state aid was somewhat weak throughout the first years of the Community, the Commission clamped down on aid from the mid 1980s onwards,[2] a consequence of the desire to create a truly liberal single market outlined in the Single European Act (SEA).

State aid control regulates member states that give market-distorting aid, rather than clamping down directly on the companies receiving such funds. For example, as discussed by Chari and Cavatorta[3], member states giving aid during privatizations can be constrained or even stopped by the Commission. This was seen, for example, when the Commission intensely scrutinized aid given during the sale of the British Rover Group to British Aerospace in the early 1990s, as well as in the case of France's Credit Lyonnais, which was massively bailed out in the mid 1990s in order to prevent its bankruptcy before its privatization.[4]

The tough stance on aid, particularly since the SEA (1986) and Commissioner Karel van Miert's leadership of the Competition Directorate during the Delors Commission, was based on producer and consumer concerns to create a truly competitive market in the global economy. From the producers' viewpoint, unfair subsidies allow recipients to maintain or increase their position irrespective of market forces. The forms of aid potentially given to either public or private companies may include direct subsidies, recapitalizations, loans below market rates, writing off debts, cash contributions, and loan guarantees given by the member state to companies.[5] From the consumers' perspective, the prices and quality of goods are not necessarily optimal because state aid prevents other competitors from entering the market or establishing a strong position.

Figure 5.1 considers the potential steps that may be taken when a state gives aid. States are legally bound to notify the Commission of aid given but, as the right-hand side of the figure indicates, this does not always occur. An example of this was seen when several tranches of aid were given public enterprises in the Spanish state holding company INI (The National Industry Institute) throughout the 1980s and early 1990s with the aim of priming the companies before they were sold for a price well below market value.[6] Because of the lack of information about such aid, the Commission did nothing. In the case where a state does

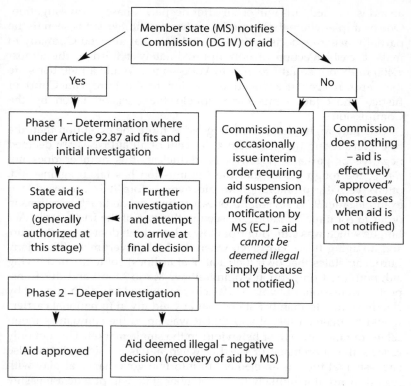

Figure 5.1 State aid policy steps at EU level

not notify the aid and the EU becomes aware of it (say, for example, through a third party complaint), the Commission may issue an interim order that the aid be suspended until the Commission has studied the case (in other words, non-notification in itself does not render the aid illegal). However, this "interim order" has rarely been used by the Commission, meaning that most unnotified aid generally goes through.

Nevertheless, it is important to note that as competition policy has gained increasing force since the early 1990s, particularly with Van Miert as the Competition Director, states have increasingly notified the Commission of subsidies. This is reflected in Commission estimates that in 1990 cases not notified represented about 20 per cent of all aid cases in the Community, while in 1996 this figure dropped to slightly over 14 per cent. This suggests that over time states have been increasingly notifying aid and complying with community regulations.[7]

The left-hand side of the figure indicates the two possible results when an aid is notified: it can be approved or deemed illegal. Most aid approval occurs in the first phase of Commission investigation. If an aid is rejected, this will occur after deeper, "Phase 2" investigation. One example where the Commission has prohibited aid is seen in the partially negative decision in the late 1990s that allowed Germany to make a cash injection of only approximately a third of the almost €400 million it sought to give to Volkswagen. While a member state may appeal against a negative decision to the European Court of Justice, most judgments have upheld the decision taken by the Commission.

One may argue that prohibiting aid is more the exception than the rule, considering that less than 4 per cent of all aid cases are deemed negative or partially negative. Nevertheless, this number does not reflect the tough stance that the Commission has taken against aid, often "verbally prohibiting" an aid even before it is proposed. For example, after 9/11 several European airlines needed cash injections in order to continue operating, as seen in the case of the Irish carrier Aer Lingus which was suffering from low sales, a high debt-to-equity ratio, and an aging fleet.[8] However, when the Irish government (like many European states that own their national airlines) contemplated giving aid, both the Competition Commissioner Mario Monti and the Transport Commissioner Loyola de Palacio pre-empted any such attempt by clearly stating to member states that any aid given to national carriers would be deemed illegal and that it was up to the companies themselves to rationalize their behaviour in the single market. This not only reflects the supremacy of the EU when aid is considered, but also suggests that there is an element of informal governance at play with regard to aid: it is unlikely that a member state will pursue a measure unless it is almost certain that the Commission, which has the final word, will give its approval.

Indeed, the idea that member states are reacting to the tough stance taken by the Commission on aid is reflected in the data in Table 5.1. The figures demonstrate that state aid as a percentage of GDP has generally decreased over the time series, suggesting that member states are giving less aid over time. The average of the EU-15 (which refers to the 15 member states of the EU before the 2004 expansion) in 2002 is less than half of the value in 1992. Table 5.1 also suggests that there are differences between the member states, although there is no discernable trend for the "north" to give less aid than the "south" as seems often to be assumed by some observers. In 2002, Denmark had the highest level of state aid as a percentage of GDP at 0.72; states such as Belgium, Italy and France hovered around the EU average; and the United Kingdom, Finland, Sweden and the Netherlands were all well below all other states.

Interestingly, we can compare the EU 15 figures from 2002 with those of new member states from central and eastern Europe that have recently joined the Community. To this end, Table 5.2 suggests that aid in new member states represents an average of 1.42 per cent of GDP,

Table 5.1 Total state aid (less agriculture, fisheries and transport) as a percentage of GDP, EU-15, 1992–2002

	1992	1993	1994	1995	1996	1997	1998	1999	2000	2001	2002
EU	0.85	0.95	0.85	0.74	0.75	0.66	0.59	0.46	0.43	0.41	0.39
Belgium	0.71	0.78	0.52	0.49	0.52	0.34	0.38	0.37	0.33	0.32	0.37
Denmark	0.33	0.52	0.54	0.50	0.59	0.60	0.64	0.64	0.82	0.77	0.72
Germany	1.39	1.75	1.62	1.19	1.05	0.92	0.82	0.74	0.67	0.63	0.56
Greece	1.59	0.87	0.37	0.82	0.66	0.77	0.47	0.37	0.50	0.36	0.31
Spain	0.41	0.38	0.51	0.88	0.73	0.69	0.67	0.54	0.49	0.62	0.55
France	0.51	0.64	0.51	0.46	0.84	0.85	0.74	0.55	0.48	0.43	0.42
Ireland	0.45	0.42	0.32	0.32	0.40	0.47	1.01	0.86	0.71	0.65	0.45
Italy	1.44	1.40	1.09	1.12	1.10	0.84	0.70	0.40	0.39	0.39	0.38
Luxembourg	0.56	0.34	0.33	0.36	0.33	0.31	0.31	0.22	0.20	0.17	0.26
Netherlands	0.21	0.17	0.17	0.18	0.19	0.17	0.16	0.20	0.17	0.15	0.19
Austria				0.27	0.28	0.30	0.27	0.25	0.21	0.26	0.21
Portugal	0.47	0.58	0.82	0.47	0.98	1.52	0.93	1.06	1.09	0.88	0.55
Finland				0.33	0.27	0.33	0.29	0.25	0.24	0.17	0.17
Sweden				0.32	0.31	0.22	0.24	0.23	0.20	0.18	0.16
UK	0.15	0.10	0.21	0.31	0.22	0.19	0.22	0.10	0.11	0.11	0.17

Source: http://europa.eu.int/comm/competition/state_aid/scoreboard/indicators/k1.html#data.

Table 5.2 State aid in the new 2004 EU members, average annual figures for 2000–03

	Total state aid less agriculture, fisheries and transport (€million)	State aid as percentage of GDP
EU 15 (2002)	34,000	0.39
New member states	5,654	1.42
Czech Republic	1,908	2.80
Estonia	7	0.11
Cyprus	285	2.85
Latvia	23	0.26
Lithuania	34	0.24
Hungary	571	1.04
Malta	159	3.86
Poland	2,409	1.29
Slovenia	139	0.69
Slovakia	118	0.51

Source: data from DG Competition and Eurostat found on:
http://europa.eu.int/comm/competition/state_aid/scoreboard/indicators/k14.html#stats1.
Note: the time period for Malta is 2000–02.

almost 1 per cent more than the EU15 average. This may reflect the type of discipline that has been demanded by the EU of its members. Yet it would be unfair to suggest that all new entrants have the same levels. While countries such as the Czech Republic, Cyprus and Malta have aid levels close to or over 3 per cent of their GDPs, states such as Latvia and Lithuania have figures similar to those found in the UK and Finland.

Liberalization: not everyone can play monopoly

For many years, important sectors of the European economy were monopolized by state-owned enterprises which faced little or no competition. Examples of such sectors included electricity, telecommunications and rail transport, all of which were services deemed essential. In the 1980s and 1990s many member states privatized state-owned enterprises in these sectors. Although this was particularly the case in Thatcher's UK, Socialist governments in countries such as Spain and France did the same. However, privatization did not necessarily mean liberalization. In fact, one may say that the opposite could be true, as seen in countries such as Spain where state companies such as Telefonica (telecommunications) and Endesa (electricity) were fully or partially privatized well before other competitors were allowed entry in the respective sectors.

Article 86, though largely unused by the Commission until the mid 1980s, served as a basis for the Commission to liberalize these key sectors which had seen little or no competition. Several member states were wary of full liberalization, especially those where the privatization process was incomplete because the state continued to own a large number of monopolies. Armed with Article 86 the Commission believed that "competition should be introduced in monopoly industries ... so as to improve the quality of the service and to bring prices down."[9] Article 86 does not require states to privatize – in fact the EC Treaty and the official Commission position remains neutral with respect to state ownership.[10] Whereas liberalization refers to the idea of increasing competition in the economy (especially in those sectors where there may be only one monopoly power), privatization refers to the idea the state selling public enterprises that that it owns. As McGowan states, Article 86 "addresses sectors of a 'general economic interest' and requires that competition rules be applied to these sectors as long as they do not prevent the fulfilment of the general interest".[11] Moreover, as noted by McGowan, Article 86.3 lays down that such rules could be "imposed directly by the Commission without reference to the Council".[12]

The heart of the Commission's argument is that one must distinguish between infrastructure and commercial activities: ownership of the former (regardless of who owns it) should not mean that other competitors cannot use it; the overriding aim is to improve services, lower prices and create a competitive European economy on the world stage. In the Commission's words:

> [M]onopolies have been in network industries – transport, energy and telecommunications. In these sectors, a distinction must be made between the infrastructure and the services provided over this infrastructure. While it is often difficult to establish a second, competing infrastructure, for reasons linked to investment costs and economic efficiency, it is possible and desirable to create competitive conditions in respect of the services provided. The infrastructure is thus merely the vehicle of competition. While the right to exclusive ownership may persist as regards the infrastructure (the telephone or electricity network for example), monopolists must grant access to third parties wishing to compete with them as regards the services offered on their networks (telephone communications or electricity consumption). This is the general principle on which the Community liberalization directives are based.[13]

In terms of process, and in contrast to the case of state aid, the Commission does not necessarily have to render a formal, final decision when it investigates a liberalization case. Rather, corrective measures may be implemented during the course of an investigation, or the Commission itself may not make any decision as Article 86.3 states that corrective measures should be pursued only "where necessary" as decided by the Commission itself.

With regard to specific examples of liberalization decisions, one sees that the Commission has over the last ten years taken a tough stance towards member states in areas such as telecommunications, airports, postal services and broadcasting. An example of a telecommunication case in the late 1990s involved the Commission and the Spanish government.[14] In the early 1990s, the Commission pursued a broad strategy of liberalization of telecom services in Europe, and in 1996 it introduced more specific measures to inject competition into mobile telephone services. In 1996 it found that the Spanish government had charged Airtel Movil over €500 million for a licence to operate in Spain, intending to direct these funds towards restructuring the infrastructure so as to allow for full mobile coverage in Spain. However, no such a charge was placed on the first mobile operator, Telefonica (a formerly public enterprise which had been partially privatized since the late 1980s). According to the Commission, this gave Telefonica a competitive advantage. As such, the Commission ruled that the state should either reimburse the payment made by Airtel or pursue corrective measures. Interestingly, similar dynamics have been seen in other EU states, including Austria, Italy, the Netherlands and Ireland, where companies seeking a second mobile licence were charged heavily. In all cases, as in Spain, member states pursued corrective measures that were subsequently accepted by the Commission.

An example of the Commission seeking to inject competitiveness in airport operations is seen in its 2000 decision to abolish discriminatory landing fees at Spanish and Italian Airports.[15] In the case of Spain, the government had issued a decree making two regulatory changes. First, lower landing fees would be charged for domestic flights, while higher fees would be charged for flights originating outside Spain. Second, "discounts" of between 9 per cent and 35 per cent would be given to airlines that landed with more frequency per month. In the case of Italy, the government had similarly legislated that domestic flights would receive discounts of up to 57 per cent and 64 per cent off the regular fee. On both counts the Commission argued that national carriers – in the case of Spain, this included Iberia Airlines, Spanair and Binter Canarias, and in the case of Italy, Alitalia – benefited. In the Commission's view, this type of discriminatory practice against competitors could not be tolerated in European air space. As in the case of mobile phone services, other EU states, such as Portugal, France, Ireland and Sweden, also maintained "uncompetitive" structures in landing fees. This behaviour was condemned by the Commission in the same way as the Spanish and Italian cases, and corrective measures were subsequently taken by the respective member states.

Anti-trust policies: watch out Bill

While one may contend that the object of regulation in state aid and liberalization remains focussed on member-state governments and/or (publicly or privately owned) monopolies functioning within the domain of protected sectors at the domestic level, anti-trust policy regulates the actions of firms and undertakings operating anywhere in the European single market. The idea here is that the negative actions of actors which distort the market's supply–demand model will eventually result in an inefficient and uncompetitive environment where there are lower quality goods at higher prices. As such, Articles 81 and 82 authorize Commission officials to prevent potential market abuses on two grounds.

First, Article 81 of the EC Treaty prohibits agreements between firms that restrict competition. A restrictive agreement, which may be one of four types, is one whereby firms:

> (1) fix purchase or selling prices or other trading conditions ... (2) limit production, markets, technical development or investments ... (3) share markets or sources of supply between competitors ... (4) apply discriminatory conditions to firms that are not parties to the agreement, placing them at a competitive advantage.[16]

Second, Article 82 prohibits firms from abusing a dominant market position. It does not state that firms cannot have a dominant position. However, it does rule that they cannot abuse it by either denying access to new competitors or intentionally attempting to put others out of business. In the Commission's words, an abuse of a dominant position is when a firm:

> may overcharge consumers, or charge prices that are excessively low so as to exclude weaker competitors or new entrants from the market for example, or it may grant some customers discriminatory advantages such as fidelity rebates provided that they agree with its sales policy.[17]

While some authors have criticized the rather informal procedural measures taken by the Commission in some anti-trust cases,[18] analysis of some of the formal decisions made by the Commission illustrates the effectiveness and strength of the Community in its ability to prevent market-distorting behaviour in various member states. Armed with almost unlimited investigative powers, ranging from simple written requests for information to raids on business and non-business premises, the Commission can impose fines of up to 10 per cent of a company's annual worldwide turnover if it is found that Articles 81 or 82 have been breached.

A recent example demonstrating the might with which the Commission can clamp down on breaches of anti-trust regulations, in this particular case an infringement of Article 82, is seen in the Commission's five-year investigation of Microsoft which terminated in March 2004.[19] It offers a clear example of how supranational authorities seek to create a competitive environment. Because it challenged one of the largest American corporations operating on European soil, the case was a clear signal that the European market would operate by its own rules in the context of the global economy. The case revolved around two main issues. First, Sun Microsystems Inc. had made a formal complaint in 1998 to the Commission stating that Microsoft, which had a monopoly position in the operating systems market, had abused its dominant position by restricting "interoperability" between its own products and those of other companies. "Interoperability" can be defined as "the ability to exchange information and mutually to use the information which has been exchanged".[20] Sun's complaint was that Microsoft refused to supply Sun with interoperability information, thereby deliberately restricting the ability to exchange information between Microsoft's Windows product and Sun's Solaris, which is a non-Microsoft work-group server. By so doing, Microsoft was abusing its position in the work-group server operating system market and seeking to slowly weed out any potential competition in it.

The second issue, based on the Commission's own concerns that arose in 2000 during its investigation of Sun's complaint, was that Microsoft had tied its Windows Media Player product (which plays digital media such as CDs and DVDs on personal computers, and which can also be used to listen to the radio on the Internet) to Windows, thereby restricting users' choice. It is interesting to note that this dynamic of "leveraging" (where a firm with a monopoly position in market A seeks to reduce competition in market B by tying products together in the same package) had previously been investigated by American authorities in the late 1990s under Section 1 of the Sherman Act. Although the original decision against Microsoft was later overturned by an appeal court, Microsoft was accused of having integrated its Internet Explorer browser into Windows in order to eliminate Netscape's Navigator from the browser market: because Microsoft enjoyed a dominant position in the operating systems market, consumers would be more likely to use Explorer, eventually sidelining Netscape. Using the same line of reasoning, the Commission considered that by tying Windows Media Player to its Windows operating system, the company was aiming eventually to drive out potential competitors, such as Real Media, from the media player market.

One may argue that the investigation led by Commissioner Mario Monti into these abuses of dominant position marked one of the most ambitious, longest, most detailed, and perhaps most technically sophisticated investigations ever pursued by the Commission, reflected in over 300 pages that constitute the final decision. Two main actors along with the Commission partook in the investigation. On the one hand, several of Microsoft's competitors in addition to Sun were asked to comment by the Commission, including Time Warner, RealNetworks and Lotus. And on the other, over 70 small and medium-sized companies in the EU were surveyed twice in a wider market inquiry in order to gauge if these users felt that Microsoft's behaviour had influenced their choices.

The final decision was a major blow to Microsoft. Given the gravity of the abuses of dominant position on two fronts, a fine of €165,732,101 was initially imposed.[21] However, this fine was then doubled by the Commission in order to ensure that it should have a "sufficient deterrent effect" on a company with the world's highest market capitalization in 2004.[22] Moreover, the Commission considered that because the abuses had started in October 1998, the fine should also take into account that it was an infringement of long duration,[23] and therefore ruled that the fine should be increased a further 50 per cent. In all, Microsoft was fined a total of €497,196,304, or, almost half a billion euros. Beyond the financial penalty, Microsoft was also ordered to immediately pursue remedies that would ensure a level playing field in both the work-group server operating market and the media player market. Although Microsoft did attempt to have the decision reversed, the European Court of First Instance upheld the Commission's decision in December 2004, forcing the company to state in January 2005 that it would comply with the Commission's judgment.[24]

Merger Control Regulation: you can dance together ... with our permission

Like anti-trust regulations which focus on the potential market-distorting activity of firms, the Merger Control Regulation (MCR) gives the Merger Task Force (MTF), which is a sub-bureaucratic actor within DG Competition, "the exclusive power to investigate (and potentially stop) mergers with a Community dimension".[25] As discussed in more detail in the next section, which analyses the formulation of this aspect of competition policy, supranational regulations on mergers did not come into force until 1990. The MCR defined a merger as the consolidation of two or more firms and can be characterized as horizontal, vertical, or conglomerate.[26] Horizontal mergers see the merging of two rivals that function in the same market. Vertical mergers witness the combining of two firms that have buyer–seller relationships. And conglomerate mergers see a consolidation of firms with little observable market relationship: they are neither sellers in the same market, nor involved in a buyer–seller relationship.

In terms of the types of mergers that are regulated by the MCR, the Commission's XXVIIth Report states that:

> The Community will ... be responsible for mergers meeting the following four conditions: (i) the combined worldwide turnover of all the companies concerned must be more than ECU 2.5 billion and (ii) the combined turnover of all companies concerned must be more than ECU 100 million in each of at least three member states. In addition, so as to ensure that mergers with cross-border effects are also included, (iii) the turnover of each of at least two of the companies concerned must be more than ECU 25 million in each of those same three member states and (iv) the Community-wide turnover of each of at least two of the companies must be more than ECU 100 million. These measures will enable economic realities to be reflected more accurately and will provide companies with greater legal certainty and increase administrative efficiency by extending the "one-stop shop."[27]

It should be noted that although the College of Commissioners theoretically has the final say on a MCR decision taken by the MTF, to date no MTF decision has ever been overturned at this level. Nevertheless, Shea and Chari[28] have argued that some decisions have led to heated debates among the Commissioners. An example of this was seen in the De Havilland case, the first prohibited merger under the MCR. The main point of contention in this case surrounded what criteria should guide merger analysis. The French delegation insisted that social and industrial criteria should be taken into consideration, and therefore that the merger should be allowed. However, the MTF and a majority of Commissioners were swayed by Commissioner Brittan's "competition only" criterion; this blocked any possibility that the MCR could be used in the future as a means to strengthen European industry by the creation of European "champions".

What exactly is the "competition criterion" that guides merger regulation? According to Article 2.3 of the MCR, the focus of the regulation is dominance:

> A concentration which creates or strengthens a dominant position as a result of which effective competition would be significantly impeded in the common market or in a substantial part of it shall be declared incompatible with the common market.

One may argue that there is an assumption here that if firms are in a dominant position after a merger, then they will be more likely to abuse their power. From this perspective, while Article 82 (discussed previously) only allowed the Commission to clamp down on firms already in a dominant position that abuse their power, the MRC went a step further by arming the Commission with tools to prevent potential scenarios of dominance from manifesting themselves in the first place.

With regard to process, the MCR states that merging firms reaching the thresholds above must first notify the Commission of their intentions. The second row of Table 5.3 shows how the number of notifications since the inception of the MCR has increased dramatically, averaging around 280 over the last five years, reflecting European companies' desire to rationalize and cut costs in an increasingly globalized economy.

Once notification has been given, a series of potential "phase" investigations are pursued by the MTF, in a similar vein to the state aid process and in some contrast to both anti-trust and liberalization cases, which do not always follow a clearly structured investigative process or necessarily require formal decisions. These investigations are usually assigned to a member of the MTF referred to as a *rappateur*. A Phase 1 investigation, which is finalized within a month after notification, may result in three main types of outcomes. First, the merger as proposed by the merging companies may be considered compatible with the Common Market as there is no perceived threat of dominance. Second, the merger may be deemed compatible as long as conditions outlined by the Commission are met by the companies. These conditions may include, for example, the need for the merging companies to disinvest in some of their activities in order to maintain a competitive environment in the sector. Or, third, the MTF may deem that deeper investigation is required, at which time a deeper, Phase 2 investigation is initiated over a four-month period. The possible outcomes for Phase 2 investigations include merger approval without conditions, approval with conditions, or prohibition.

As rows 3 and 4 of Table 3 indicate, virtually all cases are resolved in Phase 1, with a strong majority of mergers deemed compatible without any conditions being laid down by the Commission. Of the relatively small number of mergers that make it to Phase 2 investigations, rows 5, 6, and 7 indicate that a majority are approved with conditions. Over the period shown, fewer than 1 per cent of all cases have actually been prohibited.

Because most mergers are eventually approved by the Commission prima facie, it is reasonable to reflect on how powerful the EU level is in this area of competition policy. One may argue that EU governance at this level is effective on three counts. First, although numerous cases every year are approved, others are approved with conditions laid down by the Commission. This suggests that prohibition itself is not the only way that the Commission can ensure competition in the

Table 5.3 European merger control statistics, 1990–2004

I.) Notifications	1990	91	92	93	94	95	96	97	98	99	2000	01	02	03	04	Total
Number of notified cases	12	63	60	58	95	110	131	172	235	292	345	335	279	212	249	2,648
II.) Final Decisions																
Phase 1 – compatible	5	47	43	49	78	90	109	118	207	236	293	299	240	203	220	2,237
Phase 1 – compatible with commitments		3	4		2	3	2	2	12	19	28	13	10	11	12	119
Phase 2 – compatible		1	1	1	2	2	1	1	3	0	3	5	2	2	2	26
Phase 2 – compatible with commitments		3	3	2	2	3	3	7	4	8	12	10	5	6	4	62
Phase 2 – Prohibitions	1	1			1	2	3	1	2	1	2	5	0	0	1	19
Other *	2	5	13	7	12	13	15	22	19	17	21	20	20	9	8	203

Source: DG Competition http://europa.eu.int/comm/competition/mergers/cases/stats.html.

* Cases withdrawn Phase 1 + Cases withdrawn Phase 2 + (Final Decision) 6.1 (a) out of scope Merger Reg. + 9.3 partial referral to M.S. (ph I) + 9.3 full referral to member states + 8.4 restore effective competition.

single market. Rather, the fact that other measures (such as forcing merging firms to discontinue making some of goods if they produce a wide range of products) are often negotiated informally with the participation and consent of firms suggests that the Commission has a strong influence on the nature of the merger. Second, between 1990 and 2004 almost 90 cases were withdrawn by companies after merger notification had been given. Thus it is possible that firms will not seek to proceed unless they are almost certain that the merger will be approved by the Commission. This suggests that there is a type of "self-selection process" undertaken by the firms themselves if they fear that the Commission may ultimately rule against them. Third, and related to the second point, the effectiveness of the Commission may also be seen in cases where approval is made without conditions precisely because these firms have proposed only mergers that they are certain that the Commission will approve under MCR guidelines. Firms know that because they must notify the Commission of their intention to merge, they have to satisfy EU authorities. To this end, it is not uncommon to have a type of informal bargaining process between merging firms and the Commission even before formal notification is made. Such a process eventually results in notification of details to which the Commission has already implicitly agreed.

Indeed, the first of these dynamics was captured in the Nestlé-Perrier merger of 1992 as examined by Shea and Chari.[29] The multinational Swiss-based food conglomerate Nestlé notified the Commission in February that it was seeking to acquire the French bottled-water company Perrier. The merger would have left Nestlé with 48 per cent of the French market for mineral water (the next largest supplier would be BSN with a 20 per cent share). Because the MTF raised concerns regarding dominance, Nestlé proposed to sell Volvic (one of Perrier's leading brands) to BSN. Estimated post-merger market shares after the Volvic deal would have left Nestlé with 37 per cent and BSN with 31 per cent. Nevertheless, the MTF was still concerned that the merger posed significant problems for competition in the French market for bottled water: even though the Volvic deal would have eliminated the threat of a Nestlé monopoly, the MTF believed that Nestlé and BSN would become collectively dominant. As such, a deeper Phase 2 investigation ensued. The MTF outlined a remedy stating that were Nestlé to dispose of eight of its lesser brands (which represented 20 per cent of the market) to a single approved buyer who could not sell them to BSN or back to Nestlé within a ten-year period, the merger would be approved. The acceptance and concession by Nestlé help demonstrate that, even without prohibiting a merger, the Commission can influence the dimensions of a merger so as to maintain competition and prevent dominance in European markets.

Competition policy and its 1st order status

In sum, taking the four aspects of competition policy together, the evolution of the policy area means EU regulations ensure that member states are increasingly being constrained from freely giving market-distorting aid, governments and/or enterprises with a monopoly position in certain states must increasingly seek liberalization in sectors that were once in their domain, economic actors operating in the single market are increasingly put under the microscope if engaging in restrictive practices or abuse of dominant positions, and firms seeking to merge are required to have the approval of Brussels. From another vantage point, developments suggest that national governments have a relatively weaker role in regulating competition policy issues, and that major efforts to reach integration have been made. Given that one generally sees that the supranational level has the responsibility to make determining and final decisions in this area, something which member state governments have largely respected, one can thus argue that this area is representative of a 1st order policy.

We now turn to a more detailed analysis of developments to do with the formulation of the Merger Control Regulation in order to better understand which actors were involved, what motivated them, and how this can be theoretically characterized.

Formulation of the Merger Control Regulation

Policy initiation: the Commission taking the lead (again)

As discussed previously, although Articles 81 and 82 explicitly noted that restrictive practices and abuses of dominant position by firms could be regulated at the European level, there was no explicit regulation concerning firms that sought to merge. Reasons for this include the desires of many member states throughout the 1950s and 1970s to foster the creation of the "European Champions" which could compete internationally against other firms operating out of the United States and Asia, as discussed by authors such as Frazer.[30]

As Shea[31] notes, however, as early as the late 1960s the European Commission began to develop a policy for the regulation of firms that were merging, given concerns that mergers had anti-competitive effects in the European market. As early as 1973, the Commission chose what is referred to as the Continental Can case as a test case of its powers to deem mergers illegal via Article 82. Although the ECJ ruled against the Commission in this case, in its wake the Commission "proposed the first draft of the MCR to the Council where it faced major political opposition from member states ... [that] were unwilling to concede authority"[32] to the supranational level. Further attempts by the Commission to develop merger control regulations were made in 1982 and 1984, spearheaded by

Competition Commissioner Sutherland, who throughout the 1980s warned that a level playing field would not be attained if mergers were not regulated at the supranational level. Although the Council was still unwilling to cede power to the Commission in this area throughout the early 1980s, the Commission would eventually persuade the Council to consider regulation by threatening that Articles 81 and 82 would be used to stop mergers. The force of this threat was upheld by in the Philip Morris case of 1987 when the ECJ declared that regulation of some mergers could fall within the scope of anti-trust regulations.[33] As Shea argues, "the Philip Morris judgment brought home to the parties concerned the realization that control based on a new regulation might be far better than reliance on the unpredictable consequences of that case".[34] Given this evidence, one may argue that the Commission, supported by the ECJ, was primarily responsible for the initiation of merger control regulation. This indicates the importance of ideas raised by supranational governance scholars in understanding how the policy was initiated.

Policy negotiation: the Commission meets the ERT (again)

Turning to policy negotiation, it can be seen that from 1987 until late 1989 the details of the MCR would be decided by both the Commission and economic actors in a similar vein to the negotiation of the single market programme discussed in the previous chapter. When discussing the latter programme, it was argued that multinationals sought to decrease transaction costs by centralizing market regulations while the Commission welcomed the input of capital actors because of their technical expertise. Focussing on the negotiations surrounding the MCR, one also sees that, beyond immediate concerns for creating a level playing field, European Commission authorities and business leaders alike felt the need for supranational merger regulation because market consolidation went hand in hand with (neo-liberal economic) globalization and resulted in an exponential growth of mergers throughout the 1980s, as discussed by Eberlein.[35] As Garrett and Mitchell argue, the constraining policy effects of globalization throughout the 1980s and 1990s forced a re-evaluation of the need for merger control by both the Commission and economic actors.[36]

Thus, on the one hand, the Commission sought not only to ensure a level playing field as discussed above, but also "to increase its stronghold of power in a regulatory policy process which was increasingly necessary given global economic dynamics, without necessarily isolating the very object of their regulation – corporate interests".[37] In the words of Peterson and Bomberg "the Commission [could] use the MCR to set policy where it [had] been unable to before".[38] Moreover, as shown by Coen[39] and the Commission itself,[40] great weight was given by the Commission to the discussion of the nature of the regulation with the relevant firms in order to establish "credibility". By appearing to accommodate capital's demand for the creation of a "level playing field" and a "one-stop shop" for merger control, the Commission was successful in securing a "strong" policy partner and expanding its policy competence into a new area where it would be the principal EU institutional actor.

On the other hand, "European capital also realized that if the internal market was to become a tangible entity, massive corporate mergers and restructuring would become reality and thus sought to gain a foothold in its regulatory policy-process."[41] As far as capital was concerned, a codified merger directive had two advantages. First, it would help capital attain its goals of reorganization and consolidation in the global economy. Second, regulations could limit the Commission's power over economic actors that might otherwise have occurred in the absence of clearly defined rules. The ECJ's ruling on Phillip Morris potentially allowed the Commission the authority to stop mergers on the basis of the EU's anti-trust policies, something that concerned capital because the exact boundaries to deal with supranational merger control remained unclear. Rather than function in an uncertain regulatory environment, business sought to influence the details surrounding the supranational merger rules and standards.

Given the interests of both actors, throughout the late 1980s members of the Commission (led by DG Competition[42]) would negotiate the details of the MCR alongside members of the ERT and UNICE. As Shea neatly summarizes, there were three main issues on the discussion table: jurisdiction, tests and criteria, and time frame.[43]

With regard to jurisdiction, an example of a major concern for capital related to the concept of "double jeopardy": business wished to be sure that once a decision on a merger was made, it could not be reversed by a different decision taken by another (national) competition authority. While the Commission strongly held the view that the MCR should be a "one-stop shop" for merger control within the European Market, Shea demonstrates how both ERT and UNICE "lobbied heavily for clarification on the issue as seen in various position papers exchanged with the Commission". These debates led to Article 21.1 of the MCR which states that the "Commission alone has competence to examine mergers with a Community dimension, even if they only involve firms based in the same member state."[44]

With respect to tests and criteria, capital actors were concerned about which criteria would be used in order to evaluate whether or not a merger was permissible. The concern here was whether or not decisions should be primarily based on "competition aspects" or whether other issues, such as social concerns, should come into play when considering if a merger was to be allowed. The ERT's position, as set out in an internal memorandum, was clearly in favour of a "competition only" criterion, as this would allow for rapid decisions to be made by the MTF while also allowing firms the autonomy to downsize, if necessary, in the wake of a merger.[45] While countries such as the UK and Germany held similar views to the ERT, others such as France believed that social and industrial policies should be reflected when merger decision were being considered. Article 2.1 was finally agreed by both the Commission and capital, and under it competition concerns would be at the forefront of merger investigations.[46] The spirit of this article was upheld in the de Havilland decision discussed earlier, and leaders of DG Competition would later consistently state in 2001 with regard to the goals of the MCR that:

> It may be that, in the short term, efforts to improve the competitiveness of firms by means of mergers or acquisitions will involve restructuring and thus loss of jobs. However, this does not change the fact that improving firms' competitiveness on the global market is the only effective way to ensure the growth needed to create business.[47]

The third and final concern of capital related to the period within which a merger investigation should be completed. As discussed in the first section of this chapter, the MCR considers different potential phases in a merger's investigation, leading to different outcomes. However, given the concerns that especially arose during the evolution of Articles 81 and 82 over cases where there may not necessarily be a formal decision that is taken within a specific timeframe, one of capital's main concerns during the negotiations of the MCR was that a clear system be established for the investigation process. To this end, capital wished for two principles to be firmly established, arguably at both the "informal" and "formal" governance levels. With regard to informal governance, as discussed earlier, even though it is formally stated in Article 10 of the MCR that mergers must be notified to the MTF one week after they are announced publicly, both actors sought to guarantee that "pre-notification" discussions could be pursued by both parties so that, before the merger was announced, they could informally "address in a cooperative manner possible difficulties that may arise from a merger".[48] As Shea's work highlights, "there is almost always conflict between the companies and the MTF at the start, but common ground is usually reached [in pre-notification discussions]."[49] With regard to a more formal aspect relating to time period of investigation, capital wished to ensure that if a decision was not arrived at in a timely fashion, it should be considered void. As Shea intriguingly notes with regard to a UNICE internal memorandum, during the negotiations UNICE wrote that it:

> considers it essential that the regulation state the legal effect of the time limits set down. ... If the Commission makes no pronouncement within the time limit (of one month after initiation of

Phase 1 or four months after the start of in Phase 2 investigations) the decision should automatically be deemed positive.[50]

Although the Commission had not fully considered this time limit in initial drafts of the MCR, the final outcome stated in Article 10.6 that a merger would be deemed compatible with the common market if no decision were made within the proper time period. Once the Commission and capital had negotiated the details of the MCR to meet these three concerns, the package was finally approved by the European Council in December 1989.[51]

It is worth noting that "during the formal legislation process the European Parliament was consulted by both the Commission and Council in accordance with EU law, however there was minimal Parliamentary debate or feedback."[52] Furthermore, organized labour – arguably the ones who would suffer the most given the downsizing that usually occurs after a merger – was not invited to partake in the process when negotiation surrounding the MCR occurred. Even when amendments were made to the MCR in 1997 on the issue of thresholds, further evidence of labour's exclusion was seen when the Commission stated that it "followed wide-ranging consultations with Member States, the competent competition authorities and the business community."[53]

Given the overall importance of both the Commission and capital during the negotiation phase, the evidence suggests the importance of both the supranational governance perspective (with the focus on the actions of the Commission in particular) as well as the dominant class perspective, in understanding the negotiation of the policy. Conversely, considering the relative absence of other potential major players in the policy process – such as the Council and interest groups such as labour – the intergovernmentalist, pluralist, and corporatist perspectives are of relatively little importance in fully understanding how the main details of the policy were negotiated.

Conclusions

This first section of this chapter analysed the key aspects of EU competition policy. It specifically focussed on developments in: state aid control, where Brussels is empowered to ensure that no market-distorting subsidies are given by member states; liberalization, where the Commission seeks to end monopoly dominance at the domestic level in sectors such as telecommunications and electricity; anti-trust measures, where the Commission is able to penalize and fine companies that engage in restrictive agreements or that abuse their position of market dominance; and merger control, where the Commission must approve mergers which have a Community dimension in order to ensure that a competitive market environment is maintained. After analysis of the evolution of each of these four areas, it was concluded that competition policy constitutes a 1st order policy, given that relevant policy competences have been fully transferred to the supranational level. This has resulted in a strong, centralized EU in this policy area, intended to create a competitive market in the world economy. As such, member states have accepted that in issues of state aid and liberalization, Brussels regulations need to be followed and that the supranational level has the final say. For example, all aid given by national authorities has to be approved by DG Competition, and if it is not, the state is obliged to recoup such aid. Similarly, economic actors such as firms have accepted that Brussels has the final word on the acceptability of their behaviour in the Common Market. For example, companies engaging in abuses of a dominant position, even if this occurs only in one member state, will ultimately face the judgment of the Commission if the overall competitive environment of the Single Market is compromised.

The second section offered a more detailed analysis of the formulation of a specific aspect of competition policy, the Merger Control Regulation of 1990. In terms of policy processes, the section showed the importance of the Commission in the initiation stage: since the late 1960s the Commission had contemplated developing merger control regulations, used anti-trust regulation as a means to stop mergers throughout the 1970s and 1980s, and eventually, with the decision of the ECJ in the Phillip Morris case, was able to convince the Council of the need to develop the MCR. Given the above, and considering the four theoretical perspectives outlined in Chapter 3, the evidence suggests that the policy initiation phase can be best characterized by ideas raised in the supranational governance perspective, because of the importance of the Commission in initiating merger control regulation. Although the Council did initially offer resistance to supranational regulation in this area, continuous threats by the Commission as well as a positive decision by the ECJ in the Philip Morris case served as catalysts to ensure Council acceptance of the idea of supranational governance in this area.

Turning to policy negotiation, the evidence demonstrated that the Commission did not act alone in formulating the details of the MCR. Rather, the direct participation of capital actors, specifically those from UNICE and the ERT, was manifest. The ensuing policy negotiation thus saw the predominant influence of both the Commission and representatives of capital, lending strength to the idea that this phase of analysis is best informed by ideas raised in the supranational governance and DEC perspectives. For its part, the Commission sought to ensure a level playing field in the single market, while institutionalizing its power in an area not fully covered under pre-existing anti-trust regulations. At the same time, economic élites sought to influence the nature of the regulation in order to help consolidate their position in the global economy while potentially limiting the Commission's ability to act unilaterally when setting the rules.

Clearly, the Council did have the final say when the MCR had to be approved. However, the evidence suggests that in terms of initiation and negotiating the details of the policy, the Council took more of a back seat. Interestingly, it was pointed out that neither the European Parliament, nor other interest groups – such as representatives of European labour – played a significant role in either of the policy stages. In fact, with regard to the latter, it was suggested that even though issues such as social and employment ramifications of mergers could have been nominated as factors to be considered when adjudicating on a merger, the negotiating dynamics wherein capital was granted privileged access over labour resulted in such issues being of minute importance. As such, given that actors who were not representative of either capital or the Commission played a relatively minor role in negotiating the policy, one can argue that neither the intergovernmentalist, nor the pluralist nor the corporatist models are of value in explaining the policy's development.

6 Economic and Monetary Union: the making of the money tree

This chapter examines and explains economic and monetary policy in the EU. The first section considers the main objectives and evolution of Economic and Monetary Union (EMU). Analysing data across several years, including the evolution of the so-called "convergence criteria" that states had to meet in order to qualify for EMU as well as several indicators that help one gauge the evolution of the euro on world markets since 1999, the main argument to be developed here is that EMU is representative of a 1st order policy. The second section offers a more detailed analysis of the formulation of the EMU, starting with the Hanover Summit in 1988 and ending with the Maastricht agreement three years later. This section argues that in order to better understand policy initiation, particular attention must be paid to the role of the Commission, and of Jacques Delors as its president. This indicates the importance of the supranational governance perspective in helping understand this stage of the policy-making process. When turning to the negotiation phase, however, Delors' role became less relevant since the Council played a more important part in what can be referred to as an intergovernmental bargaining process led by the Franco-German axis. Nevertheless, in contrast to most mainstream works in political science that have studied the formulation of the EMU, it will be argued that the role of capital, acting through the ERT, also influenced the negotiation process, therefore pointing to the significance of the dominant economic class (DEC) perspective in explaining the EMU.

Objectives and evolution of Economic and Monetary Policy and its 1st order status in the integration process

Objectives and goals of EMU

The overall objective of Economic and Monetary Union (EMU) is the establishment of a single currency to increase the economic efficiency of the single European market and help it compete in the world economy. The European Community had previously contemplated the idea of increased monetary ties, most notably with the Werner Report of 1970, which had to be abandoned in the face of the recessionary pressures that Europe faced a few years later. The European Monetary System (EMS) was set up in 1979 with the goal of achieving monetary stability by having several EU currencies linked in order to prevent large exchange fluctuations.

The impetus in the 1980s for a single currency started with the Delors' Report of 1989, which played a crucial part in laying the foundations for the EMU, highlighting two main components: monetary union and tight fiscal control. It is important to note here that monetary policy can be defined as the regulation of interest rates and money supply by a central bank with the goal of attaining price stability (i.e. controlling inflation.) In the absence of a single currency area, national governments are able to use monetary policy as a tool to either boost economic growth or to slow down the economy. That is, on the one hand, if a country is in a recession and the state wants to spur economic growth, it may pursue reflationary (expansionary) monetary policies by lowering interest rates. On the other hand, if the state wants to slow down the economy, it may pursue deflationary (or contractionary) monetary policies, increasing interest rates (so as to decrease inflation). With a single European currency area, however, member states would transfer this power to the "centre" and thus not have this ability to control their monetary policy. Padoa-Schioppa notes that "Monetary union *strictu sensu*, is usually defined as the 'irrevocable locking of exchange rates,' the expression frequently used in the Delors' Report, or the adoption of a single currency."[1] But, Padoa-Schioppa also notes that the important feature of monetary union in the European case is that "the responsibility for monetary decisions is shifted to one single institution (namely the European Central Bank that is required to promote price stability) instead of being entrusted to a plurality of central banks. ... In other words, creating monetary union means moving from a plurality of decision-making centres to just one" in order to increase the economic competitiveness of Europe on the world stage.[2]

The 1989 Delors' Report also insisted that fiscal discipline would need to be imposed on any state that formed part of monetary union. Padoa-Schioppa notes that "fiscal discipline was required as a safeguard to ensure that monetary union was stable, that the value of money would not be threatened by fiscal disorder in the budgets of member states."[3] Without indirect control over fiscal policy in the EMU, the absence of strict limits on deficits and debts might have encouraged governments to pursue expansionary fiscal policies in order to stimulate economic growth, thus potentially increasing inflation while decreasing investment opportunities for businesses seeking to operate in the single, integrated market as discussed in Chapter 4.

Even though many would argue that the transferring of monetary policy making to the EU level would seriously decrease the "independence" of member states, especially those suffering from recession, several observers highlighted the benefits of a single currency for Europe. Authors such as DeGrauwe[4] note that these would include: decreased transaction costs within the more efficiently functioning single market; a concomitant increase in investment and trade across the Community; low inflationary economic growth coupled with lower interest rates, given the greater economic certainty in the free-market zone; and, providing that the euro was a success, a strong international currency which could rival the currency of major competitors such as the United States dollar and the Japanese yen on world markets.

Guided by ideas in the Delors' Report, one of the main aspects defined in the Maastricht Treaty of December 1991 related to the various criteria that needed to be fulfilled by states seeking to join the EMU, also referred to as "convergence criteria", The criteria outlined in Article 121.1, which were to be attained by the end of the decade, specified limits on inflation rates, interest rates, debts and deficits as follows:

- *Price stability*: The inflation rate of a given member state (MS) must not exceed by more than 1.5 per cent that of the three best-performing MSs in terms of price stability during the year preceding the examination of the situation in that MS.
- *Interest rates.* The nominal long-term interest rate must not exceed by more than 2 per cent that of the three best-performing MSs in terms of price stability.
- *Deficits.* The ratio of the annual government deficit to gross domestic product (GDP) must not have exceeded 3 per cent at the end of the preceding financial year. If this is not the case, the ratio must have declined substantially and continuously and reached a level close to 3 per cent (interpretation in trend terms according to Article 104.2) or, alternatively, must remain close to 3 per cent while representing only an exceptional and temporary excess.
- *Debt.* The ratio of gross government debt to GDP must not have exceeded 60 per cent at the end of the preceding financial year. If this is not the case, the ratio must have sufficiently diminished and must be approaching the reference value at a satisfactory pace (interpretation in trend terms according to Article 104.2).
- *Currency stability.* Normal fluctuation margins provided for by the exchange-rate mechanism of the European Monetary System must be observed for at least two years, without devaluing against the currency of any other MS.[5]

As will be seen more fully in the data presented below, throughout the 1990s member states made serious efforts to meet these criteria in order to join the Euro-zone. One example was the labour market reform of Spain in the mid 1990s. In the midst of speculation shortly after Maastricht that there would be a "two-speed" EMU (made up of those expected to join the EMU, such as Germany, France, the Netherlands and Luxembourg, and those that would be left out, such as Spain, Italy and Portugal), states such as Spain quickly pursued domestic policies to meet the criteria. The deregulation of the Spanish labour market was intended to decrease inflationary tendencies and reduce spending.[6] Some of the reforms taken up by the Spanish Socialists in the mid 1990s included: introducing less expensive forms of contracting in which the state would have no role; facilitating the use of temporary and part time contracts; decreasing the power of wage agreements to set salary bases, thus allowing more autonomy for employers to set salary structures; making it easier for employers to fire workers unilaterally without state involvement; lowering indemnity and unemployment benefits for sacked workers; introducing new instruments to enable employers to downsize easily; and giving employers more freedom to determine working hours, working conditions and place of work. Furthermore, a sharp axe was taken to social-welfare programs in Spain that would otherwise have burdened the deficit and debt; the measures included cuts to healthcare, pensions, education and unemployment benefits. Even states such as France, arguably in a relatively better position to meet the criteria, pursued deregulatory initiatives and cuts in the public sector, triggering strikes with hundreds of thousands of protestors taking the streets in the mid 1990s.[7]

It is also interesting to note that at the Dublin Intergovernmental Conference in 1996, the Stability and Growth Pact (SGP) was developed, and formalized in the Amsterdam Summit in the following year. Its main objective was to prevent states that joined the EMU from running excessive deficits. The problem was that while monetary policy objectives, particularly interest rates, would be controlled largely by the European Central Bank (ECB) for those states forming part of the EMU, if there were no formal regulations the EMU member states might be tempted to pursue national fiscal policies that ran against the objectives of controlling spending (as established by the deficit criteria). In other words, states might attempt to get around the "monetary policy straightjacket" in order to stimulate growth in the midst of a recession. As such, at the insistence of Germany and France which were concerned about the potential for smaller states in the EMU running excessive deficits, the SGP gave the Commission the power to penalize EMU states that had deficits in excess of 3 per cent of the GDP. As a result, when presenting national budgets all member states had to produce a detailed "Stability Programme" demonstrating their commitment to a tight fiscal policy in which spending was controlled and taxes would not be lowered in an attempt to fast-start the economy. While the first test for the SGP came in 2001 when the Irish government and its Finance Minister Charlie McCreevy were reprimanded by the Commission for pursuing an expansionary budget, the real test came in 2003 came when the Commission led by Pedro Solbes took on both France and Germany which, somewhat ironically, were guilty of breaking their own proposed rules, as discussed later.

In May 1998, a special Council agreed that 11 member states had met (or at least approximated) the convergence criteria and would therefore join the EMU, while Greece was allowed to enter later.[8] As such, the EMU-12 (as they are referred to in this book) would consist of the following states: Belgium, Germany, Greece, Spain, France, Ireland, Italy, Luxembourg, the Netherlands, Austria, Portugal and Finland. The other three states of the EU-15, namely the UK, Denmark and Sweden, preferred to either "opt out" (UK and Denmark) or not to join (Sweden). On January 1, 1999 the EMU was launched (with the European Central bank fixing interest rates) and in January 2002 the euro notes came into circulation.

Evolution of EMU: convergence criteria and the euro in world markets

It is useful to attempt to measure the success of economic and monetary policy by considering two main ideas, which reflect how the policy has been given priority by European institutions and actors therein. First, how committed were member states not only to attaining the convergence criteria in order to enter the EMU, but also in maintaining low levels of inflation, interest rates, debts and deficits over the last five years? Second, and also relating to the determination of member states to ensure the success of the EMU, how has the euro performed since its launch in 1999 and is there evidence to point to a favourable evolution of the currency in international markets?

Convergence criteria

Turing to the first major point, Table 6.1 considers the evolution of inflation rates of all EU-15 countries between 1995 and 2004.

When examining the EU-15, one generally sees that the trend indicates a decreasing rate of inflation over the time series. Between 1995 and 1997, inflation rates clearly fell in all member countries, with the only state not meeting the criteria in 1997 being Greece.[9] Despite a drop in rates during this time period, there were nevertheless certain local minimums and maximums throughout. For example, in some states a local minimum was reached around 1999 after serious efforts had been made to curb inflation throughout the decade so as to meet convergence criteria, despite the enormous social costs of so doing (as seen in the case described earlier of labour market deregulation which helped subdue inflationary tendencies).[10] Despite a tendency for inflation levels to rise shortly after 1999, from 2002 most countries started to converge again to lower levels, with the exception of Greece which has had historical problems in keeping inflation at bay. By 2004, the best performers were Finland, the UK and Sweden (the latter two states are actually outside the Euro-zone, suggesting that this macro-economic

Table 6.1 Inflation rate: annual average rate of change in harmonized indices of consumer prices (HICPs), EU-15

	1995	1996	1997	1998	1999	2000	2001	2002	2003	2004
Belgium	**1.3**	1.8	1.5	0.9	1.1	*2.7*	2.4	**1.6**	1.5	1.9
Germany		**1.2**	1.5	**0.6**	**0.6**	1.4	1.9	**1.3**	**1.0**	1.8
Greece		*7.9*	*5.4*	*4.5*	*2.1*	*2.9*	*3.7*	*3.9*	*3.4*	*3.0*
Spain	*4.6*	*3.6*	1.9	1.8	*2.2*	*3.5*	*2.8*	*3.6*	*3.1*	*3.1*
France	1.8	*2.1*	1.3	**0.7**	**0.6**	1.8	**1.8**	1.9	*2.2*	*2.3*
Ireland		*2.2*	**1.2**	*2.1*	*2.5*	*5.3*	*4.0*	*4.7*	*4.0*	*2.3*
Italy	*5.4*	*4.0*	1.9	*2.0*	1.7	*2.6*	*2.3*	*2.6*	*2.8*	*2.3*
Luxembourg		**1.2**	1.4	1.0	1.0	*3.8*	*2.4*	*2.1*	*2.5*	*3.2*
Netherlands	**1.4**	1.4	1.9	1.8	*2.0*	*2.3*	*5.1*	*3.9*	*2.2*	1.4
Austria	1.6	1.8	**1.2**	**0.8**	**0.5**	*2.0*	*2.3*	1.7	**1.3**	*2.0*
Portugal	*4.0*	*2.9*	1.9	*2.2*	*2.2*	*2.8*	*4.4*	*3.7*	*3.3*	*2.5*
Finland	**0.4**	**1.1**	**1.2**	1.4	1.3	*3.0*	*2.7*	*2.0*	**1.3**	**0.1**
Sweden	*2.7*	**0.8**	1.8	1.0	**0.6**	1.3	*2.7*	*2.0*	*2.3*	**1.0**
UK	*2.7*	*2.5*	1.8	1.6	1.3	**0.8**	1.2	**1.3**	1.4	1.3
Denmark	*2.0*	*2.1*	1.9	1.3	*2.1*	*2.7*	*2.3*	*2.4*	*2.0*	**0.9**
Average of the 3 best performing	1.03	1.03	1.2	0.7	0.56	1.16	1.63	1.4	1.2	0.66
Average +1.5	2.53	2.53	2.7	2.2	2.06	2.66	3.13	2.9	2.7	2.16

Source: Eurostat.

Blank spaces represent unavailable data; bold data represents one of the three best performing; italics means over the limit.

priority is of significance to them as well), while the worst performers were Spain, Greece and Luxembourg.

Interestingly, one can also see similar trends in the case of the ten new accession countries to the EU in 2004 as captured in Table 6.2. The data suggest that with regard to price stability, these countries have taken their "cue" from EMU states with the goal of becoming part of the EMU "club". With the exception of Cyprus and Latvia, which have veered between periods of high and low levels of inflation, the other states have generally reduced inflation from very high to very low levels, most remarkably in the case of Estonia and Hungary.

Turning to the EU-15 again, Figure 6.1 demonstrates that as inflation rates have gone down, interest rates have also decreased remarkably and also almost converged.

Even before the European Central Bank set rates in 1999 for the states in the EMU-12, one sees that a drastic drop in rates had occurred over the four previous years, reflecting the efforts made by these member states to

Table 6.2 Inflation rates: annual average rate of change in harmonized indices of consumer prices (HICPs), ten new entrants in 2004.

	1997	1998	1999	2000	2001	2002	2003	2004
Czech Republic	8.0	9.7	1.8	3.9	4.5	1.4	-0.1	2.6
Estonia	9.3	8.8	3.1	3.9	5.6	3.6	1.4	3.0
Cyprus	3.3	2.3	1.1	4.9	2.0	2.8	4.0	1.9
Latvia	8.1	4.3	2.1	2.6	2.5	2.0	2.9	6.2
Lithuania	8.8	5.0	0.7	0.9	1.3	0.4	-1.1	1.1
Hungary	18.5	14.2	10.0	10.0	9.1	5.2	4.7	6.8
Malta	3.9	3.7	2.3	3.0	2.5	2.6	1.9	2.7
Poland	15.0	11.8	7.2	10.1	5.3	1.9	0.7	3.6
Slovenia	8.3	7.9	6.1	8.9	8.6	7.5	5.7	3.6
Slovakia	6.0	6.7	10.4	12.2	7.2	3.5	8.5	7.4

Source: Eurostat.

meet the interest-rate criterion throughout the 1990s. One of the sharpest falls in the original EMU countries between 1995 and 1998 is seen in the case of Italy, where interest rates fell from slightly over 12 per cent to a little less than 5.5 per cent in this short period. Since 2000, interest rates have generally gone down from an average of around 5.5 per cent to one of slightly over 4.2 per cent in the EU-15. By 2004, the three countries with the lowest rates were Spain, France and the Netherlands. The three countries outside the EMU – the UK, Sweden and Denmark – had the highest rates of the EU-15 in 2004, demonstrating the importance of the ECB in maintaining low rates for the EMU-12. Although not shown in Figure 6.1, data from 2000 demonstrate that interest rates in all new accession EU states from central and eastern Europe have continuously decreased, except in Poland which saw an increase of over 1 per cent between 2003 and 2004.[11]

When turning to the debt criterion, a similar convergence is seen to that in Figure 6.1, although less acute: Figure 6.2 demonstrates an overall convergence towards the debt-to-GDP ratio of 60 per cent, reflecting many states' overall desire to pursue spending cuts.

Such cuts were seen in several policy areas across the EMU-12: decreasing welfare payments and funding for health systems, lower pensions, decreased funding for education, and privatization of both loss-making state companies (in order to not drain the budget) and financially strong public enterprises (in order to raise revenues).[12] Social costs aside, it is interesting to note in Figure 6.2 that, despite the

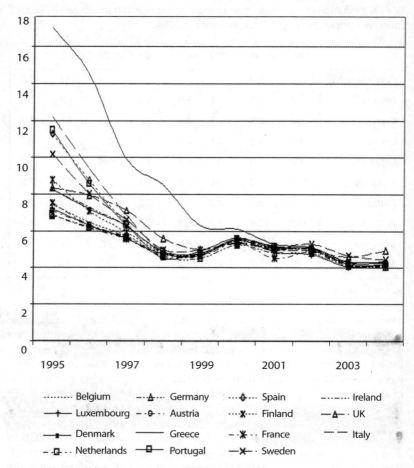

Figure 6.1 Long-term interest rates, EU-15, 1995–2004

Source: Eurostat and European Central Bank.

serious efforts made by member states to decrease debts, one can distinguish between three types of trends within the data. The first represents countries that remain drastically over the limit, although convergence is taking place: Greece (top line in 2004), Italy (second from the top in 2004) and Belgium (third from the top). Clearly, the first two of these countries have had historical problems with high debt-to-GDP ratios as seen in the late 1990s when their entrance into the EMU was questioned on the grounds of this criterion, as mentioned earlier.[13] The second trend is seen in states that are slightly over the 60 per cent limit: Germany (except 2001), France (only in 2003 and 2004), Austria

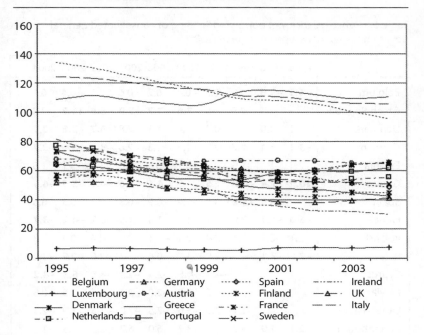

Figure 6.2 General government consolidated gross debt as a percentage of GDP in the EU-15

Source: Eurostat.

(throughout the time series), and Portugal (in 1995, 2003 and 2004). Finally, there are several countries which are well below the limit: Ireland, Luxembourg, Finland, the UK, Sweden and Denmark. The case of Ireland is particularly interesting because it had one of the highest debt levels in 1995, but has drastically controlled its debt since 1998; the result was the development of one of the weakest welfare systems in the EU, despite the growth of the so-called "Celtic tiger" that significantly increased the wealth of many economic élites in a short amount of time. Again, and in similar vein to what was seen in Table 6.1, although the UK, Sweden and Denmark are outside the EMU they have nevertheless been committed to debt reduction. Interestingly, all of the new adhesion countries (except for Cyprus and Malta) have had debt levels well below the 60 per cent target since 1997, leaving them in a prime position for future EMU entry.

Turning to the deficit criteria, one sees in Table 6.3 that while there has been an overall commitment to controlling deficits, in the years 2002–04 some of the EMU states had deficits over the 3 per cent of the GDP established in the Stability and Growth Pact (SGP) discussed earlier.

In more detail, and considering first the EMU-12 states, even though

Table 6.3 Public balance: net borrowing/lending of consolidated general government sector as a percentage of GDP

	1995	1996	1997	1998	1999	2000	2001	2002	2003	2004
Belgium	**-4.3**	**-3.8**	-2.0	-0.7	-0.4	0.2	0.6	0.1	0.4	0.1
Czech Republic			-2.5	**-5**	**-3.6**	**-3.7**	**-5.9**	**-6.8**	**-11.7**	**-3.0**
Denmark	-3.1	-1.9	-0.5	0.2	2.4	1.3	-2.8	**-3.7**	**-3.8**	**-3.7**
Germany	**-3.3**	**-3.4**	-2.7	-2.2	-1.5	1.3	-2.8	**-3.5**	**-3.9**	**-3.7**
Estonia			1.9	-0.3	-3.7	-0.6	0.3	1.4	3.1	1.8
Greece	**-10.2**	**-7.4**	**-4.0**	-2.5	-1.8	**-4.1**	**-3.6**	**-4.1**	**-5.2**	**-6.1**
Spain		**-4.9**	**-3.2**	-3.0	-1.2	-0.9	-0.5	-0.3	0.3	-0.3
France	**-5.5**	**-4.1**	-3.0	-2.7	-1.8	-1.4	-1.5	**-3.2**	**-4.2**	**-3.7**
Ireland	-2.1	-0.1	1.1	2.4	2.4	**-4.1**	0.9	-0.4	0.2	1.3
Italy	**-7.6**	**-7.1**	-2.7	-2.8	-1.7	-0.6	-3	-2.6	-2.9	-3.0
Cyprus				**-4.3**	**-4.5**	-2.4	-2.3	**-4.5**	**-6.3**	**-4.2**
Latvia				-0.6	**-4.9**	-2.8	-2.1	-2.7	-1.5	-0.8
Lithuania			-1.1	-3.0	**-5.6**	-2.5	-2.0	-1.5	-1.9	-2.5
Luxembourg	2.1	1.9	3.2	3.2	3.7	6.0	6.2	2.3	0.5	-1.1
Hungary			**-6.8**	**-8.0**	**-5.6**	-3.0	**-3.7**	**-8.5**	**-6.2**	**-4.5**
Malta			**-10.7**	**-10.8**	**-7.6**	**-6.2**	**-6.4**	**-5.9**	**-10.5**	**-5.2**
Netherlands	**-4.2**	-1.8	-1.1	-0.8	0.7	2.2	-0.1	-1.9	**-3.2**	-2.5
Austria	**-5.6**	**-3.9**	-1.8	-2.3	-2.2	-1.5	0.3	-0.2	-1.1	-1.3
Poland			**-4.0**	-2.1	-1.4	-0.7	**-3.9**	**-3.6**	**-4.5**	**-4.8**
Portugal	**-4.5**	**-4.0**	-3.0	-2.6	-2.8	-2.8	**-4.4**	-2.7	-2.9	-2.9
Slovenia				-2.2	-2.1	**-3.5**	-2.8	-2.4	-2.0	-1.9
Slovakia			**-5.5**	**-4.7**	**-6.4**	**-12.3**	**-6.0**	**-5.7**	**-3.7**	**-3.3**
Finland	**-3.7**	**-3.2**	-1.5	1.5	2.2	7.1	5.2	4.3	2.5	2.1
Sweden	**-7.0**	**-2.7**	-0.9	1.8	2.5	5.1	2.5	-0.3	0.2	1.4
UK	**-5.7**	**-4.3**	-2.0	0.2	1.0	3.8	0.7	-1.7	**-3.4**	**-3.2**

Source: Eurostat.

Note: numbers in bold show countries have gone over the 3 per cent limit established in the SGP; blank spaces represent unavailable data.

many have shown a strong commitment to controlling spending, the latter years of the time series highlight how Germany, France and Greece went beyond the 3 per cent limit. Particularly note-worthy are Germany and France, which ran deficits that exceeded the limits for three years. As discussed earlier, the SGP was set up with the intention of preventing states from dodging the tough monetary policies of the ECB by seeking to increase spending and having large deficits, something that in the long term was perceived as likely to undermine the value of the euro. In the case of Germany and France, however, the early 2000s witnessed severe recessionary tendencies: low economic growth meant a fall in tax revenues, increasing unemployment, and therefore increased government social spending. As a means to spur on growth, and against the desires of the DG Economic and Financial Affairs of the European Commission, led by then Commissioner Pedro Solbes that policed the SGP, both France and Germany decided to cut taxes, something that also received tough criticism from most other EMU states, which had made serious sacrifices to maintain low deficits.[14] While both Germany and Portugal stated later that they would take measures to bring their future deficits under control, the French government somewhat challenged the European Commission in its 2003 budget by honouring Chirac's pledge to the French electorate to cut taxes and stating that an excessive deficit would be necessary in the short term, given the economic slowdown. In the end, nevertheless, the Commission decided not to fine France and backed down as Solbes conceded that "the sprit of the Pact was being kept" and that "if the recommendation [to not cut spending, particularly in the health sector] is not satisfactorily heeded [in the future], we can call for sanctions" against France.[15]

Interestingly, turning to developments outside the EMU-12, UK Chancellor Gordon Brown supported France's position with respect to the SGP claiming that the pact "is too rigid", a support that becomes more understandable when we consider that if the UK were part of the EMU it would have failed this criterion in 2003 and 2004, as the data above show.[16] Also, it is significant to note that should the new accession countries join the EMU, many would have fulfilled this criterion throughout the time series (for which data is available), except for Cyprus, Hungary, Malta, Poland and Slovakia in 2004. This again highlights the efforts that have been made by these countries to attain the criteria in order to join the EMU club, as has also been shown in other data given earlier.

The euro in world markets

If the above evidence demonstrates that member states have in general made intensive efforts to achieve and maintain low inflationary economic growth coupled with controlled spending as outlined in the convergence criteria, what evidence is there that the euro itself has been a success as an international currency that is strong in world markets? An answer to this can be found in a recent report by the European

Commission analysing the evolution of the euro in international markets in the five years since its introduction. One of the Commission's main observations relates to the use of the euro by the private sector: in a short period of time, the currency has established itself as the second leading currency in international markets, behind only the US dollar. In the Commission's words, "the euro area accounts for about 16 per cent of global output and almost one fifth of global trade ... [and] is also one of the biggest sources and recipients of global foreign direct investment flows."[17] The strength of the euro in the global economy is reflected in the currency's use in international debt markets as captured in Figure 6.3, which highlights the euro's strength vis-à-vis its main competitors – the US dollar and the Japanese yen.

What is crucial to note is that since its introduction in 1999 the line representing the euro has shown an upwards trend versus a general decreasing one for the other two currencies, which represents the increasing strength of the euro. As the Commission stated:

> By the end of June 2003, the euro accounted for more than 30 per cent of the debt securities (bonds, notes, and money market instruments) issued in a currency different from that of the borrowers' country of residence. ... This compares to a share of 21.7 per cent in 1999, reflecting a marked increase of the euro's

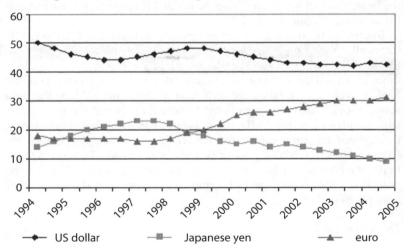

Figure 6.3 Stock of international debt securities: currency shares (bonds, notes and money market instruments, excluding home currency issuance, as a percentage of the total amount outstanding at normalised rates)

Source: ECB, review of the international role of the euro, January 2005 (two observations per year at six-monthly intervals).

share in this market segment since the launch of the third stage of the EMU. The share of the constructed aggregate of the euro's predecessor currencies was relatively stable below 20 per cent in the years prior to the introduction of the euro.[18]

Most of the significant non-euro issuers of euro-denominated bonds are based in the UK (and the USA), and it is therefore clear that economic actors in these states are making significant gains with the currency even though their states do not form part of the Euro-zone. Important examples include: HBOS plc and HBOS Treasury Services[19] (€13,900 million), Merrill Lynch & Co (€5, 450 million), Goldman Sachs (€5,187 million), Citigroup (€4,100 million), Bradford & Bingley PLC (€3,850 million), and GE Capital Europe (€3,750 million).[20]

Turning to the international use of the euro by the official sector, the Commission also notes that:

> The share of the Euro in official foreign exchange reserves held by central banks around the world is gradually increasing and stood at about 20 per cent at the end of 2003, significantly exceeding positions held by the previous aggregate of the Euro's predecessor currencies. ... Between 1999 and 2003, the amount of Euro held in foreign exchange reserves more than doubled ... [which] compares to an increase in US dollar reserves of 52 per cent. ... The increase of the euro share ... is remarkable.[21]

Finally, turning to actual exchange rate values of the euro against the US dollar and UK pound sterling, Figure 6.4 demonstrates the increasing strength of the former by considering data from 1999 until early 2005.

The graph indicates that although the euro remained weak against the US dollar in its early years, particularly between early 2000 and late 2002, thereafter it gained significant value. This positive trend is also seen in the last two years of the graph against the pound sterling. While many may think that a "strong euro" represents a success in international markets, others may argue that it has not come without social costs: those countries with important export markets outside the EU have been hard hit and may suffer low economic growth (as their products are more expensive in international markets) and increased unemployment. Critics of the strength of the euro argue that if it could be driven down against other currencies by lowering interest rates, this would stimulate growth by increasing economic competitiveness (particularly in those countries with strong export markets), by creating jobs and by potentially raising wages. However, those in favour of a strong euro may contend that a falling currency is the least preferred option during a recession precisely because it would result in increasing export outputs, an increased number of jobs, stronger demands for wage rises to

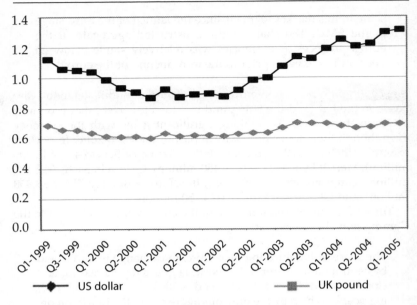

Figure 6.4 Euro foreign exchanges references rates (UK pounds and US dollar 1999–2005)

Source: European Central Bank (four observations per year at quarterly intervals).

compensate for the higher prices of imports, and a potential decrease in domestic supply: all of which add to inflationary pressures which go against the mandate of the ECB. As such, rather than devalue the euro, the preferred option of those who support a strong euro would be to attain economic growth by pursuing deeper deregulatory measures, such as further labour market "flexpoitation" and by decreasing social benefits: both of which would make investment more attractive and increase the insecurity of workers.

The EMU: a 1st order Policy

In sum, the evolution of EMU has demonstrated that EU regulations in this area are of paramount importance for several member states of the EU, particularly the 12 members that form part of the Euro-zone. All have pursued policies at the domestic level in order to meet convergence criteria in the late 1990s, and throughout the 2000s they continued to be largely committed to price stability and to controlled spending. It was also shown that even though some EU states do not form part of the EMU, they have largely aimed to maintain low interest and inflation rates and attempted to control debts and deficits in order to maintain an overall competitive European economy. In some cases, such as those of central and eastern Europe which have recently joined the Community, it may be argued that this is being done with goals of one day joining the "club". For others, such as the UK, Sweden and Denmark, who originally opted out, one may argue that they could be leaving their options open to one day join should they so desire. It was demonstrated that the priority given by the various member states to attain, and maintain, their position in the EMU is reflected in international markets, where in a very short period of time the euro has become one of the strongest world currencies. Taken together, the evidence suggests that, given a relatively weak role for national governments in economic and monetary policy making, one can conclude that major efforts to reach integration in this policy area have been successful. Furthermore, given that the supranational level has the responsibility to take the primary decisions in this area – particularly with respect to monetary policy which is led by the ECB, but also through the Commission's monitoring of the Stability and Growth Pact – this area can be seen as being representative of a 1st order policy.

Formulation of the EMU: Delors, the Council and the ERT

This section will consider EMU policy formulation by analysing developments at both the initiation and negotiation stages. It should be noted from the beginning that, as reflected in Verdun's[22] work which reviews the existing political science literature on the theme and highlights the different explanations of EMU, various accounts identify different factors of importance in EMU formulation. These include, the role of "experts",[23] supranational actors,[24] core executives[25] and intergovernmental bargaining among major states.[26] Taking from these different ideas in the literature, as well as extending them by attempting to better understand the role of capital actors during the process, this chapter will argue that several perspectives may be of value in explaining EMU.[27] Thus, this section will first argue that the initiation phase of EMU policy can be best understood as being led by the Delors' Committee, thus pointing to the importance of ideas raised within the supranational governance perspective. In the negotiation phase, however, the Council of Ministers played a prominent role, as did capital actors represented by the European Round Table (ERT) who acted in similar vein to that witnessed in the SEA and the MCR policy negotiations examined in Chapters 4 and 5. This suggests that in order to understand policy negotiation of the EMU, attention must also be paid to ideas raised by the intergovernmental and DEC perspectives.

The period between 1988 and 1992 saw the main developments of the formulation of the EMU. In order to better structure the analysis, the period between June 1988 (starting with the Hanover Summit) and June 1989 (ending with the Madrid Summit) will be denoted as corresponding to the initiation (or preparation) of the policy. From June 1989 until December 1991 was the period that witnessed the policy negotiations of the new Treaty on the EU in which EMU would be formalized at Maastricht. We turn to both of these stages in turn.

Policy initiation: Delors and his committee planting the seed

The initiation phase began with the Hanover European Council in June 1988. Although this was not the first time in the history of the Community that the idea of closer monetary relations had emerged, Article 236 of the SEA served as a starting point for more serious consideration of proposals for a single currency. It was thought that economic and monetary union was necessary in order to fully realize the potential of the integrated market in which capital could thrive. The Hanover Council in 1988 revisited the idea of closer monetary ties and charged Commission President Jacques Delors, an essential figure in the making of the SEA as discussed in Chapter 4, to set up a committee to study the options of closer monetary ties. As Padoa-Schioppa notes, however, the Council itself did not specify what needed to be studied. Rather:

> exactly what was meant by EMU was not defined at the Hanover meeting, which devoted only a few lines to the subject and really did no more than set up a committee under the chairmanship of the President of the Commission, Jacques Delors, with the task of "studying and proposing concrete stages leading towards this union."[28]

It was therefore the committee headed by Delors that would play a key role in the policy initiation phase. It was responsible for defining the concept of EMU – and setting the blueprint of what it was about – using the terms discussed at the beginning of the chapter, namely, monetary union and fiscal discipline in the context of the single market.[29] The importance of Delors at this stage of policy making is also captured in Ross'[30] work, which emphasizes how Delors was instrumental in putting the EMU on the agenda, given his view that if the single European market were to truly function effectively in the world economy, monetary integration and a single currency were necessary.

Offering more detail on the committee set up and chaired by Delors to examine the future of EMU between 1988 and 1989, Verdun[31] explains that it consisted of 16 members apart from the Chair: twelve central-bank presidents, Frans Andriessen (of DG 1 of the European Commission), and three other members from various backgrounds including Niels Thgesen (a professor of economics), Alexandre Lamfalussy (then the general Manager of the Bank for International Settlements) and Miguel Boyer (the ex-Minister of Economy and Finance of Spain's first socialist government and then president of the Banco Exterior de España).

Beyond highlighting the significance of having monetary officials from central banks on the committee, a point which is also reiterated in the work of Cameron,[32] Bernard Connolly, who was once the head of the Commission unit responsible for monitoring the European Exchange Rate Mechanism, notes the almost manipulative way that Delors took control of the committee right from the outset:

> Delors realized from the start he could play on two features of the (central bank) governors: their egos and their clubbiness. He turned their heads with the prospect of a new Super-Bundesbank at the European level, totally independent of governments and consequently able to exercise a degree of power beyond the wildest dreams.[33]

Consolidating his position as the "leader" of the committee, Delors would waste little time in setting the agenda for EMU within weeks of the Hanover Summit. As Verdun notes,

> In the summer [of 1988] he sent around a host of questions for discussion in the first meeting in September. These included questions about whether a ... single currency was necessary; ... a European Central bank would need to be created and ... what its statutes would be; what transition stages would look like; the necessary macro-economic conditions to enable a successful EMU, and, finally, what institutional changes would be required to create EMU.[34]

With regard to the dynamics within the committee, Verdun notes that although it was supposed to have produced a final report by March 1989, it was unable to do so due to the intense debate around some central issues, including the structure of the central bank and general ideas on the transition periods for EMU. After last minute meetings, Delors, with the support of the powerful Bundesbank President Karl Otto Pöhl,[35] was able to achieve consensus within the group on the outstanding issues. For example, the "Committee was surprisingly quick in deciding that it would require a federal bank system, which would need to be independent and would aim at price stability."[36] Apparently, concerns about having an unelected, unaccountable power holding such policy competences did not pose much of a problem.[37] And, without deciding on fixed dates, the committee decided on a "three stage" process in order to attain EMU:[38]

- *Stage 1.* Commencement of macroeconomic coordination between member state governments, increased ties between central banks, accelerated removal of restrictions on the movement of capital.

- *Stage 2.* Pursuit of treaty reform for institutionalization of EMU.
- *Stage 3.* Irrevocable fixing of exchange rates and management of single currency area by a European Central Bank

In mid April 1989, the Delors Committee finalized and presented its report on economic and monetary union,[39] later forwarding it to the Council of Economic and Finance Ministers (ECOFIN) in May 1989. After approval by the Council, the Madrid Summit formally accepted the Delors Report in June 1989 and decided to begin the first stage of EMU on July 1, 1990.

With this evidence in mind, one may argue that by setting the agenda of what "needed to be done", Delors and his committee would play a central role in offering a blueprint of EMU during the initiation stage of the policy process. However, as Verdun states, "the committee members were interested in creating a feasible blueprint, but they would leave the political decision to the Heads of State and Governments."[40] Or, as Dyson and Featherstone contend, "the Delors' Report provided a vital basis of technical legitimacy for EMU and set the key parameters for the subsequent Treaty negotiations."[41] That is, the specific details that were not defined in the Delors' Report, which rather presented issues that needed to be resolved and further debated among the Council of Ministers, included how long the transition periods were to be in the different stages, what were the exact definitions of the convergence criteria to be used, and how the UK was to be dealt with, given that Thatcher had balked at the idea of economic and monetary union and her view that a single currency was not necessary to complete the single market.[42] Although the Commission led by Delors did not formulate all of the specific details of the policy, however, it is important to note how the supranational institution itself indirectly set the rules of the EMU game for member state governments. As Dyson explains, "the creation of the Delors' Committee weakened the ability of national governments to act as gatekeepers and control the content of early EMU policy proposals."[43] Thus, given the evidence, the initiation stage of policy formulation can be best understood by considering ideas raised in the supranational governance perspective.

Policy negotiation: the Council and the ERT watering the money tree

When considering the negotiation stage of the policy, however, Dyson and Featherstone, who offer one of the most detailed and thorough accounts of EMU negotiations, argue that:

> In the aftermath of agenda setting, Delors' role was weaker and more distant. EMU was then located in a technical negotiating milieu dominated by national actors who were concerned to limit,

or even exclude, the role of the Commission. EC finance ministers and central banks had accumulated vast experience and reputation and had their own closeted networks with a complex infrastructure of meetings, lunches and telephone calls.[44]

From this perspective, the negotiation process can best be understood only by analysing the Intergovernmental Conference (IGC) negotiations that, authors such as Moravcsik argue,[45] demonstrate how EMU served the interests of state leaders. Important meetings of heads of state in this regard include December 1989 when the European Council in Strasbourg agreed to an IGC to discuss the institutional changes required for monetary union; December 1990 when the European Council met in Rome and launched two intergovernmental conferences on economic and political union; and, perhaps most importantly, December 1991 when the European Council met in Maastricht and agreed on a draft Treaty on European Union. By broadly considering developments in these meetings, one can ask: what were the various interests of the member state governments and how were these reflected in the final treaty?

Almost all authors focussing on the importance of member states in EMU formulation highlight the importance of the Franco-German leadership in the IGC bargaining process. As Dyson and Featherstone contend, "The most potent venue for political leadership [in the negotiation phase] on EMU proved to be the Franco-German relationship. ... Kohl and Mitterrand were vital in animating and 'engineering' the EMU negotiations, determining their pace and shape."[46] Three main issues were of importance when considering both countries: timetabling, criteria and role of the central bank.

With regard to timetable and criteria, several authors have pointed to the importance of the "economist" view of monetary union (led by Germany) and the "monetarist" view (led by France). As Connolly explains in reference to the compromise finally attained in Maastricht:

> The so-called "economist view", traditionally espoused in Germany and the Netherlands, was that economic convergence must precede monetary union, which would otherwise be damaging and unstable. France and Italy claimed on the contrary that monetary union would produce economic convergence. In the first view, monetary union was a distant goal; in the second, an instrument to be used immediately to achieve the supposed goal of convergence. The Maastricht agreement made a bow to the monetarist view by specifying fixed dates for monetary union, but also acknowledging the "economist" arguments by laying down criteria in terms of inflation convergence and budgetary good behaviour, for entry to the union.[47]

The specific convergence criteria that were negotiated[48] and agreed to by all member states were discussed earlier in the chapter. The timetable that was finally agreed was for Stage 2 to start in January 1994 and for Stage 3 to start either in January 1997 if at least seven states attained the convergence criteria, or, automatically in January 1999 for those states attaining the criteria.[49]

With regard to the role of the central bank, the establishment of an independent bank whose goal was price stability was a necessary condition for both Chancellor Kohl and the Bundesbank President Karl Otto Pöhl, who were strong supporters of what Dyson and Featherstone refer to as the "sound money paradigm".[50] Nevertheless, the Germans did accept certain conditions demanded by the French. This is seen in the final acceptance that ECOFIN would have a role in setting (by way of qualified majority voting) external exchange rate policy; that some flexibility would be allowed at the start of Stage 3 as discussed by France and Italy;[51] and that (national) central bank governors would have a role on the ECB executive board, as highlighted in Garrett's work.[52]

Beyond the specific details of timetabling and the functioning of the central bank, there were larger economic and political arguments that were of significance to both France and Germany and guided their desire to come to an agreement. Dyson and Featherstone note that while potential economic benefits were of initial importance to France, "from 1989, the diplomatic rationale of binding enhanced German power into a European framework became decisive for the French, and economic arguments were transformed into the instruments for this purpose."[53] Similarly, in the context of the German reunification and the decline of the Soviet Union, Germany had its own political reasons, as discussed by Garrett;[54] in agreeing to EMU, Germany would consolidate a place for itself in an even closer union.

Another issue that was negotiated in the Council included an "opt-out" clause for the UK. While it was perceived that the economic principles of both the Germans and the British were not completely at odds, the UK's concerns about joining the EMU were related more to views of its role within the EU and the perceived loss of sovereignty that joining the EMU club might entail. Dyson and Featherstone explain that "The Thatcher and Major governments had an ideological commitment to the protection of national sovereignty, whilst the German government sought to place EMU in the context of building Europe and overcoming historical painful legacies."[55]

A final negotiation point within the Council related to potential guarantees within the Maastricht Treaty that would aid the so-called "peripheral economies" in their drive towards EMU. This included, on the insistence of Felipe González of Spain, the development of a Cohesion

Fund that would help Spain, Portugal, Greece and Ireland – arguably the "poor four" in the Community – help meet the convergence criteria. The Cohesion Fund was set up with the view of increasing the economic growth of the poor four, without these states having to fund certain projects themselves, thereby allowing them more of an opportunity to attain the deficit and debt convergence criteria. The funds specifically supported two main types of projects: environmental protection and transport (infrastructure) networks.

It is interesting to note that, alongside the specific reasons mentioned above that motivated various member states during the negotiation process, several authors have noted the "scapegoat" argument that EMU offered to domestic level actors. Although EMU would allow for a competitive position for many European economies within the global market, it also served as a mechanism for pursuing neo-liberal economic policies that many states (even under socialist administrations) desired: in order to obtain convergence criteria the pursuit of neo-liberal economic policies could be justified. As Verdun explains:

> [M]ember states drew the conclusion that their domestic economies were too rigid, making a flexible adjustment to external changes very difficult. Politicians who needed to restructure public finances and the welfare state found themselves having to sell very unpopular measures. It was considered much easier to restructure the economy by focusing on the benefits of European integration, and by using ... integration to legitimise the need for change.[56]

Given the neo-liberal free-market environment that would manifest itself in the course of meeting convergence criteria, it seems logical that business leaders were openly committed to the EMU: not only would governments be forced to reduce spending on social welfare in order to meet deficit and debt criteria, but also businesses could be allowed more freedom in the market in the drive towards EMU. With regard to the latter point, for example, one sees that in an attempt to attain convergence criteria many Southern Europe states (which had a long way to go if they were to meet the criteria) allowed more latitude to employers from the mid 1990s on, as seen in labour market deregulation aimed at reducing inflationary tendencies, so as to control interest rates and decrease deficits and debts; making it easier for employers to set lower salaries; and taking the state out of the regulation of the labour market (in adjudicating unfair dismissals, for instance) gave employers more room to manoeuvre. Some political actors within the Euro-zone also sought to decrease corporate taxes and seek further deregulatory initiatives in order to increase investment and create "flexible" jobs;[57] the most conspicuous example is Ireland, which has one of the lowest corporate tax rates in the EU. Given the enormous benefits that capital would have in the drive towards, and eventually the establishment of, EMU, it is little surprise to see that capital acted, yet again, in its transnational form in order to influence EMU negotiations.

In more detail, Balanyá *et al* highlight the importance for EMU developments of the ERT, which was instrumental in the creation of the single market (Chapter 4) as well as the formulation of the Merger Control Regulation (Chapter 5). In addition to the ERT, Balanyá *et al* also argue that the AMUE – the Association for the Monetary Union of Europe which is representative of ERT's "financial offspring" – is also of importance in EMU negotiations, and Van Apeldoorn also supports this view.[58] Limited to members of corporate and financial services, the AMUE was founded in 1987 by five major corporations in the ERT: Fiat, Philips, Rhone-Poulenc, Solvay and Total. The "overlap" between the ERT and AMUE is shown in the fact that Wisse Dekker, then CEO of Philips and Chair of ERT (and previously one of those behind the creation of the single market as seen in Chapter 4), "was the first to chair the AMUE".[59] Balanyá *et al* argue that the "AMUE was created as a single-issue task force, to supplement the ERT's own campaign for economic and monetary union in Europe,"[60] an aim reflected in a report prepared for the ERT by Ernst and Young consultants.[61]

In terms of the political activity of both the ERT and AMUE during EMU negotiations, Balanyá *et al*'s evidence shows that during the 1990 IGC members of the ERT met "regularly with Commissioners such as Vice President Frans Andriessen (External Trade), Ray McSharry (Agriculture), Leon Brittan (Competition) and Commission President Jacques Delors".[62] The ERT also published reports that would eventually have an impact on decisions taken by the Council. In particular, it published in 1991 a report entitled *Reshaping Europe*,[63] which included several main points that are worth quoting at length:

i)   The forces pressing [business] towards a single monetary system are becoming stronger everyday. As the volume of cross-frontier trade and investment grows and grows, the costs and uncertainties of the present system are becoming an intolerable handicap.
ii) Japan has one currency. The US has one currency. How can the Community live with twelve?
iii) The direct savings are substantial – over ECU 13 billion a year [is] wasted [in operating costs].
iv) The potential of the single market cannot be realized until it has also become a single financial market. That is why industry needs to be certain of the ultimate objective.

a. We need a firm commitment to the final goal of a single currency, so that industry can start planning now.
b. We need a sense of urgency.
c. We need a clear and unambiguous timetable
d. A stable value for our currency is an overriding goal and there must be a Central Banking system sufficiently strong and independent to guarantee this.
e. Governments must commit themselves to the necessary preconditions – a firm stance against inflation, a total ban on the monetary financing of budget deficits and a steady convergence of economic policies – and they must accept binding disciplines to give credibility to these objectives.

With regard to point "iv.c" Balanyá *et al* write that in *Reshaping Europe* the ERT "proposed a timetable for EMU implementation that bears remarkable similarity to the one incorporated in the Maastricht Treaty a few months later", and that the ERT along with AMUE directly met with and pressed national governments to pursue a "well-defined time-schedule" for completion of the EMU.[64] In particular, comparing what was accepted in Maastricht and what was earlier proposed by the ERT, one can see the following similarities: the ERT called for an IGC to finally agree on the new Treaty to take place in 1991 (and this eventually took place in Maastricht in December 1991); the ERT called for Stage 2 to occur in 1994 (and the Council of Ministers later agreed to a date of January 1, 1994); and the ERT called for Stage 3, the irrevocable fixing of exchange rates, to take place in 1997 (and the Council agreed to a date of 1997, but only if a majority had met the criteria.)[65]

In summary, while supranational governance played the major role in the initiation stage of the policy , the negotiation stage suggests the importance of both the intergovernmentalist and the DEC perspectives. More concretely, the evidence demonstrated the importance of the Franco-German axis in terms of negotiating some specific details outlined in the blueprint offered by Delors in the first stage, and also pointed to the importance of the ERT and its offspring AMUE in dealing directly with members of the Council, particularly with regard to the timetabling aspects of the EMU. There is little evidence to suggest other interest groups played a significant role in the policy-making process. In fact, one may argue that organizations such as labour were intentionally marginalized, given the nature of the neo-liberal project and the negative consequences this would have for labour in general, particularly when states attempted to meet convergence criteria and pursued policies such as heavy cutbacks in social programmes. As such, both the pluralist and the corporatist perspectives are of limited value in explaining developments in either stage of the formulation process.

Conclusions

The first section of this chapter analysed the goals of EMU by considering that its main features included monetary and fiscal discipline intended to achieve low-inflationary economic growth in a single currency area. It then turned its attention to the evolution of EMU by first analysing how member states have "converged" in the drive to monetary union in terms of decreasing inflation rates, interest rates, deficits and debt. We then considered the very favourable evolution of the new currency in international markets, showing how this has consolidated a strong position for Europe in the global economy. Given that this is a policy area that has seen a large transference of power from the member state to the supranational level, it was argued that this was representative of a 1st order policy.

The second section analysed developments during the formulation of EMU, focussing on developments between 1988 and late 1991. It was contended that the evidence suggests that the policy initiation stage witnessed a leading role played by Commission President Jacques Delors who, with the Delors' Report of 1989, constructed the blueprint for EMU. Nevertheless, when the details of the policy were negotiated throughout 1990 and 1991, it was the Council of Ministers that played a leading role in terms of setting the details for convergence criteria, setting up the institutional structure needed for monetary union and drawing up the timetable with regard to completion of the various "stages" of EMU. It was also suggested that with regard to setting the timetable, capital actors in the ERT, who believed that a single currency zone would be highly beneficial for business operating in the single integrated market, played a significant role in the policy process by suggesting dates which were largely reflected in the final outcome accepted by the Council of Ministers.

Given the actions of the various actors in both policy initiation and negotiation, and following the arguments of authors such as Verdun, the main conclusion to be drawn is that a plurality of theoretical perspectives are necessary in order to explain EMU policy formulation: theories of supranational governance help inform our understanding of EMU policy initiation, while the intergovernmental and DEC perspectives help explain developments as the policy was negotiated. Given that labour did not have a fixed role in the policy process, despite the fact that labour itself had to bear many sacrifices on the road to monetary union as a result of domestic policies such as social welfare cuts and increased deregulation, one may argue that the corporatist perspective is of limited importance in explaining any stage of EMU. Similarly, because other interest groups were not allowed open and free access to either level of governance during either stage of formulation, the pluralist perspective is also of limited relevance.

7 The Common Agricultural Policy: redistributive policy in favour of whom?

In the first section of the chapter, we analyse the broad objectives of the Common Agricultural Policy (CAP). We show how the CAP is a price-support system aimed at protecting a certain sector of the European economy from both domestic and international pressures. The 1st order status of the policy will be demonstrated, by emphasizing how this policy spends the largest part of the EU budget. The second section then moves on to analyse policy formulation during the 1992 MacSharry reforms, the Agenda 2000 reforms and the Fischler reforms of 2003. These policies are significant because they represent the most recent attempts to reform the CAP. In an integrated discussion that gives an overview of the objectives of these reforms, we attempt to determine which actors were most influential in shaping EU agriculture policy, with a specific focus on the role of the Council, the Commission and farming interest groups. Given the evidence, the main argument to be developed is that the CAP constitutes a 1st order policy and, considering the actors involved in the different policy-making stages, that the supranational governance (with a focus on the Commission), intergovernmentalist and dominant economic class (DEC) perspectives best inform agricultural policy developments.

Objectives and evolution of the CAP: its "1st order status" in the integration process

The CAP attained a very prominent status in the Treaty of Rome of 1957 when the original six member states (France, Germany, Italy, Belgium, the Netherlands and Luxembourg) declared a common policy and granted it its own title in the Treaty. In particular, the five objectives of Article 33 of the TEU (ex article 39, EEC Treaty) were:

- to increase agricultural productivity, by promoting technical progress and rational development of agricultural production and optimum utilization of the factors of production, particularly labour
- to ensure a fair standard of living for the agricultural community, in particular by increasing individual earnings of persons engaged in agriculture
- to stabilize markets

- to ensure the availability of supplies
- to ensure that supplies reach consumers at reasonable prices.

The CAP represented the first redistributive policy of the EU. Redistribution refers to the idea that budgetary funds are reallocated to, or spent on, programmes that benefit various people where it is generally deemed that there is a common social good that can be achieved by so doing. At the domestic level, examples of redistributive policies may include healthcare, unemployment insurance and spending on education. Examples of redistributive policies in the EU, however, are not applied in the traditional areas of social welfare found at the domestic level. Rather, EU redistributive policies are seen in agricultural policy, and in directing structural funds towards regions in less favourable conditions and aid to developing countries. The general concept behind the redistributive mechanism in the CAP is that EU budgetary funds are given to farmers in order to subsidize production of certain products that are considered essential or whose production is seen as beneficial for the Community as a whole.

Discussing the historical rationale for the development of the CAP, Rieger highlights the importance of post-war international dynamics. He states that:

> in the inter-war period, major sections of the agrarian population had turned to radical right-wing parties to protest against governments that had tolerated the collapse of agricultural policies. This experience created a dramatic change in agricultural policies, providing income security to farmers through guaranteed prices, but at the expense of creating tensions at the international level.[1]

With this in mind, it is useful to turn to Hix's summary of the three elements of the EU price support system that were agreed in the early 1960s in order to protect farmers.

- Protection against low internal prices. Surplus farm products are bought from farmers – with funds from the European Agriculture Guidance and Guarantee Fund (EAGGF) – when prices fall below an agreed guaranteed price in the European market
- Protection against low import prices. Import quotas and levies (paid into the EAGGF) are applied on imported agricultural goods when world prices fall below an agreed price.
- Subsidies to achieve a low export price. Refunds are paid (from the EAGGF) for the export of agricultural goods when the world price falls below an agreed price.[2]

The price support mechanism clearly reveals the anti-competitive mechanism behind the CAP, whose goals were to protect the sector from international pressures. In Rieger's words, "the stated goal of the CAP is the preservation of an economic sector with supposedly distinctive institutional and social features, incompatible with the principles of industrial production and competitive markets."[3] Such a preservation was aimed at "insulating the farming sector from international competition",[4] and this can be seen as the "raison d'être the CAP, for which a really supranational policy was a precondition".[5] From this vantage point, the CAP can be seen as "a politically driven and defensive strategy to modernize European agriculture against the internal threat of an expanding industrial society and the external threat of vigorous trade competition".[6]

Of all EU redistributive policies, the CAP is the most significant because it has clearly dominated the EU central budget since its inception. Although the percentage of the overall budget devoted to it decreased throughout the 1990s, it remains to this day the policy that receives the largest amount of EU funding. Data from Rieger show that:

> CAP expenditure rose from 64.2 [million] Ecu ... in 1987, to 104.6 Ecu in 1992, and to €120.7 in 2001. Even if expenditure fell from 0.61 per cent in GDP in 1993 to 0.43 per cent of GDP in 2004, the share of agriculture in the GDP fell from 2.5 to 1.7 percent, while CAP expenditure per farm more than doubled in the same period.[7]

That agricultural subsidies remain centralized at the EU level, and that the amounts of funding that the policy continues to receive still surpass all other redistributive policies, suggests that the policy can be considered to have attained a 1st order status.

In terms of its evolution, many expected it to become a "story of action and success"[8] because of the funds that were initially earmarked for the policy. However, the policy could never be seen in the eyes of free-market liberalizers as completely fulfilling the role of an exemplary paradigm for competitive European integration. This is because the very nature of the policy was to offer advantages to one sector of the economy over others and, as will be discussed later, within this sector the CAP favours large landowners. It followed from an earlier agreement between member states, which emphasized that agriculture had to be treated differently from other economic sectors in the European single market.

The idea here was that unless a subsidy mechanism was implemented, the small and medium-sized European farmer would disappear. This would result in the decline of the rural population, an increase in unemployment and destabilization of markets in general. Thus, the CAP was set up with a welfare dimension which had implications for its functioning; it also demonstrated the role of interest groups.[9] Member states thus introduced the so-called price-support system in order to work against these possible distortions: once a year the national Ministers of Agriculture established prices for the agricultural products covered by the CAP. If market prices were below those established, the prices would be pushed up artificially through EU-intervention purchases to a level agreed upon. Conversely, if prices were too high, the EU would release the agricultural products purchased during low-price periods, thus bringing prices back down.

This policy had a twofold effect. First, there was a continuous surplus of agricultural products as the system encouraged farmers to maximize their output by setting the guaranteed EU prices well above world prices. This resulted in what have been referred to as "food mountains", "wine lakes" and "butter mountains". These terms help describe the vast quantities of products that were produced, that turned out later to be of no real use or value. The second effect was that the costs of the CAP exploded. Rieger notes that throughout the 1960s and 1970s, "high prices were institutionally guaranteed, farmers were protected against the consequences of over-production (i.e. falling prices), and import competition was offset by export subsidies."[10] The effect of this was increasing output and spiralling costs to the CAP, a system that allowed for accumulation of profits, particularly by those large landowners who were able to produce more than smaller and medium-sized farmers.

Hence, several attempts were made between the 1960s and 1980s to reform the CAP. One example was the Mansholt Plan of 1968. This tried to restructure the agricultural sector, offering small farmers financial support to set aside their land (also referred to as summer fallowing). The aim of the reform was to reduce agricultural inefficiency, which would automatically lead to a reduction of costs and a levelling-off to world prices. However, the plan collapsed due to opposition by France and Germany, who claimed that the reform would have a detrimental effect on their farming communities. A second example was seen with the entry of the UK into the European Community in 1973, where reform of the CAP was yet again considered, with only limited success. A third attempt was made in the 1980s, a time when the problems of the CAP took on a different dimension. Beyond the overproduction and spiralling costs seen before, the 1980s saw the rise of other issues, including environmental concerns and health hazards caused by various farming practices. In order to maximize their outputs, farmers pumped huge amounts of fertilizers onto their lands and used high levels of hormones in the rearing of their animals. Moreover, the EU came under fire for of its price dumping strategy at the Uruguay Round of the GATT talks in 1986. Despite recognition of the concerns by several member states, however, no firm reforms were achieved.

It thus became evident in the 1990s that the CAP had to be reformed, resulting in first, the MacSharry reforms, then the Agenda 2000 reforms and, finally, the Fischler reforms of 2003. Our integrated discussion concentrates on three major aspects of each of these: the main objectives of the reform, who was involved in its initiation and negotiation and, given these dynamics, how such developments can be theoretically characterized. The main argument to be developed is that formulation of the policies has seen the participation not only of the Commission and Council, but also agri-businesses which have ensured that profits for large farmers have been disproportionately higher than for smaller farmers in this protectionist environment. This has resulted in a policy which continues to particularly benefit a very few large landholders. Theoretically, the policy formulation can be best understood using elements of supranational governance, intergovernmentalism, and the DEC perspective.

Formulation of the MacSharry, Agenda 2000 and Fischler reforms

The MacSharry reform: objectives and actors involved in the process

What were the objectives of the MacSharry reforms?

By 1991 the need for CAP reform was twofold. First, because the outcome and continuation of GATT-negotiations were constrained by the failure of the EU to reform the CAP, the EU could no longer postpone reforms in the agricultural sector. Linking GATT negotiations to CAP issues meant that pressure emanated not only from the agrarian community, but also from other economic interests that argued CAP reform was a necessity. For example, the German government was under pressure from the industrial community who wanted GATT-negotiations to be continued, while the French faced pressure from the large-farm cereal growers who faced competition from their US counterparts who had invaded the European market at world-prices.[11] Second, examination of the budget indicated that costs for the CAP absorbed over half of the EU's budget and it would have been impossible to continue to support such a burden.

Considering these problems, Moyer and Josling discuss how DG VI (later renamed DG Agriculture) produced a paper in December 1990 which would serve to catalyze debate about reform.[12] The fact that the Commission took this first step is consistent with much of the literature's view that the Commission has been responsible for drafting legislation and administrating the CAP. The objective of the paper was to recommend "significant price cuts for which farmers would receive direct payments based on the area farmed and average regional yields".[13] The price cuts varied between 35 per cent for cereals, 15 per cent for beef, and 10 per cent for dairy produce. The result of this was a reflection paper written by the Commission in February 1991, which in turn would lead to the final MacSharry proposal of July 1991 that was put before the Council.[14]

All of these Commission documents, which reflect how this part of the dual executive initiated the reform process, also contemplated the replacement of the price support system with a direct payment support system. This model of compensation was seen as being a means of decreasing the costs of the CAP.[15] Direct payments were seen as a way to compensate small and medium-sized farmers for the loss of income that they would experience due to the substantial cuts in guaranteed prices that the Commission wanted to make. Compensation was originally not envisaged for large agrarian producers as they were considered able to compete in world markets. Other proposals made by the Commission focussed on rural development, including environmental matters such as promoting organic forms of farming, encouraging set-aside schemes and reforestations.[16]

Even though the evidence suggests that the Commission was a key player in the initiation of the policy, Moyer and Josling's work emphasized that all members of the Council would have a voice in the final decision, undermining the full impact of Commission proposals.[17] Again this is consistent with views in the literature that in terms of the legislative process, while the Commission drafts a proposal, the Council of Agricultural Ministers must in theory approve it unanimously. The Council is seen as being in a strong position: it can either reject the Commission's proposal and return it for modification, or start negotiations within the Council, with a very limited role resulting for the EP.[18] In the case of MacSharry, the Council opposed some or all of MacSharry's proposals, and would not agree to reforms on the scale he had proposed.

Thus, after ten months of negotiations in the Council of Agricultural Ministers, the European Council in May 1992 agreed to a watered-down version of MacSharry's original reforms. The main aspects of the final agreement were:

- Prices for cereals and beef decreased, but by less than the Commission had proposed.
- Set-aside rates were much lower than foreseen by the Commission and all farmers received full compensation by direct payments.
- Early retirement schemes were introduced to encourage older farmers to cease production.
- Environmentally friendly farming practices were encouraged, but not made compulsory. Lower yields would be still be subsidized.

Because better control over expenditure could be achieved through the introduction of direct payments, a side-effect of the reform was that the economic effects of the CAP became more transparent. However, some-what ironically, costs actually increased even further after MacSharry. This is because the reform did not set price support subsidies aside, but rather simply introduced another form of subvention with direct payments. Thus, the reform's objectives were not fully achieved: even though an attempt was made to moderate expenditures, prices remained too high, resulting in continued export subsidies.

Actors involved in the MacSharry reform process: commission, council and large landowners

What were the specific dynamics among the actors involved in the initiation of the MacSharry reforms? Because the Commission had the right to initiate any agricultural issues, it is not surprising that one finds an important role for the supranational institution during policy initiation. As discussed above, the new Commissioner for agricultural affairs, MacSharry, had a particularly important role in the initiation of the policy. He also had the support of the Commission's president, Delors. Both of them played significant roles in convincing the member states of the necessity for agricultural reform to resolve the budgetary constraints faced by the CAP (though some member states were already aware of CAPs problems in the aftermath of the criticisms voiced at the GATT negotiations). Hence, it can be argued that the initiation stage is best understood from supranational governance perspective.

When turning to the negotiation of the policy, however, one may argue that the predominant role was played by actors beyond the Commission. Even though the latter was responsible for initiating policy reforms, the reform process and its outcome were dominated by the member states and their policy positions. The differences between the Commission's proposal and the actual outcome clearly demonstrate that the interests of the member states differed substantially from the Commission's, as noted by a number of scholars.[19] Even though the reforms may have been considered historic for the CAP, the major points of the Commission's initial proposal were not considered acceptable or were diluted by the Council. This was primarily due to the worries of member states about the effects of the original proposals. For example, heavily influenced by the large cereal farmers in France, "French Minister Louis Mermaz questioned the need for such a drastic cereal price cut [and demanded that] domestic supplies [be given] adequate protection on the European market."[20] Britain's John Gummer "complained that the proposed reforms would penalize the excellence of and success of large, specialist farms to prop up part-time inefficient farms".[21]

The concern that member states felt about the reforms' effect on specific farming interests helps demonstrate that certain "large farm-ers" were influential when the national positions were developed. This suggests that, along with intergovernmentalism, the DEC perspective is of value in explaining policy negotiation. These "large farmers", who one may argue represented business-like interests, were able to get their way by heavily lobbying national governments through their own nationally based farming groups. An example of how such farming businesses were able to get what they wanted is seen in the negotiations over replacing the guaranteed price system by direct payments. While smaller farmers were in favour of the direct payment initiative, larger farmers argued that this constituted a welfare payment that took away from the concept of the "individual entrepreneur" by which they defined their activity. The larger farmers, who were heavily represented in the national farming organizations, argued that these new regulations should not apply to them: for élites with larger areas of land, the guaranteed price system brought more income than direct payments. France provides a specific example of the way large farmers could influence policy negotiations. As discussed by authors such as Grant,[22] French national farming organizations, including the FNSEA, have a close relationship with French governments.[23] On the insistence of large French farming interests in cereal production, it was agreed that price support would be maintained for these key producers, with future reduction envisaged at a slower rate than originally proposed by the Commission.

Given the lobbying pressure at the national level of particular farming élites whose economic activity was more reminiscent of large corporations, smaller farmers would not obtain all they wanted. This adds strength to Rieger's claim that small farmers lack an "effective voice" in the system.[24] Within national farming organizations the more dominant financial faction outweighed the minor one and one may argue that "capitalist interests" were able to take charge.[25]

With regard to other interest groups, supranational agrarian interest organizations – which are representative of all farming interests – enjoyed wide influence in the years before the MacSharry reforms.[26] The literature has noted that before MacSharry trans-national agrarian interest groups – mainly COPA–COGECA[27] which represent the European umbrella organization of national farming groups, as discussed in Chapter 2,[28] and the Coordination Paysanne (CPE) which is mainly concerned with sustainable agricultural policy – were historically influential in defining the CAP. Many have argued that COPA has been able to establish close relationships with the Commission, while CPE has enjoyed favoured access to national governments, and these organizations have influence either in the Council of Agricultural Ministers or the European Council for two reasons. First, agricultural policy forms an element of the welfare state and the input of these farming groups is therefore needed. Second, their input was considered necessary for the policy to claim legitimacy.

It is therefore surprising that in the case of the MacSharry reforms these interest groups were not involved in the preliminary stages. Certainly, they did make negative comments on the substance of the Commission's proposal on two grounds. On the one hand, COPA feared that the Commission would seek to rationalize spending in the CAP more than ever before. On the other hand, farming interest groups feared that direct payments would make the budget for agriculture more transparent, resulting in a potential back-lash from taxpayers.[29] Yet the Commission paid scant attention to the negative reaction of agrarian interests at the European level, such as COPA.

One may argue that the position of these groups was further weakened by their inability to acquire a negotiating mandate or adopt an effective position. There are three potential reasons for this. First, they simply did not want to accept changes, in general. Second, agrarian interest groups simply rejected the idea of direct payments, in particular. This left them little flexibility to manoeuvre. Third, it was impossible for such groups to agree on a European-based proposal because of the divisions rooted in differing national interests, which eventually divided the supranational groups such as COPA. For example, some French interest groups opposed direct payments and set-asides, whereas German ones were hostile to price cuts.[30] Similarly, the Italians did not like the proposals on financial transparency outlined in MacSharry, while the Belgians were concerned about the potential impact on specialized farming. In addition to national differences, other, more contextual, cleavages within the farming community emerged over MacSharry, including the interests of small farmers versus those of larger ones, and the concerns of environmentally concerned farmers versus those who were more output oriented. In the end, as discussed above, the larger agri-businesses were much more successful in working through the Council.

This success was partly also induced by the Commission itself in using the so-called Special Committee of Agriculture to assist in achieving its reform package. Special committees consist largely of senior national civil servants, and national representatives vote according to qualified majority voting. They ensure that national interests are represented in the CAP policy process: national civil servants prepare most of the meetings of the Council of Agriculture Ministers, while the management committee guarantees the representation of national interests in issues that the Council has delegated to the Commission. By choosing this institutional set-up, national interest groups and national ministries indirectly gained influence.[31] The concomitant decrease in the influence of the EU level that ensued meant that the lobbying arena moved from the European to the national level.[32] In other words, given that the focus of influence lay at the national, not European level, European-based interest groups representing all farmers would have very little influence on the process and the outcomes of the MacSharry reforms. As Gray stated, COPA's members at the time were "embarking upon more individual initiatives without the consent of COPA"[33] and relying on the traditionally strong and powerful links between the national associations and the national ministries. This would inevitably provoke disagreement within COPA over the reform of CAP while simultaneously causing major difficulties in finding a compromise within the Council of Ministers.

One may argue that this type of "re-nationalization of agrarian interest politics" makes intuitive sense precisely because final agricultural decisions are ultimately taken within the Council of Agricultural Ministers. One may also contend that the re-nationalization was also very much in the interest of the member states. A powerful role for the pan-European interest groups would have increased the capacity of the Commission to act more autonomously and to develop its own agenda, ultimately resulting in the exclusion of the member states and therefore decreasing their power. With respect to this particular reform, Kay also points out that automatic price cuts would have led to an increase in the power of the Commission, and a decrease in that of the Council of Agricultural Ministers.[34] With this in mind, it was in national actors' interests to bypass European interest groups and attempt to seek the influence of nationally based ones in order to "deflate" supranational autonomy while preserving national power.[35]

It is interesting to note that there was some potential for other interest groups beyond agricultural ones to take part in the process. As Kay states, "the access of traditionally powerful farm interest groups was no longer exclusive."[36] Rather, trade, environmental, industrial and financial interests may have also attained a place in the negotiation process because of the nature of the MacSharry reforms.[37] However, the outcomes were still roughly in line with the desires of key actors in the agriculture sector, and proposals from other interest groups, such as the environmentalist lobby, were left mostly unexplored. From this perspective, one cannot regard the agricultural policy processes as a pluralist one where all potential interests involved have a say. There are two explanations for this lack of equal access to the negotiation process and the dominance of the member state in it. First, member states sought to protect what they perceived were the interests of a minority, yet powerful, group within the agriculture sector, and subsequently disregarded other environmental and economic factors that might have been beneficial to a majority of the European public. Second, member states had an interest in largely maintaining the status quo in the CAP because many states had a state-owned service sector associated with banking that was closely linked with agrarian issues. This is particularly seen in state-sponsored agricultural credit institutions or commercial banks with special agricultural departments.[38]

To summarize: in terms of processes, the MacSharry reform witnessed how after the Commission initiated the reform, the decision-making process shifted from the European to the national level. Member states tried to restrain the Commission's move towards more autonomy. This verifies Rieger's observation that "despite the supranational, or 'common' format of the CAP, member states' preferences are the main factors driving the policy system."[39] In other words, even though the Commission may enjoy the exclusive right to initiate Community legislation, national interests heavily influenced the several stages in the agricultural policy negotiation.[40] Negotiations during MacSharry also show some evidence that the concerns of the farming élites that represented larger, agri-business interests were raised by the Council. This suggests that even though supranational governance helps explain the initiation phase of development, elements of intergovernmentalism and the DEC perspective help explain policy negotiations. The evidence also shows that a plurality of other potential interests, including transnational agriculture groups which represent the interests of all farmers as well as environmental groups, were not allowed to influence the reform's development. This points to the idea that elements of pluralism were not manifest. We now turn to the formulation of the next set of agricultural reforms, Agenda 2000, in order to capture the dynamics involved during this policy-process.

Agenda 2000

What was Agenda 2000 About?

To remedy the perceived inadequacies of the MacSharry reform and, more importantly, to prepare the EU for enlargement, the Agenda 2000 reform project was introduced for a "stronger and wider Europe". On the one hand, the price support system coupled with direct payments post-MacSharry had increased costs even further. EU budget concerns were thus again at the forefront, catalyzing another round for reform. Further, the Commission calculated that by 2005 the EU would exceed the ceilings imposed by GATT negotiations, leading again to increased international pressure. On the other hand, existing CAP rules could not be applied to the applicant states of Central and Eastern Europe without having further dramatic consequences for the EU-budget.[41]

Agenda 2000 reform plans, which were again first presented by the Commission, continued along the lines of the MacSharry reform: reducing prices and linking production to social and environmental objectives. In more detail in 1998 the Commission mentioned:

- large reductions in support prices
- compensation for farmers in the form of direct payments with a ceiling on the level of aid that any individual could receive
- reduction of market-distorting subsidies while increasing support for farmers who did not distort production
- ending mandatory set-asides.

The publication of the document was followed by demonstrations by farmers in Brussels, initially resulting in the suspension of negotiations surrounding Agenda 2000. As far the Council was concerned, it supported the need for reform. But, there was a major concern with reducing the CAP's budgetary costs, something which was to be suspended until the IGC in Berlin in March, 1999. After long and difficult negotiations dominated by French President Jacques Chirac and facilitated by German Chancellor Gerhard Schröder, a decision on Agenda 2000 was finally reached. The main issues agreed to included:

- a cut in cereal prices of 20 per cent (10 per cent in 2000/1 and 10 per cent in 2001/2) as proposed by the Commission
- a reduction of milk prices by 15 per cent over three years starting in 2003, differing from the Commission's proposal
- an increase in dairy production quotas, against the Commission's wishes
- a 20 per cent reduction of beef prices, which was only two-thirds of the cut proposed by the Commission.

One may contend that there were three shortcomings in the final outcome. First, from the Commission's perspective, apart from the multitude of changes that were half-heartedly agreed by the Council as mentioned above, the Council also resisted the Commission's proposal on direct payments (to be partly paid by the member states) and the introduction of ceilings. The Commission's idea of "modulation" foresaw the introduction of individual ceilings for direct payments to avoid uneven impacts across the EU. However, contrary to the Commission's proposal, it was finally agreed that member states should have the decision-making power on the criteria for individual ceilings. Moreover, Agenda 2000 featured a further re-nationalization of agricultural policy, in the same way as in the process that led to the MacSharry reform: in future, direct payments were to be distributed according to economic, social and environmental criteria which the member state in question could unilaterally decide.

Second, although Agenda 2000 introduced the concept of "multifunctionality", which was considered a major breakthrough, one may argue that it remained mostly rhetorical. "Multifunctionality" was in theory intended to support sustainability and environmental concerns in agriculture – a hope that had already been raised in the MacSharry reforms but had been largely dismissed. Even though this concept laid down a basis for "environmental agriculture", Agenda 2000 did not develop incentives for farmers to invest in environmentally friendly farming.

Finally, the necessary reforms of the CAP that were needed in the context of future enlargement were also not fully worked out. In order to prepare for enlargement and to reduce long-term CAP costs, further reforms would yet be needed.

Actors in the formulation of Agenda 2000: the Commission, the Council and large farmers

Turning to the actors involved in the process, one sees that as with the MacSharry reforms the initiation stage of Agenda 2000 saw the Commission acting as principal initiator. However, as was also the case in the MacSharry reform process, after the negotiation process began supranational governance was very soon replaced by intergovernmental influences: national actors and national interests would prevail.

This stage also witnessed discordance between the Commission and member states, again reflected in the divergence between the initial proposal and the final outcome. While the Commission tried to pursue drastic changes in the CAP, member states resisted this, mainly because of irreconcilable national differences. For example, the UK, Sweden, Denmark and Italy regarded the proposal as inadequate and not far-reaching enough; Germany, Spain and Ireland silently rejected it; and France openly campaigned against it.[42] Despite differences between the member states, a common position between them was finally found on the issue of re-nationalization of the CAP. The Council adopted financial "envelopes", to "allow member states ... to compensate for regional differences in production practices and agronomic conditions".[43] Contrary to the Commission's proposal, member states established an important future position for themselves. This highlights the huge impact the member states made during the negotiation process and the way they were able to subdue the Commission and prevent it from becoming too autonomous.

Analysis of the dynamics at work during policy negotiations reveals, however, that even though the Commission did take a back-seat to the Council of Ministers, this may ironically be due to the actions of the Commission itself on two fronts. First, after the presentation of the first proposals of Agenda 2000, the Commission actually introduced four major changes to its initial plans for financial measurements, the introduction of national envelopes, price cuts and increases in quotas. As such, the Commission gave away its "strongest cards in the CAP reform negotiating process, before the negotiations [had] even started".[44] Instead of using the "radical" reform proposal as a negotiation platform, with a probability of achieving substantial concessions from member states seeking to agree on a common denominator, the Commission may have reduced its chances of achieving an extensive CAP reform. In other words, the "de-radicalization" by the Commission shortly after it presented a first draft of the proposal may have lowered the common denominator that member states had to seek.

Second, the Commission established a "high-level group" which included senior civil servants from each member state. Their task was to "consult" on the technical issues of the proposal. Such reliance on national-level actors, as opposed to gaining technical information from either Brussels institutions or transnational interests with whom DG Agriculture had previously been in contact, arguably gave member states the upper hand yet again. In short, both of these actions by the Commission can be interpreted as allowing member states to maximize their power during policy negotiation.

Turning to the role of interest groups, we find similar dynamics to those at work in the MacSharry reforms: COPA was again unable to participate in the negotiation process. The shift towards re-nationalization of farming interests in general, and towards fragmentation within agrarian interests in particular, developed further and sapped the power of the European-based organizations. As an internal report from the organization reveals,[45] COPA recognized its weaknesses quite early in the process and its internal conflicts made it unable to act effectively. In terms of COPA's internal process, positions and strategies arrived at by the organization required unanimity. However, over the years internal mismanagement within it, stemming from increasing tensions that reflected national differences, meant that there was increasing lack of cooperation between its member organizations.[46] There were also ideological divisions: COPA's left-oriented faction, which was diametrically opposed to the majority group within the organization, supported the introduction of direct payments. The strategy proposed by interim Secretary-General Peter Pooley to omit controversial issues in COPA's position proposals was thus not followed. Not surprisingly, COPA broadly rejected the Commission's proposal as it implied "damaging consequences"[47] for farmers and their families, and it insisted that the Commission's budgetary figures were unrealistic, even though average farm incomes had increased since the MacSharry reform. In the end, one may argue that broad-brush analysis of the Agenda 2000 package, coupled with a fractured management system, de-legitimized COPA's role as an actor that was supposedly representative of all EU farmers: internal organizational mismanagement, and lack of clear alternatives, eventually caused difficulty in finding a common position that could be used as a lobbying proposal to be presented at the Commission and member state levels.

Nor had CPE learned from the 1992 experience. Its arguments against the Agenda 2000 proposals were also general and only focussed on maintaining the status quo, stressing that priority should be given to increasing subsidized exports and to safeguarding farm prices. Unlike COPA, however, CPE had a very clear common position on modulation, arguing in support of the Commission's initial position because it would have been favourable for small and middle-sized farmers. CPE attacked the large national farm organization's opposition to it, indicating that their objection "demonstrates whose interest they are defending".[48] Individual ceilings would have excluded many large farmers from this form of EU subsidy.

Because member states modified the Commission's proposal in favour of larger landholders, it may be argued that within the CAP the capitalist interests of a few privileged farmers found their way into the positions of member states and dominated the final outcome. Such corporate farmers did not represent the interest of the European-wide farming lobby groups who were concerned about the reform's consequences for smaller farmers. Rather, corporate farmers sought to ensure that reforms to the CAP would maintain their subsidies (a demand that was contrary to the interests of smaller farmers) and create a more one-sided mechanism by which subsidies would be redistributed under the CAP. This lends strength to Rieger's claims that "the creation of a single agriculture support system has produced an increase in social and economic inequalities, from which large farmers, with considerable political clout, have profited disproportionately."[49]

Data that support the claim that large farmers continued to benefit in the wake of the MacSharry and Agenda 2000 reforms are captured in a recent report by Oxfam.[50] This illustrates that even after MacSharry and Agenda 2000 reforms, the CAP continued to "lavish subsidies on some of Britain's wealthiest farmers and landlords" and that the "losers include small farmers, consumers, taxpayers, and the environment in the UK."[51] Investigating payments in the cereal sector in the UK during 2002 and 2003, the report's authors conclude that "the picture that emerges is one of a perverse system of social welfare, with billions of pounds benefiting some of the UK's richest families and wealthiest agriculture regions."[52]

Their data highlight the fact that there are 224 farmers with large holdings – referred to as the "224 club" – that receive an average subsidy of over £2.00 every five minutes, with an average subsidy of over £210,000 a year. These were the same farmers who heavily influenced the UK government to oppose ceiling payments to the CAP,[53] even though they represented less than 0.4 per cent of all the UK farming population, and who spoke against cuts to the price-support system. The report notes that these farms, which receive the majority of CAP support, are predominately located in Eastern England and Lincolnshire.[54]

The consequences have been twofold. The first is increasing polarization between the large and small landowners: in comparison with small farmers, large farmers win. Oxfam's data suggests that while the "224 club" continues to gain lavish subsidies, the UK's 15,000 smallest farms in the cereal sector are relatively worse off than before: the 15,000 smallest farms together receive a similar amount of support from the CAP as that provided to the "224 club". This polarization between the (few) rich and the (many) poor farmers is depicted in Figure 7.1. It shows how the slightly over 15,000 small landholdings of less than 50 acres receive an average subsidy of around £3,500. This contrasts with the 224 large landowners with over 1,000 hectares that receive over £210,000.

The second effect of high subsidy levels under the CAP is the

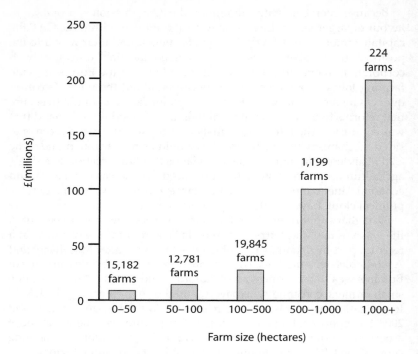

Figure 7.1 Average cereal subsidy payment in the UK by farm size (2003)

Source: Based on data and the graph found in Oxfam's *Spotlight on subsidies*, Oxfam Briefing Paper No. 55, 2004, page 14.

consequent dumping of European agricultural products onto poorer world markets. As Oxfam states, "the problem is that CAP subsidies generate vast surpluses, which are then dumped overseas, with the help of direct or indirect export subsidies."[55] Subsequently, small farmers in developing countries such as Africa, Asian and the Caribbean lose out as "the dumping of EU exports drive down world prices, costing vulnerable households income and impoverished countries foreign exchange ... [as has been seen in the case in] ... India and Jamaica."[56] Because the Fischler reforms (discussed below) did not pursue full solutions to this imbalance, the concern remains a serious one for many European citizens. This was most acutely seen when the UK government was accused of doing nothing about the dumping problem when it held the EU presidency in the second half of 2005.

Other interest groups with diverging priorities, such as environmental friendly organizations, were in theory free to join in the discussions during the Agenda 2000 reforms. However, they eventually ended up with the same negligible policy negotiation impact as they had attained during MacSharry. Although such organizations agreed with the argument that farm support should be linked to environmental performance, the Agenda 2000 proposal did not go far enough: the initiatives proposed would not seriously improve environmental quality. In the environmentalists' view, the intended reforms were much too focussed on the main sectors of the CAP, such as beef, cereal and dairy products, given that 80 per cent of the budget would be allocated to these areas. It was stated that the payments are "far too generous and cannot be justified from a taxpayers' perspective",[57] resulting in a lack of funds for the encouragement of environmentally friendly farming practices. Despite these reservations, however, the voices of the environmental groups were ignored, demonstrating that the market interests of member states and specific farmers prevailed over environmental concerns.[58] Thus, even though Agenda 2000 might potentially have seen a pluralist decision-making process involving actors with different priorities, the outcome demonstrates that it remained a largely intergovernmental process, qualified by elements of the DEC perspective as the interests of large landowners were also influential.

The Fischler reforms of 2003

The objectives of Fischler

Even though major initiatives for CAP reform were put forward through MacSharry and Agenda 2000, they were still insufficient, considering Eastern-enlargement of 2004 and the next round of WTO negotiations, referred to as the Doha round of trade talks. One of the main concerns was that the CAP budget was still very high, and might become unsustainable with Eastern enlargement. Another concern related to making the "EU farm sector more competitive in the face of increasingly open global trading regimes".[59] Thus, the European Commission put forward major new reform plans shortly after the Agenda 2000 programme.[60]

In this so-called "mid-term review" of July 2002, the Commission argued that the support of agricultural policy must go hand in hand with ensuring high-quality food, environmental protection, and the preservation of cultural heritage and landscapes. Moreover, it pointed out that agricultural expenditure must be better justified and be tied more closely to social welfare issues. More efficient distribution and allocation of CAP funds therefore needed to be introduced.

In order to obtain and maintain these improvements the Commission proposed, in a similar vein to MacSharry and Agenda 2000, to reshape and reform the CAP substantially.[61] The issues raised in the mid-term review were as follows (one can see some overlap with issues raised in previous reforms):

- The single farm payment: payments to farmers would no longer be linked to production (a change referred to as "decoupling"). Decoupling thus means that farmers were to "obtain income payments irrespective of what – and how much – they produced".[62]
- There would be a 5 per cent cut in the price for cereals.
- The price for rice would decrease.
- Prices in the areas of wheat seeds, and protein crops would be adjusted.
- Cross compliance: direct payments would be linked to compliance with environmental, food safety, animal welfare and certain safety standards for agricultural workers, and be reduced gradually to 20 per cent.
- There would be increased support for rural development: direct payments would be modified with a particular focus on preserving landscapes.
- New measures would be introduced for rural development, with a particular focus on improving production quality, food safety and animal welfare. It was proposed that the support for rural development should be paid by the national governments and no longer at the EU-level, pointing towards a partial re-nationalization of the CAP.
- There would be a new audit system to ensure the EU had more control of the budget.

The reform proposal would encourage progress for the Doha round as it was argued that the redirection of subsidies towards direct payments would have less of a distorting affect on the international trade system. Additionally, direct payments would make farmers respond to the demands of the market rather than to the availability of subsidies, while it would simultaneously ensure the preservation of landscapes and small farms, which was something European citizens strongly supported.

It initially seemed as if some parts of the reform package were well received by many member states, and it thus appeared that these reforms would be finalized within a short timeframe. However, negotiations would ultimately be prolonged due to French resistance, and by the end of May 2003 it still seemed that no compromise could be found. A main concern in this regard, as discussed below, related to the cut in cereal prices. After three weeks of negotiations among Europe's farm ministers, however, a compromise was achieved. As such, a month later, in June 2003 negotiations were concluded.

Through analysis of the final package, one sees that the reform proposals were a watered down of the Commission's initial plans, even though the plan was sold as a "truly radical reform".[63] The following elements reflect this fact:

- There was only partial disentanglement of production and direct payments.
- Although the concept of decoupling was introduced, there were exemptions for member states. In particular, France is not set to apply the new CAP decoupling agreements until 2007. Moreover, it is possible to avoid reforms in cases where a reduction in land under cultivation would take place.
- There was no change in the size of the CAP budget.
- There was no cut in cereal prices.

To observers it was quite clear that these reform steps were not sufficient either for Eastern enlargement[64] or for the Doha round, which in their eyes were doomed to fail. Another major opportunity to reform the CAP was substantially gambled away.[65] As the *Economist* puts it "[Reform] started with a proposal from the European Commission that was already cautious and complicated – and ended with a deal that was even more complex and half-hearted."[66] All member states walked away happy and none had feelings of having lost too much.[67]

Actors involved in Fischler: the usual suspects

In terms of the actors involved, once again the Commission initiated the policy process, this time by way of a mid-term review in July 2002. As in the MacSharry and the Agenda 2000 reforms, the Commission's supranational drive was quickly halted by the intergovernmental game and the actions of powerful member states, in particular France. The UK and Germany – supported by other Northern European member states and in particular by Sweden and the Netherlands – welcomed the initial reform proposal of the Commission. However, France, with its influential large cereal farmers, vehemently opposed the reduction of financial support in cereals.[68] As the *Economist* put it, "French farmers are a powerful lobby and French politicians are loath to cross them."[69] As seen in these farmers' resistance during MacSharry, cuts would have hurt the large French farmers in the cereal sector, which is one of biggest receivers of CAP funds among all sectors. Through their representative on the Council, French large farmers thus argued that the mid-term review by the Commission was unacceptable and aim to make only minor changes. They argued that the CAP budget had been fixed at the Berlin summit in 1999 and should remain untouched until the next budget round in 2006.[70] France was subsequently backed by the "southern coalition" of Portugal, Spain, Italy and Greece, as well as Ireland.

Thus, in the months after the mid-term review of 2002 was released, member states' opposition to reforms mounted. Beyond opposition to cutting cereal prices, early in the negotiations France voiced strong opposition to decoupling income support from production. This was because

French farm lobbies were strongly against not only cuts to cereal prices but also decoupling, as it was the largest farmers who would have been the biggest losers through the Commission's proposal. French farmers, in particular, therefore told the French government almost immediately that any decoupling reforms along the lines of those presented by the Commission in the summer of 2002 would damage their livelihood.[71] France was once again backed by the southern European states with their strong farm lobbies. In other words, along with France, the influence of large farmers was especially seen at work in the Mediterranean countries. These states negotiated either only minor decoupling measures or none at all, due to the strong farm lobby in which large landowners played a crucial role.[72] In order to arrive at an agreement on at least partial decoupling, sectors such as olive oil and sugar remained untouched. Similarly, Ireland proved a noteworthy ally to these "southern" states. The Irish farm minister spoke of huge damage to Irish farm families and rural Ireland if these reform plans were to be put into practice. As in France, large landholders acted through national farm organizations that strongly lobbied their national governments. This is reflected in how the Irish farm lobby ICMSA pressured the then Irish farm minister not to implement Fischler's proposal as they stood: the Irish position was influenced by the ongoing talks between the government and main farm organizations.[73] This strong opposition is not surprising when it is remembered that 80 per cent of all CAP subsidies in all sectors in 2003 went to just 20 per cent of the EU's largest farms.

Hence, full decoupling would clearly disadvantage larger farmers more than smaller ones. It is thus little surprise that many observers witnessed strong opposition from countries with larger farms, including finally the UK, which is home to some of the most lucrative large landholding operations, as discussed earlier.[74] Given this opposition from several member states, which acted in the interests of and in participation with large landholders in their country, the Commission's decoupling suggestion was watered down substantially, with exemptions being introduced in the final proposal. Interestingly, if not ironically, all national negotiators would later hail the minor agreement on decoupling as a major milestone in the reform.

In the wake of mounting opposition from member states, in January 2003 the Commission explicitly tried to override some of the member states' opposition by emphasizing the importance of the far-reaching Fischler reform proposals. It is noteworthy in this regard how the Commission came up against the private agreement between French President Jacques Chirac and German Chancellor Gerhard Schröder, who openly opposed the Commission's proposal. In October 2002 Chirac had (falsely) assured Schröder that the CAP would not be reformed until 2006. This had provoked angry reactions not only from the Commission, but also from Britain and the Northern member states that were expecting reform. This incident reflects how supranational interests were diametri-cally opposed to some intergovernmental ones, and how a clear intergov-ernmental conflict was starting to emerge due to what many perceived was the undiplomatic approach of the French. The reforms that passed in the end could therefore also be attributed to these internal cleavages precipitated by the French. The end game was an intergovernmental battle where both sides had to emerge as winners, even if this meant giving up supranational initiatives that would have helped prepare the CAP for a successful Eastern enlargement.

If the above highlights how the Commission was influential in initiating reforms in 2003, while the Council and specific large farming interests worked together in negotiating the final outcome, then what can be said of the role of other potential interest groups? On the European level COPA–CODEGA rejected the proposals as they did not reflect a balance between the demands of global trade and European society's concerns and wishes. Quite clearly their interest was in maintaining a closed European agricultural market that was not influenced "by the world's major exporters ... where values and standards are very differ-ent".[75] Moreover, COPA–CODEGA accused the Commission of not demonstrating the far-reaching impact that the reform would have had for European agriculture. Interestingly, they rigorously defended the link between production and direct payments, thereby supporting the interest of the larger farmers. They were also of the opinion that decou-pling would bring on a serious threat to employment in the agri-food chain. Environmental groups were also opposing the reform plan because they believed that concrete measures on developing and protecting the rural environment were being developed.[76]

To sum up, like the MacSharry and Agenda 2000 reforms, the Fischler reforms witnessed policy initiation led by the Commission. This was later replaced by a strong intergovernmental presence in the negotiation phase, when domestic leaders sought to remove many dimensions of the Commission's proposal. Such intergovernmental leaders were influenced by the interests of their larger farmers, and thus opposed measures that would have been to the disadvantage of wealthy landowners. Given this evidence, one can theoretically under-stand the policy initiation phase as being informed by ideas raised in supranational governance, while intergovernmentalism combined with the DEC perspective offers insights into policy negotiation.

Conclusions

This chapter has argued that the CAP is a 1st order policy because it represents a strong, centralized policy at the EU level through which subsidies are redistributed to European farmers; it represents one of the most important redistributive policies in the EU, given that it receives the largest percentage of the budget. In terms of policy processes, when examining developments during the MacSharry, Agenda 2000 and Fischler reforms, the process witnessed, at the first stage, policy initiation embarked upon by the Commission and, at the second stage, a negotiation process led by national actors who actively participated alongside large, business-like, farming interests. One may argue that of all 1st order policies studied in this book, the CAP may be considered one of the most intergovernmental policies, given that European players are left largely outside the negotiation process. Considering the theoretical frameworks of Chapter 3, the policy area suggests that ideas influenced by the supranational governance school are valuable in explaining how the policy was initiated. Yet, during the negotiation phase both the intergovernmentalist and DEC perspectives are of more value.

The findings here also help us re-evaluate some issues raised by work on EU agricultural policy, where it is often assumed that lobbying in this area takes place at two levels. The first is the national level, where national interest groups try to influence their respective governments, which are represented through their Ministers of Agriculture who make final decisions on the CAP. The second level is the supranational one, where European-based interest groups, namely COPA-COGECA, have established ties with the Commission, which has the sole right to initiate legislation in the CAP.

Though this formal description suggests that COPA has been very successful with its lobbying strategies at the European level, the evidence in this chapter suggests that this is not entirely the case. Rather, COPA, which increasingly gained in importance in the 1980s, actually lost influence throughout the 1990s and early 2000s for three reasons. First, the Commission had an interest in a weakened COPA as both actors' interests regarding the future of the CAP drifted steadily apart. COPA tried to maintain the status quo in the CAP, while the Commission sought rationalizing reforms. Second, COPA suffered from slow fragmentation at the management level. Although farming groups stood out in the 1950s as an example of a well-organized and disciplined body, the change in agricultural production, the growing cleavage between small and big farmers, the change in consumers' wishes and an increase in environmental concerns led to more heterogeneous farming groups expressing differing and contradictory interests.[77] Hence, one of the reasons for a decline in the influence of European-wide agrarian interest groups can be found in the changed internal structure of the supranational farming organization, one that inevitably reflected the changes in the profession itself. Third, member states were in favour of outflanking European-based interest organizations, fearing that strong transnational interest groups may have helped to increase the autonomy of the Commission vis-à-vis member states. This may have had the effect of changing negotiations over aspects of the CAP from being less intergovernmental to more supranational. By refocussing on the importance of national agrarian interest groups, member states were able to work alongside specific national-based farming interest lobbies. Strong national farmers' unions, with their capacity to mobilize support easily at the national level, were able to pressurize their respective governments to adopt positions that reflected the main interests within such organizations, namely, those of the large, agri-businesses. This would further erode the negotiating power of small and medium-sized European farmers, and empower almost exclusively those large landholding interests that could seek to maximize profits in the wake of the reforms.

8 Social policy: demonstrating European incapability and differences

This chapter focusses on the objectives of social policy and in particular on the goals of the Social Charter of 1989 and the Social Protocol of 1992. The first section of the chapter examines the evolution of policy, which we would claim indicates a weak and decentralized EU. The consequence of this has been fewer EU-wide norms in this issue area than in the policy areas studied earlier. Because member states retain sovereignty and EU-wide regulations are difficult to decide in this field, it is argued that this issue area represents a 2nd order policy area. In order to explain why it has developed as such, the chapter analyses those actors most influential in driving different initiatives. The second section thus pays attention to the importance of the Commission in initiating the Social Charter and Social Protocol developments, the intentions of the Council in amending Commission recommendations (with a particular emphasis on the actions of the UK), and the role of specific interest groups including trade unions and organized business. The account will suggest the significance of the supranational governance perspective (with a focus on the Commission) as well as the intergovernmental and corporatist perspectives in explaining developments in this policy area.

The objectives and evolution of social policy: a 2nd order status

Even though it is weak, the legal basis for EU social policy is provided in the Treaty of Rome.[1] Based on the insistence of the French in particular, the Treaty's general objectives were to promote high employment, the improvement of living and working conditions, equal pay for men and women (gender equality provisions), and the free movement of workers.[2] France was also concerned with the creation of a European Social fund to aid occupational and geographical mobility.[3] However, despite these broad and general goals, even from the early days of integration one could observe that member states paid less attention to social policy matters and pushed more for deeper regulation of the economic sphere. In Arnold's words, the "social dimension has [been] ... subordinated to economic and industrial goals"[4] in order to make Europe more competitive in the world economy.

The lack of a desire to strengthen EU regulation in this area is reflected in the fact that, as many observers have noted, EU social policy came almost to a standstill in the 1970s and 1980s.[5] The first "Social Action Programme" in 1974 failed not only because of the opposition of business and the British government, but also because of the Commission's policy of opting for best-practice standards.[6] Only the coordination of social security systems for migrant workers and equal pay for women were pursued in this period.

A type of "U-turn" in social policy occurred in the late 1980s. In the wake of the economic crisis at the beginning of the 1980s and the strong neo-liberal trend brought about by the 1986 Single European Act (SEA), as discussed in Chapter 4, fears grew that capital actors had too many advantages at the national and European levels. Due to the rather diverse social welfare systems in the European member states, harmonization of social policy was deemed necessary to prevent distortions of competition: without harmonization it was felt that capital might seek competitive advantages by moving to those member states with less stringent (and less costly) regulations. Hence, arguments in favour of a "social dimension" of the European integration emerged, spearheaded by Commission President Delors and French President Mitterrand, who believed that the SEA's economic and institutional dynamics made it difficult to continue to exclude social issues from the EU agenda.[7]

Therefore, the Commission pushed for a minimal harmonization in health and safety standards to be integrated in the SEA in order to contain social dumping pressures from industry.[8] Surprisingly, some viewed this regulation as having introduced high levels of standards, even though many expected only a lowest-common-denominator outcome. The introduction of Qualified Majority Voting (QMV) in the Council was pursued by the Commission for decisions on these issues, which meant that only a qualified majority of member states (i.e. not all member states) needed to agree to an initiative in order for it to be approved. Further, a corporatist decision-making procedure with regard to social policy was also introduced, under which both capital and labour would be represented when social policy was discussed. As such, the establishment of a dialogue between European labour, business and public employers' associations in the preparation of legislation was theoretically guaranteed in what has been referred to as "social dialogue".

After its first anchoring in the SEA, EU social policy was to attain what many would argue was its proper standing with the Social Charter of 1989.[9] Eleven member states –the exception being the UK – officially recognized that the EU needed a social dimension and signed the "Charter on the Fundamental Rights of Workers", better known as the "Social Charter".[10] The eleven governments declared:

> The completion of the internal market must lead to an improvement in the living and working conditions of workers in the European community. This process must result from an

approximation of these conditions while the improvement is being maintained, as regards in particular the duration and organization of working time and forms of employment other than open-ended contracts, such as fixed-term contracts, part-time working, temporary work and seasonal work. Every worker in the European community shall have a right to a weekly rest period and to annual paid leave, the duration of which must be progressively harmonized in accordance with national practices.[11]

Apart from this general declaration, the Social Charter listed a further "47 actions for the establishment of a social dimension of the single market programme",[12] an action programme which Delors largely supported. The twelve categories of fundamental social rights are:

- freedom of movement
- employment and remuneration
- improvement of living and working conditions
- social protection
- freedom of association and collective bargaining
- vocational training
- equal treatment for men and women
- information, consultation and participation for workers
- health protection and safety at the workplace
- protection of children and adolescents
- protection of elderly persons
- protection of disabled persons.

With the exception of "health and safety" and the "removal of market barriers", unanimity in decision-making processes was required by the Social Charter.[13] This requirement was soon regarded as one of the main obstacles to the fulfilment of the social dimension of European integration. A majority of member states therefore argued for a change to QMV in EU social policy issues and for incorporation of the aims of the Social Charter into the Maastricht Treaty. Unsurprisingly, the British blocked this idea whilst the other eleven member states came to a separate "Agreement on Social Policy", also called the "Social Protocol",[14] which provided the following:[15]

- QMV for areas such as working conditions, consultation and information of workers, improvement of the working environment to protect workers' health and safety, integration of persons excluded from the labour market.
- Unanimity in areas such as social security interests and social protection, representation and collective defence of the interest of workers and employers, conditions of employment for third-country nationals.

- Greater consultation of the social partners in the drafting of social legislation.

In general, the Social Protocol achieved a procedural breakthrough and an expansion of competences, which led to a series of additional directives. However, issues such as social security of workers, protection of workers after termination, worker representation and employment conditions still remained under the unanimity procedure, while wages, rights of association and rights to strike were completely excluded from the Protocol. This leads to the observation that only minor regulatory measures have been introduced under QMV, and no measures with a fiscal or redistributive character.[16]

With this evidence in mind, how can one characterize the evolution of EU directives over the last few decades? Falkner points out that there has been at least one directive per year on social policy issues since 1975.[17] In all, 79 directives have been passed since 1975, with the 1990s being the most active period so far. The changing numbers of directives are captured in Figure 8.1. One can differentiate between three issue areas where the Commission has been active: first, security and health protection at the working place; second, working conditions in general; and third, non-discrimination and equal opportunities. Most directives (38 in total) have been passed in the area of "security and health protection at the working place" because QMV has been applied in this area since the SEA.

Along with directives, non-binding measures have been pursued at the EU-level as seen in Figure 8.2. In contrast to directives, non-binding

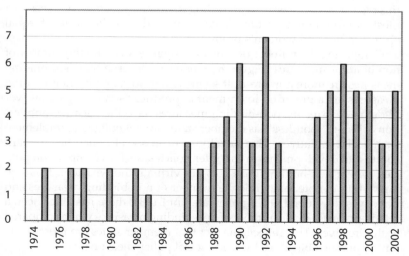

Figure 8.1 Development of social policy directives, 1974–2002

Source: Falkner, 2004.

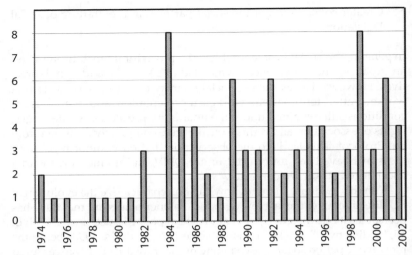

Figure 8.2 Development of non-binding measures in social policy, 1974–2002

Source: Falkner, 2004.

measures have no legal force. Up to 2002, 15 recommendations, 50 resolutions, 16 argumentations, three declarations and three memorandums – a total of 87 non-binding measures – had been issued by the EU on social issues. Figure 8.2 indicates that the rate has substantially increased since the 1980s, reaching a maximum in the 1990s. The periods after the SEA and the Amsterdam Treaty were especially fruitful in this regard. When classified according to different themes, one sees that most non-binding measures have been made on the issue of equal opportunities and women's promotion.[18]

Comparing the number of directives (Figure 8.1) with the number of non-binding measures (Figure 8.2), one can observe that non-binding measures are more numerous. It seems as if in social policy non-binding measures are a preferred instrument to produce "something", however ill-defined: in reality, non-binding measures have the negative implication of being "toothless", as member states are not obliged to implement such social initiatives. This development in social policy lies in stark contrast to developments in 1st order policies, such as competition policies, where non-binding measures are virtually non-existent. It is also interesting to note that while the number of non-binding measures and directives developed at a similar rate until 1984, there has since been a relative increase in the number of non-binding measures when compared with directives. This reflects the fact that member states are more reluctant to pursue obligatory EU-wide social policy measures.

Generally, over the course of the last decade, the number of binding actions has declined and there have been more non-binding ones, reflecting member states' unwillingness to submit to EU-wide rules in this area. Falkner describes this trend as "neo-voluntariness", with recommendations and other non-binding instruments increasing in importance in "regulating" social policy.[19] Moreover, new methods of coordination, including European benchmarks, evaluations of national action plans and recommendations based on them, have increased substantially in the last few years. The Commission and the member states hence try to govern social policy in a "modified", non-binding way, unlike the compulsory approach in other policy areas where one sees supranational regulations taking prominence over, or replacing, national-level rules, as seen in 1st order policies. Further, the weakness of EU policies in the social area prevents the individual from bringing complaints to the ECJ to enforce a claim related to social regulations.

It is interesting to note that Falkner also finds that there are more non-binding measures in certain social policy issues than in others. Non-discrimination and gender issues feature mostly in non-binding measures, while working conditions and health protection feature more in directives.[20] Why does one observe so many non-binding measures in the former areas? Falkner argues that for the promotion of information and creation of awareness (measures mostly regarded as important in non-discrimination and gender issues), non-binding measures work sufficiently well, but they are less effective for issues such as working conditions.[21] The question then arises: why are information and awareness regarded as sufficient to "promote" some policies, while in other policy areas these instruments are less used? A conclusion one could draw is that actors formulating social policy – namely political actors, economic actors and workers, as discussed in more detail in the next section – are less likely to find agreement in the different issue areas within social policy. The only instrument they could come up with has been the use of non-binding measures. Falkner observes that many recommendations result from social partner agreements between capital, labour and EU institutions. Hence, it seems as if corporatist decision making at EU level, as seen in more detail in the next section, also correlates with the use of non-binding instruments.[22]

In sum, on the basis of these observations one can regard social policy as having a 2nd order status. Even though many developments can be observed over the last decades in this area, they do not primarily come in the form of binding actions. Rather, non-binding measures have been used that allow member states much freedom to opt out of EU-wide regulations in this area. Given the lack of harmonization in the policy area, regulations from the national level remain paramount, reflecting a weak and decentralized EU in this policy area. The next section thus turns to a more focussed analysis of the role member states had in ensuring that social policy remains within the remit of the domestic level.

The formulation of the Social Charter and the Social Protocol

Before examining the formulation of the Social Charter and Social Protocol, it is important to emphasize that different actors have been regularly involved in the policy-making process in this area. The most important are the Council and the Commission; the latter has proven to be a central actor in promoting an EU-wide social policy. Despite the Commission's desire to promote a deepened social policy agenda, however, the Council remains the decisive actor in the policy area as seen in more detail below. With the change from unanimous voting to QMV for particular social issues, decisions could have been theoretically reached in an easier manner, with one single member state less likely to veto any decision. However, as will be seen below, member state governments still protect their social policy sovereignty rigorously and are sceptical of the Commission's initiatives in social policy: in the Council's view, transferring social policy issues to the European level is regarded as taking away one of the last few policies where national governments enjoy sovereignty.

It is important to note, however, that in contrast to the previous policy areas discussed in the book, one sees that the European Parliament through its Committee on Employment and Social Affairs (ECOSOC) has been much more involved in the social policy process. Beyond the EP, interest groups have also been of importance in social policy making. These include not only the representatives of business (The Union of Industrial and Employers' Confederations of Europe (UNICE) and the Confédération Européenne des Employers Publics (CEEP)), but also labour interests (European Trade Union Federation (ETUC)) that have been regularly invited to participate in the negotiation process. As discussed below, the first talks between the different social partners were strained: they could not come up with an agreement or a common statement. This was partly also due to the fact that neither of the social partners did actually possess a negotiating mandate. With regard to dynamics between these two groups, one has seen that levels of influence are unbalanced. While business interest groups have extended their power, especially due to the increased size of the single market, labour interest groups seem to be underrepresented due to their internal conflicts and organizational difficulties. In order to better illustrate these ideas, attention is paid to the formulation process first of the Social Charter and then of the Social Protocol.

The Social Charter: the Commission as initiator

As discussed earlier, SEA negotiations fuelled concerns regarding the social dimension of the European integration process. The Commission was particularly interested in developing social policy in order to offset the potential negative ramifications of a deepened integration process. In this regard the Commission's role was crucial because it fostered and linked committees of policy experts from business and labour groups at the European level. In other words, it actively promoted the development of social policy at the supranational level.[23] It also worked resolutely to break the strong opposition of governments and economic actors who were against the development of a supranational social policy. The Commission sought to give the EU a "social face" by highlighting the potential social backlashes which the neo-liberal, single integrated market might trigger. By placing the social argument at the forefront and looking for cooperation with various groups – particularly labour – the Commission forced member states to accept and to discuss the agenda of social policy. Cram therefore argues that the Commission had a significant impact on the development of EU social policy and on the actors involved in the formulation process.[24]

As Ross contends, the Commission was very active in promoting social policy during the Social Charter's initiation phase, putting considerable effort, energy and strategic thinking into finding a way to place social policy issues on the European agenda and gaining the consent of the member states.[25] Even though some national governments were aware that a single market needed a social dimension in order to prevent a distortion in favour of capital, the extension of Commission competences in social policies was viewed negatively by most member states, particularly the UK. Unsurprisingly, employers associations and industry strongly opposed EU competences on social policies. However, along with the Commission, the EP and trade unions also promoted the idea of a European social dimension: the Commission was actively mobilizing trade unions and tried to build networks with social partners and the EP. The Commission President, Delors, in particular was personally intensively involved in this process.[26]

The introduction of a social dimension on the European level was also championed by the Commission with the argument that diverging social standards at the national level could lead to distortions of competition in the single market.[27] The importance of incorporating a social dimension in the Single Market Programme was highlighted by arguments such as the claim that "leaving out a social foundation could lead not only to social dumping, but also potential relocations of corporations."[28] In this regard, Ross observes that "harmonization efforts" in the social policy area resulted from the objectives of the Single Market and not from social policy needs per se.[29] Hence, social policy developments only occurred in the aftermath of economic ones. In order to avoid a downward spiral of social standards[30] – which would give competitive advantages to some countries – the Commission believed that a re-regulation of social policy was necessary.[31]

Policy negotiation: intergovernmentalism with a touch of corporatism

The above discussion makes it clear that the initiation process for the Social Charter can be best understood by focussing on ideas raised by the supranational governance perspective, since the Commission played an instrumental role of placing the Social Charter on the agenda. However, this theoretical perspective had less importance during policy negotiation, given the significance of other actors.[32] One sees that when negotiation of the Social Charter started, the Commission sought the input of all possible interested actors in the preliminary stages. These actors included: trade unions, employers, the Economic and Social Committee, the European Parliament, the Committee of Permanent Representatives (COREPER), and national civil servants. The Commission invited the EP's ECOSOC to develop a draft charter, and simultaneously sought to deal with the reservations of states such as the UK and Denmark. From this perspective, the Commission acted quite cleverly to obtain the approval of the diverse actors that would be involved in the negotiation process. Despite its best intentions, the timeframe for developing a draft was very limited, resulting in a text that had not been agreed between the diverse groups in ECOSOC: no compromise draft between employees' and employers' representatives had been achieved and the usual conflict lines between labour and business were inherent in the document. Instead of being an effective compromise that would serve as a basis for future negotiation, the draft opened up room for the diverse conflicting positions adopted in the Council of Ministers.[33]

Abandoning the ECOSOC initiatives, the Commission therefore presented its own draft on May 1, 1989 based on the Belgian Memorandum of 1989,[34] which the EP and ETUC broadly supported. However, the latter two groups were against the idea of the Charter representing a new "legal" instrument in the EU and they wanted the traditional legislative measures (i.e. directives) used in other policy areas such as competition policy to be pursued instead.[35] As far as the Commission was concerned, it tried to find a middle ground between the different positions of the member states, with a particular concern regarding the reservations of the UK and Denmark. Moreover, the Commission expected there would be only a "ceremonial statement", not a full Council resolution.

The Commission's draft was then discussed within the Council of Social Ministers, member states approved in principle the development of a social dimension in an integrated European market. Despite many member states' support for the Social Charter, and in contrast to the EP and ETUC, in the end it was only because the Charter explicitly remained a noncommittal declaration that many member states approved it. The two countries which shared reservations about the Charter were the UK and Denmark.[36] Denmark expressed some reservations, while the UK led by the Tories simply decided against it.

Thatcher's UK, in particular, held strong reservations about Community-wide social policy regulations, for obvious reasons considering the Conservative ideological preferences against tight labour market regulations. In the Tories' view, a supranational social policy, if supported by other EU states such as Germany, France and Spain, which have comparatively strong social welfare systems, might have the effect of undercutting the competitiveness of the British economy, which is home to one of the lowest paid and most precarious workforces in Europe.

The most prominent supporter of the Charter among member states was the French government, which held the EU presidency at the time. The French hoped the Charter could be negotiated and adopted during their presidency, which coincided with celebrations of the 200th anniversary of the French Revolution. The French Presidency was strongly supported by the Commission, which remained a key actor in the negotiation process, although it clearly played a less central role than the Council. Of course, one cannot regard the Commission as a neutral actor in this process. Similar dynamics were at work as had been seen in the Merger Control Regulation (Chapter 5): apart from the desire to introduce a social dimension into the European integration process, the Commission also sought to extend it competences in a new policy field.

Next to the Council of Social Ministers, the other actors participating in the negotiation process included UNICE, ETUC, ECOSOC and the EP. ETUC[37] and ECOSOC supported the Commission's draft[38] and were seconded by member states such as Spain, France and Germany. Although UNICE traditionally held the same position as the UK in social affairs, organized business did not disapprove of the Charter as strongly as the UK government. Business clearly indicated that it was in favour of extending Brussels' competences on social policy. However, it rejected any binding character for the Charter or the far-reaching implications this might have had on increasing trade union rights. Although the position of UNICE was somewhat peculiar, it reflected how business preferred to be part of the process instead of being excluded.[39]

Once the draft had been presented, one of the crucial issues to be decided was the change from unanimous voting to QMV on some issues, such as: health and safety in working environments; worker information, consultation and participation; part-time work; parental leave; equal treatment of men and women; and measurements regarding working hours (in other words, labour-related welfare-state policies). Unsurprisingly, there was a significant struggle over the range of issues to be decided by QMV. Members of the Commission, the EP and the ETUC were in favour of extending QMV, while UNICE and other national employers' associations strongly opposed it and favoured unanimous voting. Agreement between UNICE and ETUC was difficult to reach, as neither association had a mandate to decide on binding decisions for their members. Agreement could be reached on the regulation of health and safety in the working environment, but not all working conditions were included. Unlike health and safety issues, which were to be decided under QVM, worker information and consultation were still to be decided unanimously. The agreements made on the latter two issues already went too far according to business interests.[40]

Most other changes were blocked by the need for unanimous votes in the Council of Ministers. Some changes were simply formulated in a very vague manner and many measures were adapted to specific national conditions. Other issues were simply not targeted as no consensus could be reached. In order to get as much approval as possible the lowest common denominator was the only possible basis for agreement.[41] Although the Commission fought for social issues outside the realm of the single market (i.e. not strictly related to economic concerns), their proposals were either watered down by the member states in the negotiations, or simply ignored. Similarly, the EP was excluded from the process, something that was heavily criticized. Wörgötter argues that the EP was even more disadvantaged than the "social actors", ETUC and UNICE.[42] This is even more surprising considering that the EP was a strong supporter of the Charter project; it had been arguing for a basic social rights document for a long time and reiterated its call in its 1989 "basic rights declaration".[43]

In October 1989 the Council of Social Ministers presented a final draft of the Charter, which took account of the interests of the diverse member states. Some of the original ideas included in the Commission's draft were watered down, highlighting the significance of the Council during the negotiation phase. The final draft clearly indicates how far the member states' reservations were taken into account and one can observe that the outcome was much watered down when compared with the original proposal, with a clear bias towards market-oriented social policies. This was the only basis on which a common position could be found. Despite the changes, the British government chose to opt out of the Charter – even though it remained within the negotiation process until the end.

The outcome of negotiations in 1989 was the "Social Charter", which was only a declaration with non-binding recommendations on workers' information and consultation and no legal basis. The Charter can therefore be characterized as "no longer a Community proposal but an intergovern-mental one".[44] The member states also explicitly made it clear that they did not want the Commission to extend its powers beyond the limits defined by the treaties in the social policy area. The Social Charter served as a signal that Europe had not forgotten about social standards within a European single market about which the European public was becoming increasingly disillusioned. This points to the idea that developments in social policy are mostly created as a "reaction" to the dynamics of the

European integration process. As such, there was never a "sincere" desire of member states to develop social policy instruments per se at the European level; the Charter was simply a means to help make the single market more acceptable to the public.

In summary, one can conclude that even though the Social Charter had no legal implications as it was not part of any treaty nor formulated as a directive,[45] member states could not reach an agreement above the lowest common denominator.[46] In the end the Social Charter in fact offered less than was commonly assumed by some who seem to suggest that it helps protect workers in Europe. As Ross states, it simply gathered together the social concerns announced in the Rome Treaty and set up procedures to articulate most of them.[47] As such, one must seriously question the idea that "major reforms" in social policy were actually attained with the Social Charter. The agreement that was arrived at is probably best seen as being of symbolic value: the consequences of the Charter for the deepening of the integration process are negligible because it has no binding measures and leaves (possible) implementation to the goodwill of member states.[48]

Part of the lack of agreement can be explained by considering not only the role of the Council during the negotiation phases, but also the whole range of actors that had an opportunity to participate in the process one way or the other. With this in mind, one has to classify the Social Charter process as a political failure which left the single market programme with no social dimension as such, reflecting how social policy is a 2nd order policy in terms of actual output. Although the Commission was important in initiating the Social Charter, one could argue that social policy was simply not regarded as important enough for member states to find compromises above the lowest common denominator. Nor was it considered important enough to add a legal binding character to the Charter. Given this evidence we are faced with a policy that had a clear supranational initiation process, followed by a strong intergovernmental negotiation process, with the Commission trying to achieve a symbolic output by way of a corporatist mode of negotiation. It seems that a corporatist method of dealing with policies also resulted in an outcome much lower than the desired median outcome, given the differences that existed between business and labour. This case suggests that the fewer the number of actors involved, the easier it is to reach a desired outcome.

The Social Protocol

Commission initiating calls for further reform

Because the Social Charter did not meet initial expectations,[49] in 1991 a new attempt was made to reform the Community's social provisions "along the path laid down in the 1989 Social Charter".[50] Once again, as with developments in the Social Charter, the Commission was an important actor in initiating the discussion and submitting draft articles for the Social Protocol. The most obvious difference from the way the Social Charter had developed in 1989 was that member states now agreed more fully with the idea of strengthening the social dimension, as one can observe from the diverse government memorandums. With the exception of the UK, all member states sought for community action in social policy.[51] The Council and the Commission were pulling together for the Social Protocol in a way that they had not for the Social Charter. Given this, the initiation process can be characterized as an initiative that was rekindled and taken by the Commission, while it also had the support of the Council.

Policy negotiating dynamics: more intergovernmentalism and corporatism

The draft presented by the Commission was accompanied by a more moderate proposal by the Dutch presidency, which tried to accommodate the more critical voices in the Council, such as the British. However, the Dutch proposal somewhat surprisingly did not prevail. It was rather the more "demanding" Commission proposal that was taken as a basis for negotiation. Lange argues that this was mainly due to "last minute compromise".[52] Turning to Britain, one sees that it clearly opposed the proposal, on similar ideological grounds to those that were seen during the Social Charter's development. The Dutch presidency tried to find a compromise among the different interests of the various member states. Germany hoped to promote a political union alongside an economic one (which also included a social dimension) in order to maintain the high standards set in Germany. Italy and France promoted economic union, but knew that they had to give in on the political union in order to get the consent of Germany to their own plans. Spain tried to use the negotiations on social policy issues to accomplish a broader discussion on the EU budget. More specifically, it tried to argue that political reform – including social policy issues – had to be accompanied by money transfers from richer to poorer countries in order to eradicate economic differences. Spain thus put forward its demand for a Cohesion Fund in return for its approval of economic union. In the negotiations over the Social Protocol, manoeuvring on the different economic and monetary issues played an important role. The social dimension issue was negotiated against Economic and Monetary Union (see Chapter 6) by member states mainly concerned with how to avoid competition distortions based on diverging social standards across Europe. The Commission proved to be a strategic mediator and negotiator between member states and their different positions, acting as a kind of "policy entrepreneur".

Some non-governmental actors were also involved in the negotiation process. The Commission was the driving force in terms of deciding which social partners would participate in the negotiations, as the member states – with the exception of Belgium – were not particularly interested in including them.[53] Labour interest groups were specifically invited in order to legitimize the negotiation process, while simultaneously satisfying social democratic member states.[54] UNICE and CEEP were invited to present proposals, and observers argue that business proactively sought participation because it was fearful of the consequences of self-exclusion: to be left outside the negotiations would be damaging because it would not allow business' position to be known.[55] This resulted in an agreement with ETUC to set up structures to strengthen social partnership, which were then included in the negotiation process among member states. This seemingly compromising behaviour of UNICE was also partly induced by the behaviour of the Commission towards ETUC. The Commission encouraged ETUC to behave more like a European actor, offering and establishing communication networks. This resulted in a stronger ETUC which was taken more seriously by both UNICE and ETUC's national members. Unsurprisingly, business interest groups were again suspicious of extending QMV to other areas, whereas labour interest groups, as well as the Commission and the EP, supported this.

From the beginning the Commission put heavy pressure on the social partners to reach agreement among themselves, and this also affected future dynamics within the different interest groups and social policy developments. Instead of going through the normal "organizational procedures of approval",[56] partners had to sign any agreement immediately. Social partners had thus become "formal co-actors in a corporatist policy community"[57] with regard to EU social policy, thus guaranteeing their representation at this level of governance. Although the outcome did work well for the development of a Social Protocol, in the end this type of "hasty agreement", which was reached without the backing of the various member organizations, may also help explain the limited success of social partnership as the decade continued.[58] One can observe that although a written agreement was reached among the social partners in this case, the institutional basis it was supposed to build on was not very solid.

With this in mind, one may have the impression that although the Commission wanted a "social" output in one form or another in order to claim that the EU does possess a social dimension, it was not particularly interested in how well the follow-up process would work.[59] This impression gains more strength in light of the behaviour of business groups such as UNICE, which stated that they were not fully committed to a productive social dialogue. Rather, business preferred the status quo position that existed before the Social Protocol. Thus, on the one hand, one can see that a formal instrument for a corporatist decision-making process had been created through the Social Protocol. But, on the other hand, the instrument was in reality non-existent because one of the major actors refused to play an active and productive role in it. Unlike other (economic) policy fields studied in this book, social policy was thus limited in its development right from the beginning, even though the institutional set-up had been theoretically established at the European level.[60] Given this, there was little reason to expect that the social dialogue would gain in importance after the Social Protocol.

Yet, turning to the reaction of member states to joint agreements of the social partners, we can clearly see from the British experience during the negotiation of the Social Protocol that governments do not necessarily follow the wishes of their "social partners" and may continue to adopt negative stances towards European social policy.[61] The outcome of the negotiations was that, even though member states adopted the initial proposal that the Commission presented in 1990, there was an "unusual and unpredictable"[62] outcome due to the British opt-out. In the end, eleven member states signed the separate Social Protocol, which allowed them to use EU "institutions, procedures and mechanisms to formulate and implement social policies on which they agree".[63] The Commission's competences were expanded as more issue areas became subject to EU intervention, and among these, QMV came into force for certain issues, including working conditions, the information and consultation of workers, equality between men and women with regard to labour market opportunities and treatment at work, and the integration of persons excluded from the labour market.[64] Excluded from minimum harmonization were pay, the right of association, the right to strike and the right to impose lock-outs. As such, standards on working conditions are few, and standards on industrial relations for rules on worker consultations and co-determination are non-existent.

In other words, as that the Council was reluctant to allow Brussels full control over the policy area, national sovereignty was maintained through the Social Protocol, especially when looking at the welfare dimension, including workers' rights, unemployment and social security systems. In contrast to their approach in economically relevant policy areas, the member states were not willing to give up their power, and they therefore accepted only a half-hearted EU social policy. This is reflected in Gomà's argument that "the degree of erosion of national sovereignty is much wider in the economic than in the social domain."[65] An intergovernmental logic still prevailed in social policy decisions at EU level.

One may question why it was possible to reach agreement on health and safety standards but not on working conditions and industrial relations rules. Scharpf[66] argues that the negative externalities in terms of significant market failures in the single market would be too high if health and safety standards were not pursued. However, in the case of working conditions and regulations on industrial relations, supranational rules would mean that member states would lose out because they would have to either lower their social standards, or improve them substantially.[67] Hence, developments achieved in the Social Protocol concerned issues with a potentially negative impact on the internal market. For instance, member states feared that divergent payment scales between home workers and "migrant workers" would result in competitive disadvantages; corporations not bound by national laws on worker consultation would jeopardize the national social arrangements; and national differences in welfare standards would lead to an increase in competitive pressures. Once again, economic issues had an impact on social issues. Falkner summarizes by saying that "EC-level action was intended not to overstretch economically weaker member states or prevent richer states from implementing higher standards, but to provide a bulwark against using low social standards as an instrument of *unfair competition*,"[68] and in order to avoid unfair competition only minimum standards were sought. Moreover, the introduction of the "social dialogue" – formally bringing in labour and business interests at the European "social" level – ensures that agreements in social policy will be difficult to attain, thereby decreasing the value of a European-wide social policy. It is interesting to note that the arguments raised by the Council were not at odds with the real interests of business, even though business did attempt to work alongside labour in a type of corporatist policy-making process. Industry felt that regulations on health and safety standards were much less cost-intensive than regulations on working conditions. Thus, business was willing to accept regulations in the former areas, but preferred that only voluntary codes were adopted in the latter ones.

Lange outlines another reason why social policy was given a low-priority in the negotiation process. From an interview with an EU-official he gathered "that Delors was more committed to other aspects of integration (in particular, monetary union) and would certainly sacrifice the social dimension to attain it".[69] As such, social policy really assumed only the position of a 2nd order policy where the institutional set-up of a corporatist process contributed to the minimal policy outcome that was achieved. So even though the Commission was committed to the incorporation of a social dimension in some form, it pursued changes only to those issues "where consensus among interests and member states is more likely or areas they think essential to achieving the single goods-and-services market".[70] The Commission's social dimension interests never went so far as to override its economic ones. The Social Protocol can thus be regarded as an issue that laid the ground for additional reform in economic and monetary policy. The introduction of a social dimension made if possible for further economic reforms to be put on the table and further economic integration to be achieved. From this perspective, social policy only served as a stepping stone to further economic integration.

With these dynamics in mind, one can gain a better understanding of what one may argue are the four dimensions of the corporatist negotiating process that was found to some extent alongside the intergovernmental one when social policy was negotiated. First, social partners attempt to achieve their agreements by very carefully taking into account the different member states' positions. In order to become a binding law any measure needs the Council's approval, which excludes the possibility of incorporating decisions that might be opposed by a majority of member states.[71] Second, a social partner could prefer not to obtain any agreement at all if it is believed that the Council's decision on the Commission's proposal would be more appropriate than an agreement made between social partners (for example, on sensitive economic issues on which agreement with other social partners would be difficult). Third, the corporatist process can give business groups an opportunity to present themselves as social actors who give consideration to the social dimension. This, however, may be merely symbolic and have no effective outcome.

A fourth important dimension is that social actors have to fight on two fronts: on the one hand, they have to reach consensus within their own organizations, taking the different national contexts, positions and interests of their members into account; on the other, they have to find a consensus with the other social partners. We thus find the peculiar situation that in order to agree on a common position, unanimity at the social partner level is necessary. Taking into account the heterogeneous interests of the different organizations themselves, the corporatist process thus involves the risk that only the lowest common denominator can be achieved at the level of the social partners.[72]

As a result of these various factors, the corporatist social policy processes became quite restricted due to the multiple positions and interests of different actors. This led to not only a lower output efficiency, but also a "worse" policy output, or at least one whose impact was limited. This lies in contrast to other policy areas where the range of actors was quite small and manageable – such as in competition policy and EMU, as discussed earlier. In such areas, compromises did not have to be considered: unlike in economic issues, we argue that this kind of policy process is permitted because social policy is regarded as being of less importance by national and European authorities. Experience beyond the Social Protocol has subsequently shown that negotiations between social partners have not been very successful, giving the Commission the possibility to present its unmodified proposals to the Council without the consent of the European-level social partners. Hence, introducing a social partner is a valid idea on paper but does not work very well in practice.

In conclusion, we can state that member states agreed to changes in social policy at the European level as they expected "to gain (in terms of net benefits) in the social policy regime with the more centrally determined workplace and labour market regulatory standards likely to result from the extension of qualified majority voting than in the current social policy regime".[73] As Lange states, even though a slight improvement has been obtained on the social dimension with the Social Protocol, the impact of European-wide social policy will remain insignificant and it will therefore not become a prominent "issue" at the European level. Rather, "the interest of governments, the fragmentation of social interests, and the policy-making rules of the Community itself militate against anything [so] broad in the social dimension."[74] This clearly distinguishes it from EU 1st order policies. This can also be seen in the fact that European-level social policy did not tackle the classical issues of social policy such as education, health and pensions. Although one may argue that member states did take a step forward with the Social Protocol in limiting their sovereignty to determine social policies, some competences were only transferred to the European level because of the progress and developments in other, more important, economic policy areas. Had it been for social policy alone, no change would have been observed: unlike economic policies that have been put on the negotiation table by the Commission and the member states, social policy only came in as a "add-on".

Conclusions

This chapter has argued that EU social policy remains weakly developed: it only relates to general standards, such as those on health and safety, and has had little success in significant issues such as working conditions, industrial relations and labour market policies. If there are rules in certain social policy areas, these normally reflect the lowest common denominator among member states, resulting in only basic requirements and a flexible design for application. In other words, European social policy offers only a minimalist EU involvement and is far from the traditional "social policy" found at the domestic level which is concerned with the "major" social issues such as education, health, pensions and unemployment benefits.[75] The principal mechanisms for redistribution of resources remain in the hands of member states, and EU social policy only addresses market failures.

This chapter has shown that EU-level social policy has proved to be more complicated than other policies studied in this book because of:

- institutional obstacles, where national institutions make reform difficult as there are widely divergent institutionalized national social policies
- limited fiscal resources at the European level
- member states resistance to loss of sovereignty in social policy areas, leaving social policy one of the few key areas of policy competence where national governments still appear to reign supreme

- the weakness of social democrats and trade unions in the EU up to the mid 1990s, combined with an increase in the power of business
- the unequal distribution of power among interest groups
- the British opposition towards an EU social policy in general
- the rhetorical nature of most commitments to the construction to a social dimension.

Unlike the 1st order policies studied in this book, the EU social policy formulation process showed elements of corporatism. Nevertheless, the impact of the measures has been disappointing in terms of actually protecting and safeguarding EU workers. As Streeck puts it: "community jurisdiction on social protection was a consequence limited from the beginning to work and employment-related matters, excluding such classic social policy issues as pensions, unemployment, housing, family and the disabled and the young."[76] In Leibfried and Pierson's words: "generally, only narrow, market-related openings for social legislation have been available."[77] As a result, social policy has been given low priority. We have argued that this can be explained partly because of member states' desires to maintain sovereignty in this area. Further, social policy has always been seen as an add-on: unlike other policies at the EU-level, social policy developments were not a consequence of active initiation from policy actors. Rather, any social policy initiative has been a consequence of other efforts to unify Europe economically. Not being considered an important issue in its own right, social policy has yet to receive the same priority as economically relevant issues such as single market, competition, and monetary policies. This clearly shows that social policy as such can be rated as a 2nd order policy. It would not have made it to the European level on its own accord, but must be seen in the context of other policies.

In terms of theoretical perspectives that help explain the formulation of the Social Charter and the Social Protocol, one sees how the initiation phase can be best explained on the basis of supranational governance logic. The negotiation phase, however, is best understood by taking into consideration ideas raised by intergovernmentalism, given the importance of the Council. Because harmonizing all aspects of social policy is of secondary importance to member states, social policy formulation still remains in the realm of national sovereignty, regardless of the Commission's efforts in the initiation phase. Moreover, the evidence also suggests that there are some aspects of corporatist decision making at play in the formulation process. Beyond the Commission and member states, social partners consisting of transnational employers' associations and labour groups were invited to participate in the negotiation process.

9 Policies of freedom, security and justice: a limited role for the EU[1]

This chapter seeks to examine and explain what are referred to as "freedom, security and justice" policies of the EU. The first section of the chapter pays specific attention to the main objectives of this broad policy area by considering in more depth the issue areas that fall within the rubric of freedom, security and justice. These include immigration, asylum and EU citizenship, as well as criminal and justice policies. The section then considers whether or not this overall area can be thought to be 1st or 2nd order in nature by evaluating its evolution over the relatively short period of approximately 20 years. The main argument to be developed in the first section is that this area is representative of a 2nd order policy: replacing of national norms with European regulations in the various policy areas has been very gradual, while some states even continue to exercise their ability to opt out of any Brussels-led initiatives with regard to issues such as immigration. The second section pays more attention to the formulation of a specific Brussels-led immigration initiative in order to better understand the policy process at play. In particular, it will focus on the development of one of the first legal instruments pursued at the supranational level: the directive on the right to family unification of 2003. It will be argued that in order to understand the policy initiation stage, attention must be focussed on the actions of the Commission; thereafter, however, policy negotiation also witnessed some influence of other interest groups and, perhaps more importantly, the Council. Given the evidence, it will be argued that policy formulation in the area can be best explained by focussing on arguments raised by the supranational governance, intergovernmentalist and pluralist perspectives.

The objectives and evolution of freedom, security and justice: a 2nd order status

There have been three main stages in the development of this wide-ranging policy area. The first began with the Single European Act of 1986 which, along with the single market reforms outlined in Chapter 4, affirmed the theoretical idea of the free movement of citizens throughout the Community. The second main stage began with the Maastricht Treaty of 1992. Beyond the EMU as discussed in Chapter 6,

Maastricht institutionalized justice and home affairs (JHA) as falling within the remit of the EU, although the procedural aspects outlined clearly highlighted that any JHA initiative would have to start with, and be finalized by, the Council of Ministers, leaving a only subsidiary role for EU-level institutions. Nevertheless, the third main stage, which was attained with the Amsterdam Treaty of 1997 and which came into effect in 1999, saw the Commission being able to take a more proactive role in JHA affairs by initiating relevant legislation. Shortly after the European Council agreed in Tampere (Finland) in 1999 on goals for the establishment of common immigration and asylum policies, the importance of the Commission would be under-lined with the institutionalizing of DG Justice and Home Affairs within the European Commission under the leadership of Antonio Vitorino, later to be renamed DG Justice, Freedom and Security and presently directed by Franco Frattini.

As the name suggests, the main objective of this policy area is to promote freedom, security and justice within the EU by way of seeking to develop supranational regulations in related policy areas that touch on these themes. These areas include: immigration, asylum, EU citizenship, freedom of movement, police cooperation, action against organized crime and judicial cooperation between member states. We consider the specific objectives and developments in each of these areas in turn.

Immigration policy: towards a centralized policy? Not really ...

With regard to immigration policy, the main theoretical goal of an EU-wide policy in this area is to regulate immigration flows to member states at the supranational level. Clearly, a comprehensive EU-wide immigration policy does not exist at present given that member state politicians seek to retain almost exclusive power in this area, as exam-ined by Luedtke.[2] Nevertheless, in its quest to develop EU-based immi-gration regulations, the Commission distinguishes between regulations surrounding "legal immigration", which seek to regulate admission and residency of third-country nationals (i.e. those who are not citizens of an EU member state), and means to combat "illegal immigration", including guidelines on the "return" of illegal immigrants.[3]

Concentrating on "legal immigration" regulations, which have been comparatively more fully developed at the EU level, the data in Table 9.1 help illustrate the importance of immigration into the EU-15 states by showing the crude rate of migrants entering between 1990 and 2002.[4] The second column of Table 9.1 shows that rates have been positive for the EU-15 throughout the time series: more people have generally been immi-grating to EU-15 states than emigrating from them. This perhaps reflects the trend observed by some, such as Cornelius, Martin and Hillified, that increasing globalization results in increasing immigration into "more

Table 9.1 Crude rate of net migration 1990–2002, per 1,000 population, EU-15

	EU-15	Belgium	Denmark	Germany	Greece	Spain	France	Ireland	Italy	Luxembourg	Netherlands	Austria	Portugal	Finland	Sweden	UK
1990	2.6	2.0	1.7	8.3	7.0	-0.5	0.5	-2.2	0.4	10.5	3.3	7.6	-5.6	1.7	4.1	1.2
1991	3.0	1.3	2.1	7.5	8.5	0.8	0.6	1.4	0.1	10.6	3.3	9.9	7.2	2.9	2.9	1.3
1992	3.5	2.6	2.2	9.6	4.7	0.7	0.6	0.5	3.2	11.0	2.8	9.1	-1.0	1.8	2.3	0.8
1993	2.7	1.8	2.2	5.7	5.4	0.8	0.3	-1.0	3.2	10.6	2.9	4.2	1.0	1.8	3.7	1.5
1994	2.0	1.7	2.0	3.9	2.6	0.7	-0.1	-0.8	2.7	9.9	1.3	0.4	2.0	0.7	5.8	1.4
1995	2.0	0.2	5.5	4.9	2.0	0.9	-0.3	1.7	1.7	11.2	1.0	0.3	2.5	0.8	1.3	2.0
1996	1.9	1.5	3.3	3.4	2.1	1.2	-0.3	3.6	2.7	8.9	1.4	0.5	2.5	0.8	0.7	1.8
1997	1.3	1.0	2.3	1.1	2.1	1.5	-0.2	5.6	2.2	9.0	2.0	0.2	3.0	0.9	0.7	1.5
1998	1.7	1.1	2.1	0.6	1.2	3.2	-0.1	5.0	1.9	9.4	2.8	1.1	3.5	0.9	1.2	3.6
1999	2.5	1.6	1.8	2.5	3.4	5.2	0.8	5.4	1.7	10.9	2.8	2.5	3.9	0.7	1.5	2.8
2000	3.0	1.3	1.9	2.0	1.2	8.8	0.9	6.9	3.1	4.3	3.6	2.2	4.9	0.5	2.8	2.8
2001	3.1	3.5	2.2	3.3	3.2	6.0	1.1	11.9	2.2	6.2	3.5	2.2	5.7	1.2	3.2	3.1
2002	3.3	3.9	1.8	2.7	2.9	5.5	1.1	8.3	6.1	5.9	1.7	3.2	6.8	1.0	3.5	2.1

Source: European Commission Justice and Home Affairs.

desirable" countries (i.e. western liberal democratic states) over time.[5] Nevertheless, there has been a type of cyclical pattern throughout the time series: between 1990 and 1993 there were relatively high levels, followed by a drop between 1994 and 1998, only to see a rebound post-1998 to a rate of 3.3 per 1,000 population by 2002 (the highest level since 1992).

Table 9.1 also shows how specific countries have seen relatively higher rates during various periods over the time series. These include: Germany between 1990 and 1995, largely a consequence of dynamics relating to German unification as well as increasing immigration from states such as Turkey; Ireland between 1998 and 2002, which can be explained by opportunities that arose in that country with the Celtic tiger economic boom in this period; and Spain between 1998 and 2002, largely as a consequence of increased immigration from Latin America. As the work of authors such as Joppke has indicated, many EU states actually seek immigrants as it is felt that they are needed to maintain the strength of future workforces given declining birth rates and an increasingly elderly populations.[6]

Interestingly, Table 9.2 shows somewhat of a different dynamic when considering the same data, but focussing on movements of the ten central and eastern European countries that have recently joined the EU.

Except for Cyprus, Hungary and Malta, the new entrants generally see low to negative immigration rates. The most pronounced negative rates within the sample are Latvia, Lithuania and Poland (which are all negative throughout the time series) as well as Estonia (except 2000–02).

Although Tables 9.1 and 9.2 do give a good picture of migration flows, they fail to distinguish fully between the types of non-nationals that live in the different member states. The term "non-nationals" refers to those who are either from another EU member state or from a third country outside the EU who would be precisely the object of regulation in a supranational immigration policy. Although migration statistics are not fully available, a snapshot of Eurostat data from 2001 provides a picture of the three types of citizens that live in the different member states: nationals (those who are citizens of the country they live in), other EU-nationals (who have moved within the EU to another member state), and third-country nationals (those born outside the EU and who do not hold EU citizenship).

Table 9.3 suggests that among non-nationals, third-country nationals generally represent a higher percentage of the total population than other EU nationals. The exceptions to this general trend are Luxembourg (where over 31 per cent of all residents are other EU nationals), Belgium and Ireland. The states at or above the EU-15 average proportion of third-country nationals are Denmark, Germany, Greece, Luxembourg and Austria.

Given the significance of third-country nationals in all EU states, the EU has recently developed two main regulations in the area of legal

Table 9.2 Crude rate of net migration 1990–2002 per 1,000 population, new entrants

	Czech Rep.	Estonia	Cyprus	Latvia	Lithuania	Hungary	Malta	Poland	Slovenia	Slovakia
1990	0.1	-3.6	16.5	-3.3	-2.4	1.8	2.9	-0.3	-0.2	-7.8
1991	-5.5	-8.0	19.2	-4.1	-2.9	1.7	4.1	-0.4	-1.7	0.0
1992	1.1	-27.1	17.6	-17.9	-6.6	1.8	3.0	-0.3	-2.8	-0.5
1993	0.5	-18.9	13.9	-10.8	-6.5	1.8	3.6	-0.4	-2.3	0.3
1994	1.0	-14.3	12.1	-7.4	-6.6	1.7	3.2	-0.5	0.0	0.9
1995	1.0	-10.9	10.2	-4.2	-6.5	1.7	0.2	-0.5	0.4	0.5
1996	1.0	-9.5	9.0	-2.9	-6.5	1.7	2.4	-0.3	-1.8	0.4
1997	1.2	-4.9	6.1	-2.8	-6.2	1.7	1.6	-0.3	-2.8	0.2
1998	0.9	-0.8	6.1	-1.3	-6.2	1.7	1.6	-0.3	-2.8	0.2
1999	0.9	-0.8	6.1	-19.1	-5.9	1.6	3.1	-0.4	5.5	0.3
2000	0.6	0.1	5.7	-1.5	-5.8	1.6	3.5	-0.5	1.4	0.3
2001	-0.8	0.1	6.6	-2.2	-0.7	1.0	5.7	-0.4	2.5	0.2
2002	1.2	0.1	9.7	-0.8	-0.6	0.3	4.8	-0.3	1.1	0.2

Source: European Commission Justice and Home Affairs.

Table 9.3 Nationals and non-nationals (either other EU-nationals or third-country nationals) as a percentage of the total population, 2001

	EU-15	Belgium	Denmark	Germany	Greece	Spain	France	Ireland	Italy	Luxembourg	Netherlands	Austria	Portugal	Finland	Sweden	UK
Nationals	94.6	91.6	95.2	91.1	93.1	96.7	94.5	95.9	97.4	63.1	95.8	91.2	97.9	98.3	94.7	95.8
Other EU nationals	1.6	5.5	1.0	2.3	0.4	1.0	2.0	2.7	0.3	31.8	1.3	1.3	0.6	0.3	2.0	1.5
3rd-country nationals	3.8	2.9	3.8	6.6	6.5	2.3	3.5	1.4	2.3	5.1	2.9	7.5	1.5	1.4	3.3	2.7
Total	100	100	100	100	100	100	100	100	100	100	100	100	100	100	100	100

Source: Eurostat, migration statistics.

immigration. The first, whose formulation will be examined in more detail in Section 2 of this Chapter, is the directive on the right to family unification adopted in September 2003.[7] The objective of this regulation was to outline how, and under which conditions and circumstances, third-country nationals legally living in the EU could reunite with direct family members who are living abroad. In November 2003, a second Directive on the Status of Long Term Residents was approved, intended to ensure equal treatment of all legal immigrants who have resided in a member state for more than five years.[8]

Asylum policy: we'll fingerprint them, but that's about it

Asylum policy is concerned with protecting those who flee their countries due to the persecution that they may face. Or, as the Commission puts it:

> Asylum is a form of protection given by a State on its territory based on the principle of *non-refoulement* and internationally or nationally recognized refugee rights. It is granted to a person who is unable to seek protection in his/her country of citizenship and/or residence in particular for fear of being persecuted for reasons of race, religion, nationality, membership of a particular social group or political opinion.[9]

As Figure 9.1 shows, although numbers have ebbed and flowed since 1986, in general there is a rising trend in the number of people seeking asylum in the EU over time. According to this data, this number reached a peak in 1992, slightly diminished thereafter, but generally increased after 1998.

In terms of where such asylum applications are made within the EU, using aggregate data between 1999 and September 2003, Figure 9.2 highlights the variations across the EU.

Figure 9.2 suggests that while Germany, the UK and France are the leaders in terms of receiving new applications, with well over 10 per cent of all such applications in each state, states with relatively smaller populations such as the Netherlands, Belgium, Austria, Sweden and Ireland have also received a substantial percentage. The four "not-asylum-friendly" countries (corresponding to "others" in the graph) that together received around 5 per cent of all applications are Denmark, Greece, Finland and Portugal. The main states from which asylum seekers have come during the same time period include Iraq (8 per cent), Turkey (7 per cent), Serbia and Montenegro (7 per cent) and Russia (6 per cent), as well as China, Nigeria, Somalia and Afghanistan (all at 4 per cent).[10]

Various regulations have been prescribed in an attempt to harmonize procedures with regard to asylum in the EU. The Dublin

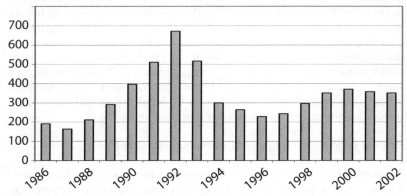

Figure 9.1 New asylum applications in the EU, 1986–2002 (thousands)

Source: Eurostat.

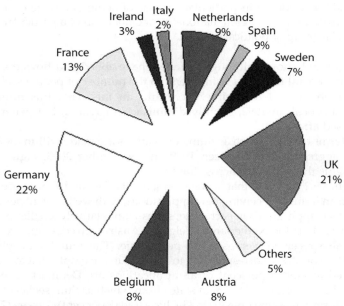

Figure 9.2 Distribution of new asylum applications between the member states, between 1998 and September 2003

Source: Eurostat (figures have been rounded).

Convention of 1990 and the Dublin II regulation of 2003 seek to prevent situations where an asylum application can be made in more than one member state. This was based on the difficulties faced by member states in making decisions on asylum seekers who had made applications to two or more states. Second, and in order to better determine which member state should process an asylum application, EURODAC – the fingerprint database – was established in 2003. Although some may contend that a European wide fingerprint database which is used with the sole purpose of identifying asylum seekers may itself be discriminatory, the justification for the centralized database is stated by the Commission as follows:

> All applicants over the age of 14 now have their fingerprints taken as part of routine procedure when they ask for asylum – either within or from outside the EU. These are sent in digital format to a central unit at the European Commission, where they are automatically checked against other prints stored on the database. This enables the authorities to see if the applicants entered the EU without the necessary papers, and if they have already applied for asylum in another member state. ... [The system] helps speed up the asylum application procedure by directing genuine refugees straight to the country they should be dealing with, and it also prevents fraudulent applicants from "shopping around" in other member states after one country has turned them down, or clogging up the system with multiple applications.[11]

European citizenship, fighting crime and judicial cooperation

European citizenship, which was introduced into Maastricht after being conceived and framed by leaders such as Spain's Felipe Gonzalez, has four main principles.[12] These include:

- All citizens of the EU have the right to move, reside freely within, and work within any member state.[13]
- EU citizens have the right to vote and to stand as candidates at municipal elections, as well as European Parliamentary elections, in the member state in which they reside.
- EU citizens have the right to petition the EP and complain to the European Ombudsman.
- When in a country outside the EU where his or her state is not represented, an EU citizen has a right to protection by diplomatic or consular authorities of any other member state.

In relation to the first main point, it is significant to note that several of the EU-15 states (except for Ireland and the UK) as well as Norway and Iceland signed up to the Schengen Agreement, which was incorporated within the Amsterdam Treaty. Schengen eliminates passport controls between the states, thereby helping facilitate movement of persons within the Community.

When turning to police cooperation and the fight against cross-border crime, it is fundamental (if not obvious) to note that a European police force, or a European-wide customs administration, does not exist at present. Nevertheless, on the basis of Article 29 of the EU Treaty, Europol was developed in 1994 to strengthen cooperation between the national forces. Staffed by member-state police and customs officials, this centre serves as means to gather, coordinate and exchange information. The development of the European Police College (CEPOL), coupled with the creation of the European Crime-Prevention Network in 2001, was also seen as a means to help fight crime across Europe.

Finally, policies of increased judicial cooperation have recently been developed as seen in EUROJUST and the European Arrest Warrant. EURO-JUST, which came into being in 2003, aims to increase cooperation between not only law enforcement officials, but also, more importantly, senior judges and prosecutors with the goal of prosecuting serious cross-border crimes more efficiently. The European Arrest Warrant of 2004 seeks to eliminate barriers to extradition between EU member states and facilitate the transfer of a suspect who may be seeking refuge in another member state.

Freedom, security and justice policies: four reasons for their 2nd order status

Despite what one may claim has been the development of several policies related to freedom, security and justice in a relatively short period of time since the free movement of persons was enshrined in the SEA in 1986, there are four main reasons why this area remains of 2nd order status: there is a lack of full harmonization of the policies between member states, member states themselves still have the final word in adapting and adopting policies, reasonably extensive regulations are not fully developed in several of the policy areas, and there remains a lack of efficiency and centralization in the coordination of the policies. We consider each of these in turn.

With regard to the first point, the lack of harmonization of the policies is evident when one considers that states such as Denmark, Ireland and the UK have retained the right to not accept and implement EU legislation in freedom and security issues, particularly immigration and asylum policies. This results in a situation where, for example, an EU-wide regulation on family reunification may exist at the Brussels level, but it has no impact in these three states. Similar dynamics are seen with the Schengen accord: although free movement of persons has definitely been facilitated by the

Schengen agreement, the fact that two member states (the UK and Ireland) have not signed up due to their own concerns for security, coupled with the fact that any Schengen member state actually has the right to opt out temporarily from the Agreement if it feels that it is necessary to do so for national security reasons, demonstrates that member states ultimately retain full power in controlling who enters their territories. The importance of the member state in regulating who enters its territory has resulted in a situation where the ideal of free movement of persons is not as fully developed as the ideal of free movement of goods, services and capital that was analysed in Chapter 4. A final example is seen in the case of the European Arrest Warrant. Despite its potential, it has yet to be transposed into national law in Italy; nor has the Czech Republic implemented the policy either.

Given that member states still retain a significant amount of power in justice and security issues, and given that there has not been a full transfer of power from the member state to the Brussels' level, it is not much of a surprise to see some states trying to continue to define for themselves fundamental concepts in the area, thereby leaving developments at the European level almost irrelevant. This was seen most clearly in the recent Irish citizenship referendum in 2004. Even though Maastricht guaranteed that EU citizenship rights extend to all who are citizens of the EU's member states, the treaty also copper-fastened the position that the each member state has the sole power to determine national citizenship laws. According to Irish regulations since 1921, anyone born in Ireland was granted citizenship, a system not particularly different from the one in France, where children born to third-country nationals would receive citizenship (albeit after 18) but somewhat in contrast to most other EU countries, which do not automatically grant citizenship to children of third-country nationals born in the respective country. However, since the early 2000s, there was an increasing perception in Ireland, among government officials and citizens alike, that there was a significant number of third-country national women (especially from Africa) coming illegally to Ireland during the late stages of pregnancy to give birth there: as long as the children were born Irish citizens, their parents could not be forced out of the country and would remain as an increased burden on the social welfare system. In wake of these concerns, the Irish government decided to hold a referendum on citizenship. Despite civil liberty groups' claims that there was no fundamental basis to the perception that large number of immigrants were coming to Ireland in the late stages of pregnancy and that any change to Irish citizenship laws was unconstitutional,[14] over 80 per cent of the population surprisingly voted that children of third-country nationals born in Ireland should not be allowed Irish citizenship and, therefore, they should be deemed illegal immigrants. Hence, such children and their parents could also be extradited to their country of origin. The Irish experience helps demonstrate that even though a person may be born on "European" soil and even though European citizenship rights may theoretically exist, member states still control who can finally become an "EU citizen".

The third reason that freedom, security and justice issues are of 2nd order status is the limited scope of the supranational initiatives: detailed and extensive regulations have not been fully developed in several of the policy areas. For example, with regard to immigration policy, there is a lack of supranational regulation surrounding the entrance of third-country nationals who are students, trainees or volunteers. Nor are there common rules on the conditions surrounding entrance and residence of third-country nationals who are self-employed. Another example is seen in respect of European citizenship: although EU citizens are allowed to vote and stand as candidates for municipal and EP elections regardless of the member state they reside in, an EU national living in another EU state does not have a right to vote in national elections of the state he/she is living in unless the government of that state has specific provisions to allow this.[15]

Finally, the 2nd order status can be seen in the overall lack of efficiency and centralization in the administration of several of the policies. This is clearly seen in the asylum process: while an attempt has been made to prevent applicants from making applications in more than one state, there is no single authority at the supranational level that takes the lead in making a decision on whether or not asylum protection should be granted. This leads to unequal measures being used across the EU-15 when examining asylum cases, meaning that some (more lenient) states may have higher numbers than others, while others that have a relatively less sympathetic view towards asylum seekers may continue to reject such applications.

The formulation of the right to family reunification of third-country nationals

This section analyses the formulation of the European Directive 2003/86/EC on the right to family reunification of third-country nationals living in the EU that was adopted in September 2003. This policy is significant because it represents the first legal instrument in respect of immigration adopted at the EU level. After analysing in more depth what the regulation entails, the section considers the two main phases of policy formulation. In the first, the Commission played a key role in the initiation of the policy, driven by its view that fair treatment of third-country nationals was a key step in the drive towards the harmonization of EU immigration policy. In the later phase, even though one saw some influence of interest groups, the member states played the most prominent role in the negotiation of the policy. Given the dynamics, it will be argued that the supranational governance, intergovernmentalist and pluralist perspectives are of value in explaining EU policy development in this area. Before analysis of the process of policy formulation, it is useful to examine the main ideas behind the directive. As there is little academic work done on this relatively recent regulation, it is necessary to go over the details of the directive in some detail so the reader is fully aware of its objectives and scope.

What is the initiative about?

The directive on the right to family unification approved by the Council on September 22, 2003 – with the exception of the UK, Ireland and Denmark who opted out[16] – has as its main purpose, as stated in Article 1, to "determine the conditions for the exercise of the right to family reunification by third-country nationals residing lawfully in the territory of the member states". In other words, it regulates the joining together of family members of non-EU citizens legally living in the EU. Article 3.1 states that the directive applies

> where the sponsor [defined in Article 2 as the person who is applying for the family to join him/her] is holding a residence permit issued by a member state for a period of validity of one year or more who has reasonable prospects of obtaining the right of permanent residence, if the members of his or her family are third-country nationals of whatever status.

Articles 3.2a and 3.2b specify that the directive does not apply to those still applying for refugee status or whose situation in the EU is based on temporary protection. Article 4.1 states that the right to unification is limited to the "nuclear" family members of the sponsor. This includes the sponsor's spouse (Article 4.1a) and their minor children (those who have not reached a member state's age of majority) including any adopted children of either the couple, or the sponsor, or his/her spouse (4.1b, c, and d). Nevertheless, Article 4.2 and 4.3 state that reunification of dependent first-degree relatives in the direct ascending line of the sponsor (i.e. a sponsor's mother and father) as well as unmarried partners does not come within the remit of the directive, and their unification with the sponsor is thus left to the discretion of the member state. Article 6 states that a member state may "reject an application for entry and residence of family members on grounds of public policy, public security or public health". Articles 7.1a, b and c stipulate that when an application is made, the member state must be assured that the sponsor has "adequate accommodation", health insurance and "stable and regular resources to maintain him/herself and the members of his/her family, without recourse to the social assistance system of the member state concerned" in order to prevent the reunification imposing a burden on national social welfare systems. Article 12.1, however, states that the housing, insurance and income requirements outlined in Article 7.1 are not applicable to those holding refugee status who are seeking family reunification. Article 14.1 outlines the rights of immigrating family members – including the right to education and training – while Article 14.2 states that the member states can limit the right to work of family members. Article 16 finally discusses circumstances in which member states can refuse or withdraw a family residency permit. These include: if the sponsor is unable to have/obtain sufficient resources to support the family (Article 16.1a); if it is found that there is a divorce or evidence that either the sponsor or his or her partner "is married or is in a stable long term relationship with another person" (Article 16.1c); if false documents were presented during the application (Article 16.2a); or if a marriage was undertaken solely in order to immigrate to Europe under the family reunification scheme (Article 16.2b).

Policy initiation: a push from the Commission

Keeping these main points of the directive in mind, in order to better understand the policy formulation process, analysis must begin with the initial proposal by the Commission on 1 December 1999[17] for a directive on family unification. Although the Commission had for some years previously been concerned about harmonizing regulations with regard to family reunification of third-country nationals, it was in a difficult position in pursuing any initiatives until the Amsterdam Treaty. As the Commission stated in its 1999 proposal on family reunification:

> Following the entry into force of the Amsterdam Treaty and the insertion of the new Title IV ... relating to visas, asylum, immigration and other policies related to the free movement of persons, the Commission feels the time has come to give practical form to the commitment entered into in 1997 and present a new proposal regarding family reunification in the form of a Community legal instrument.[18]

In the Commission's view, harmonizing the situation with regard to third-country nationals was "indispensable if these people are to lead a normal family life and will help them integrate into society".[19] As such, the 1999 Commission proposal consisted of over ten pages of an explanatory memorandum on the lack of harmonization with regard to third-country nationals and the need for a common European policy in the area, as well as over 20 articles that ought to be incorporated by the Council in a directive regulating family unification.

Analysis of the different articles of the Commission's 1999 proposal demonstrates how many of the main points seen in the final directive adopted by the Council in 2002 were actually broadly outlined by the Commission some three years earlier, clearly indicating how policy initiation came from the supranational level. For example, the 1999 Commission proposal highlights the objective of the policy (Article 1[20]); the various definitions and concepts of importance, such as what constitutes a "sponsor" (Article 2); to whom the regulation applies (Article 3); which family members are eligible for reunification (Article 5); how an application is to be processed (Article 7); under which circumstances a family member may be refused entry (Article 8); evidence that must be provided by sponsors when making an application (Article 9); the rights of family members when they are reunited (Article 12); and the circumstances under which a residency permit may be revoked (Article 14).

Because many of these themes were reflected in the final directive adopted by the Council as discussed above, one may argue that the broad ideas encapsulated in these various articles illustrates how the Commission did provide a blueprint for the directive that was eventually adopted by the Council. Given the prime role of the Commission in terms of policy initiation, the supranational governance school is of value in explaining this stage of the formulation process.

Policy negotiation: a pull from the Council

However, when one compares the specific details of the Council directive in 2003 with those originally formulated by the Commission in 1999, one sees how the Council was crucial in the negotiation process in terms of pursuing changes. Such changes were discussed throughout the different negotiating phases between 2000 and 2003. There are three key conjunctures in this regard. The first relates to negotiations with the Council in September 2000, which resulted in a first amended proposal by the Commission in October 2000.[21] That was discarded by the Council, which was unable to arrive at an overall agreement on the desire for an EU-wide regulation on family reunification. The second regards a renewed drive by the Council for a directive on family reunification as a consequence of the Laeken European Council in December 2001, which resulted in another invitation to the Commission to re-draft earlier proposals. The Commission was required to keep in mind the negotiation points raised by the Council, including the need to limit those eligible to come over, tighter application procedures and the goal of ensuring public security. The third conjuncture relates to the Commission's second amended proposal,[22] which was tabled in May 2002, debated between the Commission and the Council as well as various interest groups over the next year, and finally adopted by the Council in September 2003.

The changes made by the Council to the original Commission proposal during the almost three-year negotiating period help demonstrate that the Council played a major role during policy negotiation. Upon comparison of specific clauses in the Commission's 1999 proposal and what was finally agreed to at the Council level in 2003, one sees at least seven issues that were of concern to the Council. We will consider each in turn.

The first related to which family members could qualify. In its original proposal of 1999, the Commission had stated that family members who could seek reunification should also include: "unmarried partners living in a durable relationship with the applicant if the legislation of the member state concerned treats the situation of unmarried couples as corresponding to that of married couples".[23] In its draft proposal of 1999, the Commission also considered children of unmarried partners to be eligible for unification. However, conservative elements within the Christian Democratic governments in power, such as Aznar's Partido Popular in Spain, opposed the proposal to include unmarried people in a regular relationship, which they feared might legitimize the concept of same-sex couples. Under their influence, the Council took the view that the Commission's interpretation was defining "family" too broadly. The Council thus preferred to allow reunification of only "the sponsor's spouse" and children of a married couple, whether biological or adopted.[24]

Second, with regard to application procedures, the Commission's 1999 draft proposed that, in exceptional circumstances and on humanitarian grounds, the member state concerned should consider an application submitted when the family member seeking permission was already residing in its territory.[25] However, fearful that this clause might actually spawn illegal immigration, the Council declared that "the application shall be submitted and examined when the family members are residing outside the territory of the member state in which the sponsor resides."[26]

Third, with regard to public security, in its original proposal the Commission specified that a member state might "refuse the entry and residence of a family member on the grounds of public policy, domestic security or public health".[27] However, in the Council's view, this clause did not do enough to prevent security problems should they arise after a family member had come to reside within a member state. As such, the Council supplemented the Commission's original proposal by adding that the member state had a right to "withdraw or refuse to renew a family member's residence permits on grounds of public policy or public security or public health".[28]

Fourth, with regard to the evidence that the sponsor had to supply when making an application, in its original proposal the Commission laid down the same criteria as outlined in the final Council directive that every sponsor was obliged to demonstrate that he/she can provide "adequate accommodation", "sickness insurance" and "stable and sufficient resources". However, in its original proposal of 1999 the Commission also clearly defined stable and sufficient resources as "resources which are higher than or equal to the level of resources below which the member state concerned may grant social assistance".[29] In the Council's view, however, this interpretation seemed to be somewhat of a straightjacket and it decided, instead, to phrase it in a way that was ambiguous enough to allow each member state a certain degree of freedom. The wording was that each member state "shall evaluate these resources by reference to their nature and regularity and may take into account the level of minimum national wages and pensions as well as the number of family members".[30]

Fifth, with respect to facilitating the movement of family members who had been granted reunification status, the Commission originally proposed that member states should grant family members coming to Europe "every facility for obtaining the requisite Visas, including transit Visas where required. Such visas shall be issued without charge."[31] However, the final Council Directive reflects the belief that such costs were deemed unacceptable to member states, and the line "such visas shall be issued without charge" was deleted.[32]

Sixth, with regard to rights of family members coming to Europe, the right to education and training are granted in Commission's 1999 proposal.[33] Nevertheless, with a view to allowing each member state to control entry of such immigrants into the labour market, the Council directive explicitly mentions that states have the right to decide whether or not family members will have the right to work.[34]

Finally, with regard to penalties and redress, the Commission's original proposal was that member states could reject or withdraw a residence permit related to family unification either if entry and/or residence were based on fraudulent information, or if the main reason for a marriage or adoption was to enter or reside in Europe.[35] However, the Council added two extra scenarios in which permits could be refused or withdrawn. The first is what can be referred to as an economic clause, to be invoked if the sponsor is unable to have/obtain sufficient resources to support the family.[36] The second one may argue is a type of "moral" clause: permits could be revoked if there were a divorce or evidence that either the sponsor or his/her partner "is married or is in a stable long term relationship with another person".[37] Adding these two extra dimensions ensured that the member states would not lose all power in the regulation of the policy area.

In the negotiation process, the Council was able to successfully amend the original blueprint offered by the Commission in accordance with the views of member states and to limit the loss of states' power in this policy area. In addition to this intergovernmental aspect, there is some evidence to suggest that there was participation by various interest groups in the process, which points to some elements of the pluralist perspective at play in this policy area. These interest groups included the European Council on Refugees and Exiles (ECRE), Christian groups such as Caritas, as well as the European Region of the International Lesbian and Gay Association (ILGA-Europe), who all participated and offered their opinions throughout the various negotiation phases described above.

One group that was successful in shaping some elements of the directive was the ECRE. This group, whose main concern is related to the status of refugees, was originally disposed to favour the Commission's original 1999 proposal. Although the question of regulations applying to refugees was mentioned throughout the proposal, there was a lack of clear guiding principles with regard to how all aspects of refugee status should be dealt with. To this end, the final Directive clearly established what is referred to as "Chapter 5" on refugees (which contains articles 9 through 12) that were absent in the original proposal. The ECRE would later state that it:

> welcomes the special consideration given to the situation of refugees and in particular, the exception provided to refugees from having lived in a country for two years before their family can join them (Art 12.2). ECRE further welcomes the exemption provided to refugees who apply for family reunification within three months of being granted refugee status, from satisfying housing, health insurance or income requirements as a precondition for reuniting with family members (Article 12.1).[38]

Furthermore, in the original proposal by the Commission, children of refugees were considered in the same way as any third-country national: consent of both partners was necessary for family unification. However, there are situations when the consent of a partner is difficult, if not impossible, to attain. The ECRE therefore sought exception for refugee children from this provision, as later reflected in Article 10.1 of the directive. ECRE stated that "ECRE welcomes the exception for refugee children from the provision under Article 4.1 subparagraph 3. As a result, member states cannot limit the right to family reunification to refugees' children who are under 12 years old."[39]

Other interest groups whose views helped influence the final outcomes included Caritas Europa, the Churches' Commission for Migrants in Europe (CCME), and the International Catholic Migration Commission (ICMC), all of which published their position on the directive under the banner of the Conference of European Churches (CEC). These groups had pressed for special consideration for refugees and would later state that "we appreciate that the special needs for family reunification for refugees are recognized."[40] They would also state that they agreed with the clarification in the new directive that (non-refugee) children under shared custody would be admitted providing that the other parent explicitly agreed.[41]

Nevertheless, even though these groups did exercise some influence, they were not without their criticisms of the final directive. For example, ECRE expressed reservations about Article 3.1, which states that the directive is applicable to third-country nationals who have "reasonable prospects of obtaining the right of permanent residence". In ECRE's words, "this additional condition allows for considerable discretion by individual member states regarding the interpretation of what constitutes 'reasonable prospects' and risks undermining the purpose of the directive as a whole."[42]

ECRE was also concerned about Article 3.2, which stated that those seeking refugee status cannot make an application for family reunification until their refugee application has been approved. In ECRE's words, "Governments should seek to facilitate the reunification of family members forced to apply for asylum in different European countries."[43]

The Conference for European Churches also lamented the increased power of member states in the final directive compared to the original proposal tabled by the Commission. Criticizing the 2nd order nature of the policy, the Conference would state that: "We are convinced that the wide discretion left to Member states in the application of this Directive will not serve a harmonized approach and understanding of family reunification as a right and obligation."[44]

But, perhaps the harshest criticism of the directive came from the European Region of the International Lesbian and Gay Association (ILGA-Europe), whose ideas were completely ignored throughout the negotiation process. IGLA-Europe found the final Directive unacceptable because it institutionalizes "unequal treatment of unmarried partners".[45] In their view, by limiting family reunification rights to married partners, the European Union would entrench discrimination on grounds of sexual orientation and gender identity.[46]

In sum, the evidence suggests that during the policy initiation stage, the Commission played a key role in terms of defining the blueprint for the directive in 1999. During the policy negotiation stage, however, the Council was of prime importance in setting the specific details of the policy. Of less importance than the Council, but interestingly of some significance, different interest groups did play a role during the negotiation of the policy, which contrasts somewhat with the other policy areas studied in this book. Given this evidence, and in order to better characterize the policy-making process in this area on the basis of the formulation of the family reunification directive, one may argue that a supranational governance perspective is of some value in understanding the policy initiation phase. During the negotiation process, however, the Council was of primary importance, pointing to the idea that intergovernmentalism is of greater value in studying this stage of policy formulation. Although interest groups were of clearly less importance than the Council, there is some indication that elements of pluralism were also in play: different interest groups expressed their opinions throughout the process and were able to exert some, albeit limited, influence on the final policy outcome.

Conclusions

This chapter has examined and explained freedom, security and justice policies in the EU. The first section not only analysed the main objectives within this policy area by focussing on the goals of immigration, asylum, citizenship, and criminal and justice policies, but also demonstrated that this issue area remains of 2nd order importance. This is due to four related reasons: the lack of full harmonization as seen in some states opting out of EU initiatives, the role of member states in defining key concepts, the lack of deep integration initiatives in several areas, and a lack of centralization in the coordination of the policies.

In order to better understand policy formulation in the area of freedom, justice and security policies, the second section paid detailed attention to the policy process during the formulation of the family reunification directive of 2003, which represents a landmark first Community-wide regulation in the area of legal immigration. The evidence uncovered suggested that the Commission was vital in the policy initiation stage, in terms of providing an overall blueprint for the regulation. During the policy negotiation phase, however, the actions of the Council were more significant in terms of setting the specific details of the regulation including, among other things, determining who was eligible for reunification, setting regulations for application procedures, adding specific clauses with respect to public security, and outlining regulations revoking residency permits, all with the view to consolidating the powers of the member state in immigration policy. Some states, such as the UK, Ireland and Denmark, even opted out of the directive, illustrating how member states continue to act in their own interests in this policy area. Such was the ability of the Council to maintain a prominent state role in the process, that some interest groups claimed that the family reunification directive hardly represents a harmonized approach to immigration policy at all.

Beyond the Council, there was also some evidence suggesting that some interest groups were able to exercise some, even if modest, influence in the process as seen with developments related to the European Council on Refugees and Exiles (ECRE). Given this evidence, it was argued that while the supranational governance theoretical perspective is of value in explaining the policy initiation aspects, the intergovernmentalist and (to a lesser extent) pluralist perspectives are of greater value in explaining policy negotiation. From this perspective, and given that there is little evidence suggesting that either business organizations or organized labour participated in the process, the dominant economic class and corporatist perspectives do not seem to be relevant for an understanding of policy making in this area.

10 External policies: divided we stand, united we fall

This chapter examines and explains the EU's external policies. The first section analyses how these policies can be divided into those of a political and those of an economic nature. Thus, the first section considers the political dimension of the EU's external political relations, through an examination of European political cooperation (EPC), the establishment of the EU's Common Foreign and Security Policy (CFSP) in the Maastricht Treaty, and the changes pursued in the Amsterdam Treaty. It then considers the evolution of the EU's external economic relations, including the dynamics surrounding multilateral and bilateral agreements. With respect to the latter, and in order to gauge whether or not external economic policies have been broadly successful in attaining their overall objectives, the chapter offers an in depth analysis of the Euro-Mediterranean Partnership (EMP) agreement which has as its objectives, on the one hand, to increase trade with countries on the southern coast of the Mediterranean and, on the other, to promote values such as democracy and human rights in the area.

The first section concludes that despite the EU's increasing trade in the global economy, the EU has been largely unsuccessful in effectively speaking with one voice in the area of external political policies. It has also fallen short of attaining all of its trade-agreement objectives, especially with respect to promoting values such as democracy in some areas with which it deals. Both of these developments can be understood in the context of the divergent interests of member states, which prevent the development of strong supranational external policies. As such, it will be suggested that external policies remain a 2nd order policy area, or one that does not see a full harmonization at the supranational level.

The second section turns to a more focussed analysis of the developments during the 2003 Iraq War, demonstrating more fully why the EU was incapable of speaking with a unified voice. It argues that in order to explain the EU's debacle, focus should be concentrated on the Council, which showed the impacts of the divergent interests of national governments. Given the member states' lack of desire to seek a unified policy position towards Iraq, it is concluded that developments in external policies can best be understood from the intergovernmental perspective.

The objectives and evolution of external relations: a 2nd order status

The objectives and evolution of external political relations: forever united?

Smith[1] points to two key conjunctures in the evolution of the EU's foreign and security policy. The first is the development of European political cooperation (EPC) and the second is the replacement of EPC with the Common Foreign and Security Policy (CFSP) in the Maastricht Treaty, representing the 2nd Pillar of the Community whereby foreign and security policy became institutionalized within the EU policy framework.

With regard to EPC, Smith first points to dynamics in the 1950s which saw the development at the EU level of "civilian power ... [where] diplomacy [was] carried out mainly in the [external] economic register with none of the implications of 'hard' security or even high diplomacy that were central to member state foreign policy",[2] such as the deployment of troops to support EU initiatives. The late 1960s saw the emergence of EPC which, although being formally outside the EU institutional structure, offered a quasi-institutional opportunity for foreign ministers of the EU member states to discuss matters in "low" policy areas where agreement could be reached.[3] Useful here is the distinction made by Hoffmann[4] between "high" and "low" politics, where "high" politics refers to the areas of national security and defence, while "low" politics refers to external agreements that are more diplomatic or economic in nature. Examples of where the EPC was successful include elaborating a common EU position on the Middle East in the 1970s and attempting to gain cohesion between EU members voting in the UN on different issues. Various international factors in the late 1980s and early 1990s, including the first Iraq War, the end of Communism in central and eastern Europe, as well as developments in Yugoslavia, forced the Community to re-evaluate the future of EPC. Not only were "new patterns of diplomatic security necessary", but also the Community would put "emphasis on what became known as soft-security" including economic sanctions.[5]

In the wake of this new-found desire to go beyond the simple diplomacy offered by EPC, Article 2 of Treaty on the European Union called for the EU "to assert its identity on the international scene, in particular through the implementation of a common foreign and security policy including the eventual framing of a common defence policy, which might in time lead to a common defence". Accordingly, the EU's Common Foreign and Security Policy was established in Maastricht. There were five main elements of the CFSP as later outlined in the Amsterdam Treaty:

- to safeguard the common values, fundamental interests, independence and integrity of the EU in conformity with the principles of the UN Charter
- to strengthen the security of the EU in all ways
- to preserve peace and strengthen international security, in accordance with the principles of the United Nations' Charter
- to promote international cooperation
- to develop and consolidate democracy and the rule of law and respect for human rights and fundamental freedoms.[6]

Although commentators such as Ginsburg[7] noted that the CFSP initially gave the impression that the "EU would be poised to adopt new kinds of higher profile foreign policy actions previously not thought possible," one may argue that from the beginning one of the main weaknesses of the CFSP related to the ambiguity, or lack of precision, regarding its main elements. For example, what exactly does "strengthen common values and security" refer to; how is international security to be preserved in context of the UN's Charter; and where exactly do democracy, rule of law and human rights need to be preserved and by using which means?

Given these ambiguities, it is not much of a surprise that, as Smith[8] argues, the evolution of the CFSP throughout the 1990s can be considered a failure as it was handicapped by the divergent views of different member states. Moreover, in terms of institutional dynamics, since the Council is the exclusive actor when CFSP decisions are made, no common positions with regard to major international conflicts were arrived at. In other words, without a clear, unifying EU framework, many states with their own views of different security issues did not place the CFSP principles in the forefront when making security decisions. Rather, many either remained neutral with regard to international crises (as was the case with Ireland) or favoured other alliances with different international security agreements such as NATO, as in the case of the UK. This was seen most acutely in the Kosovo crises where the United States, under the cloak of "military humanism" as discussed by Chomsky,[9] led the attack under the auspices of NATO and took the lead in preventing Serbia's ethnic cleansing of the Albanians in Kosovo. The implications of this for the EU are best summarized by Smith who states that:

> As was demonstrated in the post-Cold War crises of 1990s Europe, not only was the EU handicapped by the intergovernmentalism of the CFSP; it was also still dependent on the muscle provided by the USA and its allies in NATO (many of them EU Member States) for the measures entailed in "hard security" and coercion beyond economic sanction.[10]

With this in mind, in the wake of the crisis in Yugoslavia where the EU was unable to act in a coordinated and coherent fashion, the Amsterdam Treaty of 1997 attempted to strengthen the CFSP and make it more effective. One of the main means by which this was to be achieved was to establish a High Representative of the CFSP. The High Representative, Javier Solana – the ex-Foreign Minister under the Spanish Socialists of the 1980s and later Head of NATO during the 1990s – would work alongside both the Commissioner for DG External Relations and the Minister of Foreign Affairs holding the Council Presidency to attempt to better define and coordinate an EU foreign and security policy. However, the ability for the EU to speak with a unified voice even after the Amsterdam Treaty, is still questionable in light of recent events in Iraq which Section 2 examines in more detail.

The objectives and evolution of external economic agreements: we like democracy, but...

Trade between the EU and other economies is regulated by Articles 131 and 133 of the EU Treaty that seeks to develop a common commercial policy (CCP) in order to improve the EU's position in the global economy. While Article 133 sets out the scope, instruments and decision-making procedures, Article 131 states that the principles of the CCP are to "contribute, in the common interest, to the harmonious development of world trade, the progressive abolition of restrictions to international trade, and the lowering of custom's barriers."

In terms of policy process, external economic policy making sees the involvement of both the Commission and the Council. Prima facie, one may argue that this somewhat contrasts to external political relations, where the Council remains the effective power, with virtually no policy formulation involvement by either the Commission or EP. Despite the Commission being involved in the negotiation of trade agreements, however, one may argue that the Council is the dominant decision maker. This is particularly seen when one considers Article 300 of the EU Treaty, which outlines the inter-institutional procedure for international agreements. In the Commission's words:

> The external trade administration of the European Commission – so called DG Trade – is the negotiator, responsible for conducting trade negotiations, and the enforcer, responsible for ensuring compliance by third countries with international trade accords. The Council, where each of the 25 Member States is represented at the ministerial level is *the* decision-maker. It issues "directives for negotiation" to guide the Commission in its work and decides, unilaterally, whether to adopt an accord. The European Parliament ... is kept regularly informed by the Commission. [Emphasis added.][11]

From this perspective, authors such as George and Bache[12] have likened EU external economic policy making to a type of three-level game, where the Council plays primary roles at both the first and third levels. At the first level, the Council decides what type of agreement is to be pursued and delegates the Commission to negotiate on behalf of the Council.[13] At the second level, the Commission negotiates the trade agreement with trading partners along the lines outlined by the Council. And at the third level, the Council accepts, amends or rejects the agreement negotiated by the Commission. The Commission will subsequently monitor the development of the agreement and report back to the Council, so that the Council can either initiate new agreements, or amend or suspend existing ones.

What are the different types of trade agreements that the EU makes? The two broad types are multilateral and bilateral (and developmental) trade agreements. Multilateral agreements are those with an international dimension, involving what it is referred to as the World Trade Organization (WTO). Such agreements with the WTO represent regulations agreed to by 148 countries. Bilateral regulations are established between the EU and either individual countries or groups of countries that form a trading bloc. There may be developmental aspects to such agreements if trade is also linked to aid from the EU. After drawing out some aspects of these two main types of agreements, we will evaluate the evolution of external economic policy by focussing on one such agreement: the Euro-Mediterranean Partnership.

Turning first to multilateral trade agreements, the WTO was established in 1995 in the wake of the General Agreement on Tariffs and Trade (GATT) Uruguay Round that lasted from 1986 to 1994. GATT had been established in order to ensure that states engaged in trade would abide by regulations agreed by all. With a similar overall goal of regulating international trade, the WTO has 148 members that account for 95 per cent of all world trade. With regard to WTO positions taken by EU states, the European Commission negotiates on behalf of all EU states on the basis of guidelines previously outlined by the Council. In terms of principles that guide the WTO, the European Commission has emphasized that:

> no country may apply quantitative restrictions on trade; an advantage granted to one country must be extended to all WTO members (Most Favoured Nation); no country may discriminate between its own products and imported products; all rules and laws affecting trade must be public; and rules and commitments are binding on member countries and enforceable through the dispute settlement system.[14]

The last point emphasizes the importance of what is referred to as the WTO Dispute Settlement System. Since its inception, the EU has taken

73 cases to the WTO, of which 25 have been lodged against the United States. Of these 25 cases, 16 have been won – a success rate of 64 per cent.[15] In the same time period, the USA has taken 76 cases to the WTO, of which 18 have been lodged against the EU. Ten of the 18 cases have been won, giving a success rate of 56 per cent.[16]

With respect to bilateral agreements, one of the EU's strongest preferential trade agreements is with the European Economic Association (EEA) states – Norway, Iceland and Lichtenstein. Although these countries do not form part of the EU, their access to the single market is on a par with that of all EU member states. Other agreements exist with central and east European states that are seeking to join the EU, and with southern countries in Latin America through the Mercosur.[17] The accords between the EU and African, Caribbean and Pacific (ACP) states constitute agreements which can be considered more "developmental" in nature as trade is combined with grants and loans which represent some of the highest levels of aid given by the EU (over a billion euros between 2001 and 2004). The 48 ACP states involved in the agreement are countries that have had a past (colonial) association with an EU member state. These states have suffered from marginalization in the world economy based on the "rich North–poor South" divide that has historically characterized the global economy. By the Commission's own admission, a main concern that has plagued the First, Second, Third and Fourth Lome Agreements (1980–98) that were negotiated between the EU and ACP states is that they have been too limited in scope, ambition, and perception.[18] To this end, Economic Partnership Agreements were pursued in the early 2000s in order to strengthen partnership, increase regional integration into the world economy, and increase aid to the ACP states.

How can one assess the evolution of the EU's trade agreements? One which has received little academic attention, but which is worth focussing on because the dynamics of this agreement over the last ten years help us understand the evolution of external economic policies, is the Euro-Mediterranean Partnership (EMP), also referred to as the Barcelona Process. The EMP reflects how the EU seeks to target certain areas not only to increase potential economic benefits but also, theoretically, to promote normative issues such as democracy and human rights.[19] This type of objective is also at play in bilateral agreements with states such as China, where there has been serious concern over human rights issues. The EMP, a policy towards the countries of the Mediterranean basin[20] formally launched in 1995, has three main pillars. The first is a political and security partnership that emphasizes the rule of law, democratization, respect for human rights and pluralism; the second is an economic and financial partnership; and the third is partnership in social, cultural and human affairs.

In terms of measuring the success of the Agreement with regard to economic objectives, Figures 10.1 and 10.2 document the trading intensity of some of the Euro-med states with the EU between 1995 and 2004.

Figure 10.1 demonstrates that, on average throughout the time series, the three main Euro-med states from which the EU imports are Algeria, Israel, and Morocco. The latter is of particular importance since it is the only one of the three that has not seen fluctuations in trade levels over the time series. Rather, there has been a consistent growth, suggesting that its economic ties to the EU are becoming increasingly stronger over time. Similarly, Figure 10.2 suggests that Morocco is one of the leading states to which the EU exports its goods and that there has also been an overall increase in trade over the period. Taking both graphs together, this suggests that, within the EMP, Morocco is a country with which the EU seeks to develop a strong trading relationship, a fact that is consistent with increased aids that are given to Morocco.[21]

Nevertheless, despite the increased trade and aid to the region in general, and Morocco in particular, there is evidence to suggest that states such as Morocco have not been committed to the universal values of democracy and human rights as enshrined in the EMP. Certainly, the Commission is of the opinion that there have been a "continuation of the democratization process, transparent and democratic general elections in September 2002 and an increase in the number of female members of parliament".[22] Nevertheless, both democratic governance and respect for human rights have yet to become strong features of the Moroccan political system. With regard to democratic governance, the holding of elections has not resulted in a concomitant power for elected officials in the decision-making process: the Constitution states that the king is the supreme decision maker and is not accountable through reliable democratic mechanisms.[23] And in terms of respect for human rights, the country's recent history of abuses is considered appalling by many. Even one of Morocco's closest allies, the United States, has severely criticized Morocco's record on human rights.[24] Such abuses have worsened since the 9/11 terrorist attacks, which gave Moroccan authorities the pretext for resorting to more forceful measures to deal with the opposition. Similarly, Amnesty International has recently highlighted Morocco's poor record.[25]

Given this evidence, the evolution of the EMP has in this respect been a failure. Countries such as Morocco do not satisfy the criteria of good governance, leading one to ask the question: why does the EU continue to trade with a country that respects neither democracy nor human rights, even though the EMP maintains that this should be the case? One explanation, sometimes called "the EU takes time" explanation, is that there is a delay in the transmission of the EU's normative values to the partner country.[26] The argument here is that the Commission, in particular, prefers not to force normative values because this might lead to a backlash in countries such as Morocco. Thus, the EU prefers to keep the partner "engaged" over a long period of time in order for the "osmosis" of norms to take place. This explanation, however, is unconvincing for two reasons. First, the EU has been directly and substantially engaged with

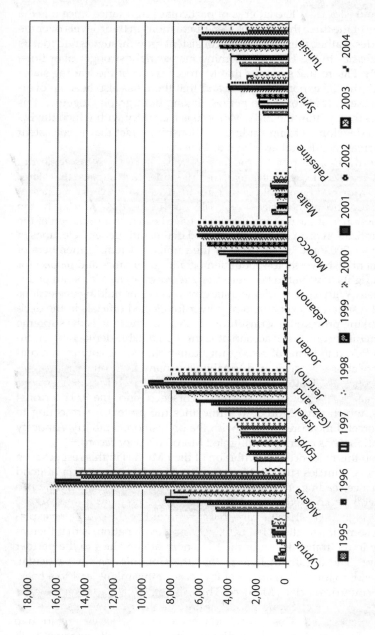

Figure 10.1 EU imports from main Mediterranean states, 1995–2004 (€million)

Source: Eurostat.

Legend: ■ 1995 ■ 1996 ■ 1997 ■ 1998 ∴ 1999 ⋇ 2000 ■ 2001 ◆ 2002 ▨ 2003 ■ 2004

Axis categories: Cyprus, Algeria, Egypt, Israel (Gaza and Jericho), Jordan, Lebanon, Morocco, Malta, Palestine, Syria, Tunisia

Axis values: 0, 2,000, 4,000, 6,000, 8,000, 10,000, 12,000, 14,000, 16,000, 18,000

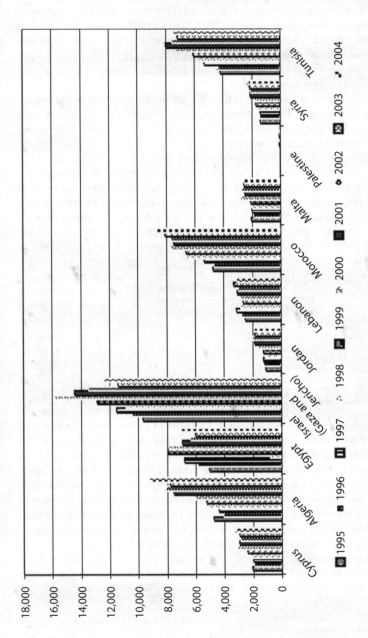

Figure 10.2 EU exports to main Mediterranean states, 1995–2004 (€million)

Source: Eurostat.

Legend: 1995 · 1996 · 1997 · 1998 · 1999 · 2000 · 2001 · 2002 · 2003 · 2004

Countries: Cyprus · Algeria · Egypt · Israel (Gaza and Jericho) · Jordan · Lebanon · Morocco · Malta · Palestine · Syria · Tunisia

Morocco for ten years and little has been achieved in terms of positive change. If anything, the human rights situation seems to have worsened; elections were less "democratic" in 2002 than in 1997, despite the fact that trade with the EU significantly increased over the five years between them. Second, the absence of forceful action during this period may signal to the partner country that human rights and democracy concerns are not actually that important.

A second explanation, termed the "the relatively nice dictators" explanation, is that human rights abuses in Morocco pale in comparison with those found in countries such as China and North Korea.[27] Therefore, Morocco should be treated differently, or with less severity. This sentiment is implicitly seen in EU documents, as well as interviews with some EU officials, which appraise Morocco's efforts to improve its governance despite clear evidence pointing in the opposite direction. Given that Morocco has "relatively nicer dictators" than those found in other states, the EU feels impelled to refrain from "lecturing Morocco" about democracy and human rights. The idea here is that compared with what else is seen in the world, the king is not so bad after all. However, this explanation fails on two grounds. First, the very core of normative values is that all abuses should all be treated and dealt with in the same way.[28] Second, the EU cannot operate by using inconsistent reasoning. For example, as seen in the cases of Turkey and Croatia, the EU does lecture countries about human rights abuses and specifically sets out strict criteria for admission into the EU. The argument that Morocco is not in the same category because it is not a prospective member does not hold much weight, given that the EU also lectures countries as different as Cuba and the Ukraine.

A more cogent explanation is that specific member states have their own reasons for seeing the EMP evolve as it has even though, in terms of fulfilling all of its principles, its evolution may be considered an overall failure. As discussed earlier, in terms of procedures the Council sets the mandate for the Commission, and then has the final say on the appropriateness of the policy's implementation. With this in mind, one may argue that under the Council's guidance the EU acts as a rational actor, paying attention to material benefits and to the regional stability that will underpin such benefits, regardless of human rights abuses and the lack of democratization in Morocco. In order to demonstrate this, we consider in more detail what we refer to as the "regional stability" and "economic" reasons that guide specific member states.

Turning to the "regional stability" considerations that guide the policies of some EU member states, it is important to note from the outset that in terms of political reforms in Morocco, the best outcome for the EU would be a process of democratization that brings to power a popularly elected leader who is both secular and keen on continuing a similar type of economic relationship with the EU. This would entail the emergence of a very strong, liberal opposition that is able to both marginalize the

king politically (forcing him to cede substantial powers) and to out-
manoeuvre the very popular Islamic movements, whose democratic
credentials are not proven. However, it is reasonable to suggest that such
an outcome is unlikely to occur at present. The largest opposition party
at the moment in an emasculated parliament is the Islamic Party of
Justice and Development, and the most popular civil society movement
in Morocco is an even more radical Islamic formation led by Sheikh
Yassine. The popularity of the secular opposition has been constantly
diminishing, because it is perceived as illegitimate by many Moroccans.

There is substantial evidence to demonstrate that an Islamic party in
government might want to adopt policies that may be perceived as being
antagonistic to the EU's economic interests.[29] Morocco has been "forced"
to introduce a number of significant market-oriented reforms that have
led to the further pauperization of the population. The economic and
social costs of such reforms are enormous, and have entailed the emergence of a small class of *nouveaux riches*, while the vast majority of the
population struggles to survive.[30] Capitalizing on the negative effects of
such reforms, the Islamist movement can play the social justice card.
Sheikh Yassine, in particular, is very vocal on this point, and he is
concerned with the international environment and the constraints that
derive from it when it comes to the choices that Morocco faces.

In these conditions, because member states are unable to attain the
outcome they really favour, they settle for the second-best option: a
fairly stable and relatively friendly authoritarian regime that seeks a
stable economic relationship. It is far better to help King Mohammed VI
to stay in power than to force elections that might throw up a leadership that questions many of the policies hitherto beneficial to states
such as France and Spain. The risk of an Islamic party coming to power
through democratic means is not worth taking if it sacrifices the
perceived stability of the region.[31] Further, regional instability might
also lead to more Moroccans leaving the country and emigrating to
states such as Spain that have historically experienced difficulties when
dealing with increased immigration from the area. This was seen in the
conflicts between the locals and immigrant agricultural workers in
Southern Spain during the late 1990s and early 2000s.[32] Taking these
points together, if stability is essential in order to continue to derive
benefits for certain member states, the Council can be seen as acting
rationally from self-interest rather than normatively in accepting the
evolution of the EMP: otherwise, democracy would be promoted
irrespective of the consequences this might have on economic relations.

With regard to the economic reasons, Figures 10.3 and 10.4 show that
there are certain key member states that are principle beneficiaries of
the EU trade agreements with Morocco.

Figure 10.3 shows that in 2003 four of the top five countries from
which Morocco imported goods and services were EU states: France

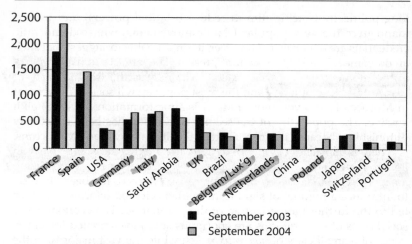

Figure 10.3 Morocco's imports by main partners, 2003 and 2004 (in thousand milliards of Dh)

Source: Office des Changes.

(the former colonial power of Morocco) was ranked first; Spain was in second position; Saudi Arabia held third spot; Italy was fourth and the United Kingdom was last of the top five. In 2004, the top four were again from the EU (France, Spain, Italy, and Germany), while China took over fifth spot and the only non-EU state in the top three the year before, Saudi Arabia, was relegated to sixth. In both years a majority of the top ten countries from which Morocco imported goods were EU members. Similarly, Figure 10.4 makes it plain that the top five countries to which Morocco exported in 2003 were France, Spain, Saudi Arabia, the Netherlands and Italy; in 2004 the first three remained the same while Brazil and India replaced the Netherlands and Italy. As in Figure 10.3, a majority of exporters in the top ten were EU member states.

With this data in mind, one sees that particular EU states have significant material interests in Morocco. The main thrust of the EMP's second pillar, despite the rhetorical commitment to more normative values in the first and third pillars, is the economic integration of southern Mediterranean states into the European economic sphere of influence. For states such as France and Spain, the area is a very significant market for European consumer goods, and also an area with significant potential for growth.[33] This supports H. Smith's argument that the EU is effective in promoting domestic economic interests abroad.[34] Given these material interests, therefore, it is in some EU states' interests to marginalize issues of democracy and human rights. In their calculation of interests, there is a perceived zero-sum game: either ignore issues such as human rights abuses in the hope of consolidating economic

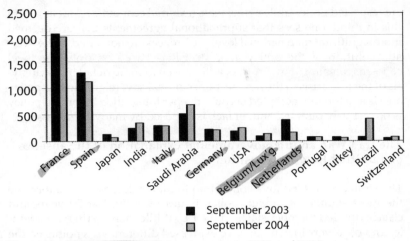

■ September 2003
□ September 2004

Figure 10.4 Morocco's exports by main partners, 2003 and 2004 (in thousand milliards of Dh)

Source: Office des Changes.

gains for EU states; or attempt to pursue such issues and potentially lose the support of the Moroccan administration, which may subsequently seek trade with other non-EU member states, and thereby decrease economic benefits.

External policies: a 2nd order status

In sum, analysing the evolution of both types of political and economic relations in the EU, it is reasonable to argue that EU foreign policy overall constitutes a 2nd order one. The evolution of the CFSP clearly shows a lack of harmonization at the supranational level, given that member states still seek to retain the final word when dealing with security issues. The evolution of economic agreements, as seen in the EMP, reflects how not all EU objectives are attained: while global economic trade has increased, European "norms" such as democracy and human rights, which are linked to some trade agreements, have been ignored and have therefore had very little force. This is because of the ability of certain member states to control the agenda for their own benefit: it is not a priority for either the Commission or member states to "uphold" the normative values embodied within the EMP, for example, because the concerns of certain member states about issues such as regional stability will always be deemed more important. Considering these dimensions of EU external policy, the evolution of the policy illustrates that it is difficult to either achieve EU-wide consensus on security issues (external political relations) or ensure that all the normative EU values

[203]

are respected under trade agreements (external economic relations). With this in mind, one sees that supranational agreements that are deemed more significant than national level preferences are not found in the over-all evolution of the policy area: decisions based on domestic level concerns remain paramount. As will be seen in more detail in the analysis of the Iraq crisis in the next section, national sovereignty in this policy area is still broadly accepted because deeper integration in foreign policy is not actively pursued and, in fact, is opposed by many member states.

The Iraq War: an intergovernmental explanation of the absence of a unified European position

The United States led invasion of Iraq in March 2003 was arguably one the most significant foreign policy issues over the last 50 years and clearly divided member states in the EU. While many writers, academics and observers in general have expressed different viewpoints on the war, it is sufficient to say for the purposes of this book that the attack remains for many critical observers an act of injustice while, for the less critical, it was something that needed to be done.

The latter view was held by US President George Bush, who had taken a tougher stance on Iraq since September 11, 2001, as discussed by authors such as Ismael and Ismael,[35] and who had the support of special pro-Israeli lobbyists and domestic groups when it came to foreign policy making in the Middle East, as discussed by Terry.[36] The Bush camp justified military intervention in Iraq on three main grounds. The first was the apparent existence of weapons of mass destruction. This was a major issue, despite calls from UN's Chief weapons inspector Hans Blix that more evidence was necessary. The second factor related to the abuse of human rights in Iraq under President Saddam Hussein. However, the United States actually failed to recognize that such abuses were similar to those pursued by states such as Chile that the US had supported in the past as documented by Dorfman.[37] The third reason was the overall threat to regional stability posed by the Hussein administration, a regime that, ironically, had received the support and backing of the United States in the 1980s. Bush's call for war, as opposed to attempting a peaceful resolution through the United Nations, was supported by what was referred to as the "coalition of the willing", including most notably Tony Blair of the UK, Silvio Berlusconi of Italy and José María Aznar of Spain.

On the other hand, several states throughout the world – presumably the "coalition of the unwilling" – opposed the lack of any attempt by the United States to seek a peaceful resolution, and they therefore heavily criticized the eventual invasion and occupation by the United States as being illegal under international law, as highlighted in Mandel's work.[38] This criticism would escalate as the insurgency continued, with the revelations that there were no weapons of mass destruction to be found, that the US had instigated its own style of human rights abuses by torturing and killing suspected terrorists in Iraq, and that those states that had cooperated in the invasion were the first to receive lucrative contracts. The most significant EU critics of the war were Gerhard Schröder of Germany and Jacques Chirac of France, two EU states that are not historically known for seeing eye-to-eye on foreign policy and security issues. The critical stance against the invasion that was held by some states is shared in the sentiments of authors such as Ismael and Haddad,[39] as well as Anrove,[40] who have argued that sanctions and war against Iraq have centred around issues of consolidating the position of states such as the USA, who have been more interested in the strategic oil reserves in the Middle-East than in human rights violations and the existence of weapons of mass destruction.

The Iraq war was not only a divisive issue amongst the leaders of the EU; Kritzinger[41] has examined and explained what a divisive issue it was amongst the élites and the masses by focussing on developments in France, Germany, Italy and the UK. As seen in Table 10.1, data collected shortly before the war show vividly how EU citizens from all these states (and indeed all EU states) were clearly opposed to any war that was not sanctioned by the UN, while in January 2003 a majority of Germany citizens were against even a UN-backed war.

By February 2003, a month before the invasion, 69 per cent of all Germans wanted their government to vote against any UN resolution for war, 71 per cent of all Italians were unsupportive of a military intervention even if authorized by the UN,[42] and 45 per cent of all British rejected war even with a second UN resolution.[43]

Kritzinger[44] argues that in order to understand the apparent divergence between the mass publics in the UK and Italy and their leaders, attention must be paid to the "war" dimension that guided most EU citizens during the period, as opposed to the "democracy" dimension that guided "conservative" political élites in the UK[45] and Italy. The "war dimension" refers to the idea of a deep-rooted rejection of war

Table 10.1 Public opposition to war in January 2003

Opposed	Without UN support	With UN support
France	87 %	29 %
Germany	89 %	51 %
Italy	88 %	32 %
UK	69 %	16 %

Source: EOS Gallup poll January 2003, published by the BBC, as presented in Kritzinger (2003).

for political and religious reasons along with the belief that diplomatic strategies should first be pursued in order to deal with the international crisis (as was felt by leaders of France and Germany as well). This was coupled with fears that pursuing military intervention might result in either increased terrorist activity, something later manifest during the Spanish general elections of 2004 as discussed by Chari,[46] or increased economic uncertainty in Europe due to the negative consequences of further terrorist activity. Added to this, many European citizens did not trust the United States which seemed to be pursuing an imperialist strategy[47] that was aimed not at preserving peace,[48] but rather at promoting war and controlling oil. The "democracy dimension", most particularly seen in some domestic leaders, such as Blair and Berlusconi, not to mention Bush, was that unless military intervention in Iraq was pursued, there would in their view be a threat to "democratic values" that western states had the obligation to uphold.

With the above dynamics between various member states in mind, how can one attempt to evaluate the failure of the EU to act with a unified voice during the Iraq crisis? From the outset, it is important to note that this analysis is not based on examination of the initiation and negotiation of policy per se that has guided policy formulation analysis in the previous chapters: after all, the EU did not officially formulate a policy position with respect to the Iraq War. Rather, this analysis seeks to explain why there was no formulation of a common position towards Iraq despite the principles laid out in the CFSP.

Chari and Cavatorta[49] argue that in order to understand the failure of the CFSP during the Iraq crisis, attention must be focussed specifically on the actions of the Council, pointing to the importance of the intergovernmentalist perspective in explaining the EU's failure in Iraq. The theoretical ideas for this argument are grounded in the work of those such as Hill,[50] who state that foreign and security policy matters remain issues of "national sovereignty" which member states are unwilling to see developed at the supranational level, as mentioned in the first section of this chapter. Extending on arguments raised by Hoffman,[51] Chari and Cavatorta argue that notions of national sovereignty as discussed by Hill are also:

> coupled with other factors that have (historically) played a part of the states' calculation of foreign policy interests: states such as the UK have favoured "Atlantic" ties; those such as France and Germany have sought to solidify links with each other in order to become leaders on the world stage within Europe; and smaller states such as Ireland remained ambivalent about the future of CFSP based on pure cost-benefit analysis and concerns regarding the loss of foreign policy "neutrality."[52]

These factors became particularly relevant during the Iraq Crisis. The UK under Blair was clearly in favour of acting in line with its so-called "special-relationship" with the United States, presumably guided by the "democracy-axis" discussed above. It is significant to note that, historically, UK leaders such as Thatcher have sometimes distanced themselves from the United States on some of its foreign policy stances, as seen in the US invasion of Grenada in the 1980s. Interestingly, in the case of Iraq, the United States was joined not only by the Italians but also by José Maria Aznar of Spain, who sought to increase the country's international profile. The idea here, as outlined by Heywood,[53] was for Spain to flex its muscles on the world stage by allying itself more firmly with the United States, while also appearing to be strong in the face of domestic terrorist threats represented by the Basque organization ETA, which seeks independence for the Basque Country. Although France and Germany did prefer to seek resolution of the crisis through the United Nations, they, too, arguably had their own interests in trying to seek to consolidate their positions as the leaders of Europe by exploiting their positions as being representative of that of all citizens of the EU. Smaller EU states such as Ireland, that have historically remained neutral during international conflicts, similarly felt that openly taking a position for or against war in Iraq would betray their policy of neutrality, which they maintained even if it meant that this would also prevent a European solution from emerging.[54]

All in all, EU member states were guided by divergent interests. Institutional leaders of the EU such as Commissioner Patten ultimately concluded that member states "do not accept that Europe could have "occupied the [foreign policy] space",[55] and that the policy area was therefore controlled by differing national interests. Given the lack of unity, supranational actors such as Javier Solana could not be in a position to develop a EU strategy. As Chari and Cavatorta argue:

> there is little doubt that the institutional procedures governing CFSP are cumbersome and that the Commission is not fully relevant in this policy area. It is also true that ... Javier Solana, is perceived as being controversial [given his previous U-turn on Spain's joining NATO in the 1980s] and being biased [in light of his Atlanticist ties as General Secretary of NATO in the 1990s]. Yet, the real issue seems not to be the decision-making structure of CFSP itself, or Solana's role in it, but the political will of the domestic actors. ... For example, during the crisis [EU President] Prodi acknowledged that better instruments and improved decision-making mechanisms are needed to create a real political Union, but he also strongly pointed out that the MSs failed to decide if they wanted the project crystallised. ... Indeed, a stark reminder of the failure of the EU to speak with one voice is the

absence (bar a very general statement) of any strong CFSP statements during the crisis. Its presence could have allowed Solana
to pursue concrete measures, but the lack of agreement between
the MSs made his position irrelevant.[56]

To conclude, examination of developments during the Iraq War demonstrates how external political relations remain the concern of member
states. As such, they are best characterized from the intergovernmentalist perspective. In this specific case, member states were unable to come
to an agreement on a common European position due to their own
incompatible interests: the UK's priority was to maintain its so-called
special ties with the USA; Spain's tough stance was motivated by its
desire to increase its ties to the United States while also helping thwart
its own domestic terrorism; in France and Germany there was a desire to
avoid confrontation at all costs while still being representative of "European" views and being perceived as the "true" leaders of Europe; and
countries such as Ireland did to want to abandon their historical policy
of military neutrality. Nor was the supranational level able to spearhead
an agreement between the different states, given that its jurisdictional
powers were limited in terms of being able to initiate a policy position.

Thus, in order to explain the EU's failure during the crisis, ideas
raised by intergovernmentalism are crucial: member states with differing views had the final say and they did not have the will to attempt to
formulate a common position. From a different vantage point, ideas
raised by supranational governance theories are of limited value in
explaining the failure of the EU to act decisively in Iraq. This is because,
as discussed above, the institutional power of the Commission is
limited given the omnipotence of the Council in foreign and security
issues, and other EU institutions such as the EP and the ECJ have no
codified role in the policy area. Similarly, the other theoretical perspectives discussed in Chapter 3 are of limited value in explaining why the
EU did not speak with one voice. There was no decision-making role
for potential interest groups, especially those concerned about human
rights abuses, which suggests that ideas raised by pluralists are irrelevant. Although all of the EU's trade union organizations were against
the attacks, their concerns were not afforded any forum at the EU level,
which suggests that corporatism is of little value in explaining the EU's
inability to take up a stance. Similarly, the DEC perspective is of little
explanatory value since no privileged position was given to economic
interests in terms of developing the EU position.

One might hypothesize that some EU businesses in the UK, Italy and
Spain may have had vested interests in winning the war in Iraq, given the
potential for lucrative contracts, and that businesses therefore exerted
direct pressure on these member states as they had in the CAP negotiations (Chapter 7) where economic actors attempted to influence the

Council. But there are two main problems with this argument that economic élites played an important role during the Iraq crisis. First, there is little "on the record" evidence to suggest that there was direct participation by economic élites when countries such as the UK, Italy, and Spain were choosing to go to war with Iraq. In fact, several European businesses with direct trading links to the Middle East were arguably concerned about going to war with Iraq on account of the regional instability that might ensue. Second, even if there were such evidence pointing to the importance of business influence, one may reasonably argue that if business pressure were so strong, one would have also expected that states such as France and Germany, arguably home to businesses with the same interests as those found in the UK, Italy and Spain, would have succumbed to these economic interests and pursued a "pro-war" policy. Yet, this did not happen. With this in mind, arguments from the intergovernmentalist camp that member states formed their positions primarily by considering their national security goals, as well in some cases their relationship with the United States, seem to be more convincing.

Conclusions

The first part of the chapter examined the key aspects of EU external policies. It first dealt with the evolution of foreign political relations by an examination of the EU's Common Foreign and Security Policy. It contended that the divergent security interests of the different member states have resulted in the CFSP being rather toothless, resulting in a weak and decentralized EU in this issue area. It then considered the evolution of external economic policies through an analysis of different bilateral and multilateral agreements. Attention was focussed on the Euro-Mediterranean Partnership, which seeks to promote trade between the EU and countries of the southern shore of the Mediterranean, while simultaneously promoting democracy and human rights in these countries. It was argued that, in terms of reaching its overall objectives, the EMP can be considered a failure: even though there is increased economic integration with the southern Mediterranean, the EU has failed to promote its normative values of human rights and democratisation, partly because of the "economic" and "regional stability" interests of some member states such as France and Spain. Given the lack of anything approaching full harmonization at the EU level, it was argued that this issue area remains one of 2nd order status.

The second part analysed in more detail the dynamics surrounding the Iraq War of 2003, seeking to explain why the EU was unable to formulate a policy position on this international crisis. It was argued that the intergovernmentalist school is most convincing in explaining developments in this policy area: member states had divergent views and were unable to agree to a common position. This, coupled with the weak institutional structure at the supranational level (which would help explain why ideas raised by supranational governance scholars have little explanatory importance in this case), meant that the EU could not speak with a unified voice. Nor is there strong evidence to suggest that different types of interest groups were consulted during the process of trying to attain a common EU position, pointing to the irrelevance of ideas raised by pluralist, corporatist, and DEC perspectives when seeking to explain the EU's inability to arrive at a common position towards the Iraq War.

11 Conclusions: understanding the present, changing the future

The first chapter started with the idea that politics is policy. Policy consists of decisions made by leaders that significantly affect the daily lives of all citizens. The chapter ended with the idea that policy is politics: the way policy is made, the people who make it and the ambitions that drive such actors, all help determine the nature of policies and, therefore, their eventual impact on citizens. With these ideas in mind, this book has been concerned with understanding and explaining EU policy outputs and the politics behind them. Certainly, many books have been written on the EU over the last 20 years. However, with increased world instability in the wake of the Iraq crisis, future enlargement questions over states such as Turkey and the apparent demise of the European Constitution in the wake of the French and Dutch referendums in 2005, there has never been a more salient and urgent time to better understand EU pubic policy. The challenge we face is to answer a range of questions. These include: what are the objectives and the evolution of EU public policies? Which actors have had more power when formulating them? How can the formulation process of the various policies be comparatively and theoretically characterized? And what are the consequences of how policies have developed (and how policies have been made) for those living in European political space today?

This book has attempted to rise to this challenge by offering readers the tools and the evidence to better understand the "policy and politics" of the EU. In this regard, Chapter 1 first outlined what was meant by the terms 1st and 2nd order policies. On the one hand, 1st order policies represent issue areas where one sees a centralized and strong EU that seeks to make its mark in the global economy vis-à-vis major players such the United States and Japan. In such areas, there has been a smooth transfer of power from the national to the supranational level in order to create a strong and internationally competitive Europe. On the other hand, in 2nd order policies there is a decentralized EU where member states are reluctant to give up their power. Thus, national governments have maintained their sovereignty in these issue areas and Brussels' policy competences in such areas remain weak and ill-defined. It was argued in the first chapter that a main goal of this book was to test whether or not the 1st and 2nd order classification was a valid one and, if so, to explain why this has developed by focussing on the actions and interests of those involved in policy making. A further goal was to theoretically characterize such developments in order to gain a more nuanced view of European integration.

Chapter 2 offered the first set of tools needed to better answer these questions by identifying the different actors involved in EU policy making. Here we elaborated on the role of EU institutional players that are of particular importance in policy initiation. One main EU institution is the European Commission, which is the EU's administrative arm, headed by Commissioners that are appointed from each member state. The Council of Ministers represents the other half of the EU's dual executive and consists of the ministers of the national governments of member states. The other main EU institutions are the European Parliament, which consists of elected Members of Parliament, and the European Court of Justice, which is the EU's highest judicial body. Non-EU institutional players involved in policy negotiation, largely referred to as interest (or lobby) groups, were also examined. These include specific corporate interests (such as the European Round Table of Industrialists and UNICE), transnational trade union organizations, and other social groups.

Chapter 3 then developed the second set of tools by presenting the reader with conceptual frameworks to better understand the interaction between these different types of actors in the policy-making process, as taken from the comparative politics and European integration theory literature. The five main theoretical perspectives that were discussed were intergovernmentalism, supranational governance, pluralism, corporatism and the dominant economic class (DEC) perspective. Intergovernmentalism argues that in order to understand EU policy making, the focus should be on the Council of Ministers. The supranational governance approach contends that power resides not in the Council, but in the main supranational institutions such as the Commission, EP or ECJ. Pluralism holds that the policy process can be best explained as a consequence of interaction between a plurality of interest groups, all of which have roughly equal access to policy making. Corporatism holds that policy making is best understood as a process involving the semi-institutionalized positions of labour, capital and political system representatives. And the DEC perspective contends that public policy is a consequence of the goals and actions of capital interests who exercise disproportionate policy-making influence compared to any other actor.

Chapters 4 through 10, which constituted the empirical heart of the book, then turned to analysis of specific EU policies. The first section of each policy chapter analysed the policy's historical development in order to better understand whether its evolution sees either a strong, centralized EU (1st order policy), or a weak, decentralized one (2nd order policy). The second section of each chapter then focussed on the different actors that have been involved in the formulation of different directives, regulations or initiatives in the various policy areas. Based on this evidence, the process was characterized, using the theoretical perspectives presented earlier. Chapter 4 first examined single market policies, which are concerned with the establishment of a neo-liberal free-trade area for Europe. Chapter 5 then paid attention to competition policy, which has as its objective the creation of competitive conditions in the single market. Chapter 6 focussed on Economic and Monetary Union, or the establishment of the single European currency. Chapter 7 analysed the Common Agricultural Policy, whose main objective is to redistribute EU budgetary funds to farmers. Chapter 8 turned to the analysis of EU social policy, including the Social Charter and Social Protocol. Chapter 9 focussed on freedom, security and justice policies, which are concerned with areas such as immigration and asylum. And finally Chapter 10 studied EU external policies, including the Common Foreign and Security Policy (CFSP).

Seeking to summarize our understanding of the policies that have been pursued at the EU and the motivations of the actors that have driven them, this chapter offers answers to the two principal questions behind this book. First, is there cogent evidence to support the idea that there are 1st and 2nd order policies in the EU? Second, if so, why and how do policies become of 1st or 2nd order nature? After turning to these two questions, the chapter elaborates on the usefulness of the different theoretical perspectives that have been used here to understand policy making in the EU. We conclude by considering how these findings may help students and European citizens reflect on their future.

1st and 2nd order policies in the EU?

In order to answer the first main question – namely, whether or not there is evidence of 1st and 2nd order policies in the EU – the first part of each empirical chapter focussed on the objectives and evolution of specific policy areas. Taking all the evidence together, one can conclude that there is evidence that points to a hierarchy between EU policies as demonstrated in the second and third columns of Table 11.1.

The second column of Table 11.1 indicates that single market, competition, economic and monetary and agricultural policies constitute 1st order policies, reflecting a strong and centralized EU in these areas that is seeking to exert itself as a unified entity on the world stage. It is useful to recall the specific developments in each of these policy areas that support this idea. In terms of the evolution of single market policy, it was felt by political and economic élites in the mid 1980s that the only way to recover from the economic decline of the 1970s was to pursue a single, integrated capitalist market which would allow for the free movement of goods, services and capital between borders. The 1986 Single European Act therefore had as its priority to remove physical, fiscal and technical

Table 11.1 Summary of main findings

Policy area	1st order	2nd order	Main actors involved in policy formulation		Theoretical perspective of value in understanding policy formulation	
			Policy initiation	Policy negotiation	Policy initiation	Policy negotiation
Single market	√		ECJ and Commission	Commission and ERT[1]	Supranational governance	Supranational governance and DEC
Competition	√		Commission	Commission, ERT and UNICE[2]	Supranational governance	Supranational governance and DEC
Economic and Monetary Union	√		Commission	Council and ERT	Supranational governance	Intergovernmentalism and DEC
Common Agricultural Policy	√		Commission	Council and large landholding farmers	Supranational governance	Intergovernmentalism and DEC
Social policy		√	Commission	Council and capital and labour	Supranational Governance	Intergovernmentalism and Corporatism
Freedom, justice and security policies		√	Commission	Council and social-based interest groups	Supranational governance	Intergovernmentalism and Pluralism
External Policies *		√	Council		Intergovernmentalism	

Notes: ERT = European Round Table of Industrialists; UNICE = Union of Industrial and Employers' Confederations of Europe

* As discussed in the chapter on external policy, analysis of a specific policy was not made per se; rather there was an analysis of developments during the Iraq War.

barriers between member states through what was known as the 1992 Programme. Data showing how member states have increasingly transposed single market directives from Brussels formed the heart of the evidence demonstrating a strong, centralized EU in this policy area. The success of the single market was also illustrated by data highlighting the increase of trade and investment in the single market since the early 1990s. Evidence of the subsequent development of a strong single integrated market that is internationally competitive was also seen in Eurostat trade integration data.

Competition policy's 1st order status was reflected in member states' active implementation of supranational competition initiatives relating to issues such as state aid control and liberalization. Member states have also given Brussels a strong role in regulating mergers and investigating whether or not European firms are engaging in restrictive practices. Given these developments it was argued that a transfer of competences from the national to the supranational level has taken place very smoothly in competition policy, allowing the supranational level significant power in ensuring the functioning of an internationally competitive single market.

With regard to EMU, economic and political leaders believed that if a single, competitive market were to be fully efficient and allow a strong role for Europe in the world economy, then a single currency was necessary. In such a currency zone, interest rates could no longer be controlled by national administrations and fiscal discipline would also be imposed. To show how the EMU was considered a priority, specific attention was paid to the evolution of the so-called convergence criteria outlined in the Maastricht Treaty. The evidence highlighted how member states made serious efforts to decrease deficits and debts throughout the 1990s by pursuing cuts to social welfare programmes. States also pursued initiatives to promote low-inflationary economic growth, such as deregulation of labour markets.[1] The priority given by the supranational and domestic leaders to the EMU is also reflected in international market data, where the euro has become one of the leading world currencies in little over five years.

Finally, the Common Agricultural Policy is a redistributive policy aimed both at ensuring the livelihood of a specific economic sector, namely farmers, and stabilizing the supply of strategic agricultural products. Such a policy not only safeguards specific (large) farmers' livelihood, but also protects them from potential international shocks, while allowing for the dumping of subsidized EU goods in international markets such as Africa and Asia. It was argued that the CAP is a 1st order policy for two main reasons. First, it is a centralized policy at the EU level which gives subsidies for all European farmers, thereby resulting in a relatively minimal role for national administrations in the policy's implementation. Second, of all redistributive mechanisms of the EU, including structural funds, cohesion funds and research and development, the CAP receives the largest percentage of the EU budget.

If the above demonstrates how some policies could be characterized as 1st order ones, the third column of Figure 11.1 shows that social policy, freedom, security and justice policies, and external policies constitute 2nd order ones. In these issue areas, the EU generally does not speak with a unified voice and the member states still retain sovereignty. In other words, one sees a weak and decentralized EU in these policy areas where member states still retain their power. There has been a generally weak development of EU social policy because strong EU-wide norms in issues such as wages and working conditions are absent. In addition, lack of harmonization in this policy area is also evident in the various non-binding agreements between member states, which are quite numerous compared with the number of directives that have been passed over the years. This means that many social policy agreements lack any real force, given that member states have the freedom to abrogate the (non-binding) EU regulations in the area. This results in national regulations remaining paramount in importance.

It was argued that freedom, justice and security policies were of 2nd order status for four related reasons. First, many states retain "opt-outs" for several of the supranational initiatives in this area, as seen in recent immigration initiatives, the Schengen Accord and the European arrest warrant. This results in EU policies lacking any real force, while national regulations maintain their importance. Second, the development of fundamental policy approaches still remains the prerogative of member states, thereby nullifying any related supranational initiatives. This was particularly seen in the case of citizenship: even if someone is born on European soil, the member state still decides on his or her nationality and, therefore, whether or not he or she can become a European citizen. Third, these policies remain of 2nd order importance because the scope of supranational initiatives remains limited. For example, even though there have been policies for the reunification of families of third-country nationals living in the EU, not only have some countries opted out, but also there are still no supranational regulations on the entrance of third-country nationals who are students, trainees, volunteers or self-employed. Finally, there is a lack of centralization in freedom, justice and security policies. This was seen in the case of asylum processes where there is no centralized European authority that can oversee all cases, resulting in a plethora of different national rules being applied to those seeking asylum in the EU.

Finally, EU external policies remain of 2nd order status for various reasons. At the political level, the EU has been unable to speak with a unified voice during international crises, as most recently seen in the Iraq War of 2003. States such as the UK and Spain desired to align themselves with the United States and attack Iraq; those such as France and Germany preferred a UN-led solution; while others such as Ireland and Austria remained theoretically neutral throughout the crisis. The Iraq crisis helps illuminate how the evolution of the CFSP points to a lack of harmonization at the supranational level, given that national governments seek to maintain the final say with respect to security issues. At the economic level, it was also argued that although there are increasing bilateral and multilateral trade agreements between the EU and parts of the developing world, the principles of such agreements are not always followed. This was particularly seen in the Barcelona process, which seeks to promote not only trade between the EU and the southern shore of the Mediterranean, but also respect for human rights and democratization in the area. Specifically focussing on the case of Morocco, it was suggested that although trade with the region has increased, the EU's normative values of human rights and democratization are not respected. In order to understand why such EU agreements have not therefore been rescinded, attention must be paid to the preferences of some member states who seek regional stability coupled with increased economic and security benefits. Taking both dimensions of external policies together, it was concluded that national level preferences have been more important than strong supranational initiatives in this issue area.

In summary, one sees evidence over the last 30 years that creating a neo-liberal, single-currency, free-market area in order to make the EU competitive vis-à-vis economies such as Japan and the United States was of 1st order priority. Efforts have also been made to protect this market from international pressure in certain sectors, such as agriculture. These policies – on the single market, competition, economic and monetary union, and the CAP – can thus be demarcated as 1st order policies. These policies, which are largely economic in nature, have been strongly developed at the EU level in order to allow the EU as a whole to be a strong, centralized economic power in the global economy while benefiting capital actors in the process. Such policies have been deemed a priority to develop in European political space. In pursuing such initiatives, however, other policies, referred to as 2nd order policies, have been largely ignored at the EU level. In these areas, which include social, immigration and external security policies, one sees that national governments have maintained their sovereignty and have been cautious about pursuing EU-wide norms. Thus 2nd order policies do not form a key part of EU policy making and the EU remains weak and decentralized in these policy areas. In order to understand why this two-speed policy space has developed, the next section considers who has been involved in the policy formulation process.

Explaining the policy hierarchy: the role of capital actors

In order to shed light on why policies become 1st and 2nd order in nature, the second part of each empirical chapter offered evidence on the processes by which different rules, regulations and directives were decided on in the specific policy areas. The initiatives that were examined were the Single European Act (single market policy), the Merger Control

Regulation (competition policy), the Economic and Monetary Union (economic and monetary policies), The MacSharry, Agenda 2000 and Fischler Reforms (Common Agricultural Policy), the Social Charter and Social Protocol (social policy), family reunification of third-country nationals (freedom, security and justice policies) and the European position towards the Iraq War[2] (external policies). Analyses were made of the actors involved in the policy formulation process of these different initiatives and which factors drove them. Taking all the evidence together we can therefore ask: is there a relation between the existence of a hierarchy of policies and the actors involved in their formulation?

An answer to this question starts with examination of the fourth and fifth columns of Table 11.1. Summarizing the evidence presented in the book, these columns indicate which actors have been involved in the two main stages of policy formulation: policy initiation and policy negotiation. It is important to recall that policy initiation refers to the EU institution responsible for first conceiving and drafting the regulations, rules or directives that were pursued. Policy negotiation refers to the stage where policy is shaped and bargained over by potential actors, including those such as interest groups that are outside the EU institutional structure. The fourth column shows that the Commission was the predominant actor when policy was initiated. In contrast to this, the fifth column indicates that different actors along with the Council were involved in policy negotiation in a majority of the public policies studied. The different actors may include capital actors and socially based interest groups, depending on the policy area.

Comparative analysis of the second and third columns of Table 11.1 (which show whether or not a policy is of 1st or 2nd order status) with the fourth and fifth columns (which show which actors were influential in the respective stages of each policy's development) indicates that what binds all 1st order policies, and distinguishes them from 2nd order ones, is that capital actors have been involved in their negotiation. 1st order policies have had the active support and influence of business actors who have negotiated alongside either the Commission (as seen in the Single European Act and the Merger Control Regulation) or the Council (as seen in Economic and Monetary Union and the Common Agricultural Policy reforms throughout the 1990s and 2000s). This correlation may go a long way in explaining why such policies have been considered a priority to develop at the EU level. No other policy-making actor has been consistently involved in the formulation of 1st order policies. The Council and Commission, for example, are sometimes – but not always – involved in the negotiation process of 1st order policies.

Of all capitalist organizations, the European Round Table of Industrialists (ERT) has been one of the most influential in assuring that there is a strong centralized EU in 1st order policies. The ERT was originally formed to push for and develop a model for a neo-liberal European market; it was heavily involved in the development of merger control regulation, and it was instrumental in setting the timetable for economic and monetary union. The ERT worked alongside different actors in the EU institutional structure – whether at the Council or Commission level – pressurizing them to iron-out policies which would allow for conditions of capital accumulation within a single, integrated, free market. As far as European political leaders were concerned, this agenda that was promoted by business would also consolidate the position of the European market in the world economy.

The views of supranational and domestic political actors were in part structured by the capitalist economic framework in which the EU political system functions. In order to develop an efficient market that is competitive in the world economy, policy input from economic actors – the major drivers of the economic system – was vital. A barrier-free market, as promoted by the SEA, would increase trade and investment both from within and from outside Europe. A completely liberalized market which would take the state out of the economy, as promoted by competition policies, would increase the market's international competitiveness and foster growth. And a single currency zone would consolidate a position for Europe in world currency markets, not to mention decrease transaction costs incurred when business was operating in the single market. The input of large farmers also ensured that their sector would be protected, while allowing for increased profits for large farmers: in comparison with small farmers, large farmer won out. Farmers in third world markets have also been forced out of business by the dumping of EU products on their markets. The development of all of these policies has therefore seen the direct participation of economic actors who wanted regulations and rules that would serve their own interest. This has gained the enthusiastic support of both supranational and domestic policy makers wanting to make Europe competitive economic vis-à-vis regional competitors in North America and Asia.

In contrast, capital actors have not played a significant role in the formulation of 2nd order policies. In fact, economic élites remained either indifferent or uncommitted during the development of what become 2nd order policies. For example, organized business has largely remained indifferent to the implementation of the CFSP, while they have also refrained from voicing too strong an opinion about issues such as immigration and asylum. In both of these issues, member states have expressed their desire to maintain their sovereignty and capital has not reacted against this. One may argue that this is because development of these policies is not directly related to increasing profits for business. Nor would development of 2nd order policies make Europe more competitive in the global economy. In fact, as social policy shows, development of some 2nd order policies might prove costly to business and have the end result of potentially decreasing trade and investment. For example, economic élites have little desire for fuller labour market re-regulation at the European level because it would increase costs to business and therefore not offer greater profits or opportunities for expansion.

Given this evidence, one may argue that the role of EU institutions such as the Council or Commission, while important, are not essential in explaining whether or not a policy will become of a 1st or 2nd order status. This does not mean that EU institutions are insignificant in the policy process. In fact, this book has shown that policy is initiated at the EU institutional level and in this respect the Commission has played a crucial role. It does mean, however, that irrespective of where policy formulation starts, "who" is involved in the negotiation process does matter. If certain actors are (or are not) involved in policy negotiations, this has implications for whether or not a policy will be deemed important. More particularly, the general rule is that the inclusion or exclusion of capital actors in the negotiation stage of a policy is fundamental in determining whether or not it will become a priority for Europe.

When there is unified capitalist interest in harmonization, this will be crucial in influencing the status of the policy: when economic élites are involved and fully committed to developing an initiative, it is more likely that it will become of a 1st order nature. Developing these 1st order policies, which are mostly economic in nature, will help foster a strong centralized EU that will make its mark against others in the world economy. Such conditions concomitantly allow business to work in optimal operating environments conducive to increasing accumulation. Furthermore, supranational officials will promote harmonization, while member state governments are rationally willing to cede a certain amount of power, in these areas because this will help strengthen the economic system within which the political system operates. Or, from a different vantage point, a strong economic system assures the survival and longevity of the political system wherein supranational and domestic political officials operate.

The indifference or absence of capital actors in policy negotiation means it is more likely that a 2nd order policy will develop. In addition, in these policy areas the issues are likely to be seen as impinging on territorial integrity and, hence, affecting a crucial part of traditional sovereignty. With regard to such policies, which are largely non-economic in nature, member states will retain sovereignty and the EU will remain decentralized. The diversity of the member states' positions in these areas will lead them to be characterized by non-harmonization and weak, non-mandatory recommendations.

Supranational governance or intergovernmentalism?
Not really – it's just a matter of class

What are the implications of these findings for the theoretical study of European integration? Given the significant role of capital actors in shaping a two-speed policy space in Europe, a theoretical argument that stems from this work is that students of EU politics are somewhat misguided in paying attention solely to EU-based theories in understanding EU policy making. This study has shown that EU-based theories such as supranational governance or intergovernmentalism, while remaining very useful, are of limited value in explaining the hierarchy of policies in Europe and the subsequent development of policy priorities. Rather, a plurality of theoretical perspectives is needed to understand EU integration and how EU public policy has evolved.

Certainly, the sixth column of Table 11.1 indicates that supranational governance is significant in explaining policy initiation in many areas. In this regard, the Commission played a key role when compared with other EU institutions such as the EP or ECJ in many cases. This suggests that supranational governance is important in explaining policy initiation. Column seven, in contrast, demonstrates that the Council rather than the Commission enjoyed a primary role during policy negotiation in several areas. This lends to the idea that intergovernmentalism is important in explaining some elements of policy negotiation. However, when columns two and three of Table 11.1 (which indicate whether or not a policy is 1st or 2nd order) are compared to columns six and seven (which show the theoretical perspective which best characterizes policy initiation and negotiation), one sees that there is a strong relationship between the DEC perspective and whether or not a policy is 1st or 2nd order.

The DEC perspective is the only theoretical school that helps characterize all 1st order policy negotiation processes, and at the same time the DEC element is always absent in the policy negotiation of 2nd order policies. This perspective is therefore of strong explanatory value in understanding why deeper integration has been achieved in some policy areas than in others. This emphasizes the importance of economic actors in driving European public policy in a direction that seeks to allow business the freedom to operate while consolidating Europe's place in the global economy. Corporate Europe has been given a privileged EU policy-making role in economic policy making, in a similar vein to that described by authors writing within the DEC perspective. Corporate actors have been allowed an almost exclusive position to negotiate alongside different EU institutional actors such as the Council and Commission when deciding the economic dimensions of Europe. This leads to a somewhat complex policy-making process that allows elements of the DEC to exist alongside those of the supranational governance and intergovernmental actors when policy is negotiated. Such a role for capital has allowed the development of public policies that promote the interests of business: a neoliberal, single-currency, highly competitive market in the global economy in which the state plays a limited role in economic development.

In contrast to the DEC perspective, pluralism and corporatism are of no value in characterizing 1st order policies. However, elements of both theories were found in 2nd order policies. In particular, pluralism was evident during the negotiation of immigration initiatives, while corporatism was manifest to some degree during social policy development. One may argue that labour and other social organizations were allowed representation in these 2nd order policy areas precisely because they were issues that were of limited importance in European political space. Because the EU would remain decentralized and weak in these policy areas, these groups were allowed to participate in the policy-making process. By appearing to be open and receptive to labour and social groups in these 2nd order policy areas, the EU institutional structure would appear to be pluralistically "open" to various interests. This perception would increase the EU's legitimacy in the eyes of many citizens. Yet, because these policies were of secondary importance, these social actors' participation was actually of limited impact. Furthermore, social groups were not allowed representation in the 1st order policies that really mattered: they were not represented in the formulation of the SEA, they were absent in MCR negotiations, they were not consulted during EMU negotiations, and they were largely sidelined in recent CAP reforms, including the Fischler ones of 2003. But one may argue that allowing social actors participation in policies such as the Social Charter and Reunification of third-country nationals was intended to appease such groups. Any potential discontent arising from not participating in the major EU deals would be quelled by allowing symbolic policy participation in issues of minor importance to the EU. From this perspective, if there are elements of pluralism and corporatism in the EU formulation process, this is simply a symbolic gesture to social groups, allowing them to participate in a process that will have no major consequence for the future of the EU in the global economy.

Understanding the present, changing the future

Returning to the reference made to Orwell's *Animal Farm* in the beginning, this book has demonstrated that all EU policies are equal, but some are more equal than others. The result is the emergence of a two-speed policy space that is pushed and pulled by a combination of 1st and 2nd order policies. The existence of this hierarchy can be understood in the light of the desires of supranational and domestic leaders to situate Europe in the world economy, while allowing economic actors an almost clean slate to create a "profitable" Europe within which they can thrive.

There is no doubt that this points to a democratic deficit in the EU. The issue is not just that elected officials in the European Parliament have little influence in the policy process while unelected Commissioners and Brussels' bureaucrats initiate and help determine the content of policies. In fact, analysis of the different policies here underlines how limited the EP's role is in EU policy making. The issue seems to be that the desires of unelected and unaccountable economic élites drive public policies that affect every European citizen's life. These actors are guided by their own self-interest. And they seek to influence policies in order to benefit themselves.

The consequences for those living in European political space are twofold. On the one hand, creating a Europe which is competitive in the global economy means that the social face of Europe is slowly being replaced with a neo-liberal smile. Deregulation, liberalization, and fiscal discipline brought about with 1st order policies are often associated with a weaker social safety net and more precarious workforce. In other words, a strong centralized EU that is economically competitive at the global level will result in the erosion of social security elements that form a rich part of the continent's historical tradition. On the other hand, granting corporate capital a privileged policy-making position – and keeping this fact generally out of the limelight – may result in an unaware, perhaps even apathetic, mass public. This public will know little about, and care even less about, policy. In that case, citizens will not be in a position to change politics. Time will tell whether or not Orwell will be proved correct.

Notes

1. A supranational or a decentralized EU?

1. The original six members of the European Community were Belgium, the Netherlands, Luxembourg, France, Italy and (West) Germany. In 1973 the UK, Ireland and Denmark joined. Later the "southern" expansion saw Greece (1981), Spain (1986) and Portugal (1986) join. In 1995 Austria, Sweden and Finland became members. And the most recent enlargement round in 2004 witnessed Estonia, the Czech Republic, Cyprus, Latvia, Lithuania, Hungary, Malta, Poland, Slovenia and Slovakia become part of the EU.
2. These texts include: H. Wallace, W. Wallace and M. A. Pollack, *Policy-Making in the EU*, 5th edition, Oxford: Oxford University Press, 2005, and J. Richardson (ed.), *European Union Power and Policy-Making*, London: Routledge, 2001.
3. J. Peterson, "Decision-Making in the EU: Towards a Framework for Analysis", *Journal of European Public Policy*, Vol. 2, No. 1 (1995).
4. As discussed by Peterson, "Decision-Making in the EU"; and S. George and I. Bache, *Politics in the EU*, Oxford: Oxford University Press, 2001.
5. As discussed by authors such as W. Sandholtz and A. Stone Sweet (eds.), *European Integration and Supranational Governance*, Oxford: Oxford University Press, 1998.
6. As discussed by those such as A. Moravcsik, "Negotiating the Single European Act: National Interests and Conventional Statecraft in the European Community", *International Organization*, Vol. 45, No. 1 (Winter 1991).
7. As discussed by R. Dahl, *Who Governs*, London: Yale University Press, 1961.
8. As discussed by those such as N. Hardiman, "From Conflict to Coordination: Economic Governance and Political Innovation in Ireland", *West European Politics*, Vol. 25, No. 4 (October 2002) and S. Royo, "A New Century of Corporatism? Corporatism in Spain and Portugal", *West European Politics* Vol. 25, No. 3 (July 2002).
9. These neo-Marxist scholars include, for example, R. Miliband, *The State in Capitalist Society*, London: Weidenfeld and Nicolson, 1969. As with all authors mentioned briefly here with regard to the theoretical perspectives, the full arguments of each will be presented in Chapter 3.
10. Wallace *et al*, *Policy-Making in the EU*.
11. J. Greenwood, *Interest Representation in the EU*, London: Palgrave, 2003.
12. S. Hix, *The Political System of the European Union*, 2nd edn, London: Palgrave, 2005.
13. B. Balanyá, A. Doherty, O. Hoedeman, A. Ma'anit and E. Wesselius, *Europe Inc. Regional and Global Restructuring and the Rise of Corporate Power*, London: Pluto, 2000.
14. This includes the European Currency Unit (ECU) and later the euro (which came into circulation in 1999.)

2. Who's coming to play? Policy-making actors in the EU

1. P. Heywood and V. Wright, "Executives, Bureaucracies and Decision Making", in M. Rhodes, P. Heywood and V. Wright (eds.), *Developments in West European Politics*, London: Macmillan, 1997, pp. 75–92. Also, R. Elgie, *Political Leadership in Liberal Democracies*, London: Macmillan, 1995.
2. R. S. Chari, "Spanish Socialists, Privatising the Right Way?" *West European Politics*, Vol. 21, No. 4 (October 1998).
3. See for example, T. J. Lowi and B. Ginsberg, *American Government: Freedom and Power*, New York: Norton, 1991, Chapters 3 and 4.
4. A. Stone Sweet, "Constitutional Courts and Parliamentary Democracy", *West European Politics*, Vol. 25, No. 1 (2002).
5. P. B. Evans, D. Rueshemeyer and T. Skocpol (eds.), *Bringing the State back in*, Cambridge: Cambridge University Press, 1985.

6. R. Dahl, *Who Governs*, London: Yale University Press, 1961; J. Greenwood, J. R. Grote and K. Ronit (eds.), *Organized Interests and the European Community*, London: Sage, 1992; J. Greenwood, *Interest Representation in the European Union*, London: Palgrave, 2003.

7. R. Miliband, *The State in Capitalist Society*, London: Weidenfeld & Nicolson, 1969.

8. For a detailed account of the EU's institutions see J. Peterson and M. Shackleton, *The Institutions of the European Union*, Oxford: Oxford University Press, 2002.

9. Helen Drake, "France on trial? The challenge of change and the French Presidency of the European Union, July–December 2000", *Modern and Contemporary France*, Vol. 9, No. 4 (Nov. 2001); A. Ortega, "A mitad de la presidencia Espanola", *Política Exterior*, No. 87 (May–June 2002); A. Macchi, "Il semester di presidenza belga dell' Unione Europa", *Civilta Cattolica*, No. 3639 (2 February, 2002); G. Edwards and G. Wiessala, "Conscientious resolve: the Portuguese Presidency of 2000", in G. Edwards and G. Wiessala (eds.), *The European Union: Annual Review of the EU 2000–2001*, Oxford: Blackwell, 2001, pp. 43–46.

10. A. Moravcsik, "Preferences and Power in the European Community: A Liberal Intergovernmentalist Approach" *Journal of Common Market Studies*, Vol. 31, No. 4 (December 1993).

11. T. Christiansen and S. Piattoni (eds.), *Informal Governance in the EU*, London: Edward Elgar, 2004.

12. The specific wording here is that the "European Council shall provide the Union with the necessary impetus for its development and shall define the general political guidelines thereof."

13. N. Nugent and S. Saurugger, "Organizational Structuring: The Case of the European Commission and its External Policy Responsibilities", *Journal of European Public Policy*, Vol. 9, No. 3 (June 2002).

14. Pascal Lamy, "L"administration exterieure de la Comission europeenne et les defies de la mondialisation", *Revue francaise d"administration publique*, No. 95 (July–Sept 2000).

15. R.S. Chari and F. Cavatorta, "Economic Actors' Political Activity on 'Overlap Issues': Privatisation and EU State Aid Control", *West European Politics*, Vol. 25, No. 4 (October 2002).

16. A. MacMullen, "Political Responsibility for the Administration of Europe: the Commission's Resignation March 1999", *Parliamentary Affairs*, Vol. 52, No. 4 (October 1999).

17. A. Stevens, "La Chute de la Commission Santer", *Revue francaise d"administration publique*, No. 95 (July–Sept 2000).

18. E. Vos, "Les Agences et la reforme de l"administration europeenne", *Revue francaise d"administration publique*, No. 95 (July–Sept. 2000); S. Tihonen "Continuita e cambiamento nell"amministrazione della commissione euopea", *Amministrare*, Vol. 31, No. 2 (August 2001).

19. L. Metcalf, "Reforming the (European) Commission: Will Organizational Efficiency Produce Effective Governance?", *Journal of Common Market Studies*, Vol. 38, No. 5 (December 2000).

20. M. Horeth, "Neither Breathtaking nor Path-Breaking: The Europe Commission's White Paper on Governance", *Journal of International Relations and Development*, Vol. 5, No. 1 (March 2002).

21. See for example S. Hix, *The Political System of the European Union*, 2nd edition, London: Palgrave, 2005, pp. 27–59.

22. According to Hix, Ibid., pp. 70–1.

23. As discussed by authors such as H. Wallace and W. Wallace, *Policy Making in the EU*, Oxford: Oxford University Press, 2000, pp. 3–38.

24. P. Pennings, "The Dimensionality of EU Policy Space: The European Elections of 1999", *European Union Politics*, Vol. 3, No. 1 (March 2002).

25. S. Hix, "Legislative Behavior and Party Competition in the European Parliament: An Application of Nominate to the EU", *Journal of Common Market Studies*, Vol. 39, No. 4 (November 2001).

26. M. Gallagher, "Electoral Systems and Voting Behaviour in 1997", in M. Rhodes, P. Heywood and V. Wright (eds.), *Developments in West European Politics*, London: Macmillan, 1997.

27. Hix argues that the EP's increasing powers under the Amsterdam Treaty can be explained by the idea that the EP was a "constitutional agenda setter" that allowed it to increase its power with regard to legislative reform (of "co-decision" procedure reform) and executive appointments as discussed below. See S. Hix, "Constitutional Agenda

Setting through Discretion in Rule Interpretations: Why the European Parliament Won at Amsterdam", *British Journal of Political Science*, Vol. 32, No. 2 (April 2002).

28. G. Wiessala, "European Union in a Changing World: Trompe l'oeil or Revolution? Reform of the European Commission on the Eve of 2000", *World Affairs*, Vol. 3, No. 4 (October–December 1999).
29. Taken from http://curia.eu.int/en/instit/presentationfr/cje.htm.
30. E. Bomberg, L. Cram and D. Martin, "The EU's Institutions", in E. Bomberg and A. Stubb (eds.), *The EU: How Does it work?* Oxford: Oxford University Press, 2003.
31. A. Stone Sweet, "Constitutional Courts and Parliamentary Democracy", *West European Politics*, Vol. 25, No. 1, (January 2002).
32. R. Dahl, *Who Governs*.
33. S. Mazey and J. Richardson (eds.), *Lobbying in the European Community*, Oxford: Oxford University Press, 1993; R. H. Pedlar and M. P. C. M. van Schendelen (eds.), *Lobbying the European Union: Companies, Trade Associations and Interest Groups*, Aldershot: Dartmouth, 1994.
34. R.H. Pedlar and M.P.C.M. Van Schendelen, *Lobbying the European Union*.
35. J. Greenwood, J. R. Grote and K. Ronit (eds.), *Organized Interests and the European Community*, London: Sage, 1992; Greenwood, *Interest Representation*.
36. R. Watson and M. Shackleton, "Organized Interests and Lobbying in the EU" in Bomberg and Stubb *The EU: How Does it work?* p. 89.
37. The literature also refers to regional and local groups. Such actors may have vested interests in lobbying the Commission, the Council, or the EP. A policy area of importance to such interests is seen with respect to structural funds (which are not studied in this book, as discussed in Chapter 1). The distribution of these funds, which are administered by the Commission in accordance with the needs of different "objective regions" in the Community with relatively low socio-economic status, has witnessed active lobbying by different regional governments who have acted against the desires of national administrations. In the creation of the Committee of the Regions, the Maastricht Treaty also institutionalized the role of regional and local governments in the regional policy process. Beyond their influence in regional policy, however, the literature has paid scant attention to the role of these lobby groups in the formulation of other public policies, which suggests that such actors are not particularly important interest groups in the formulation of public policy.
38. D. Coen, 1997, "The Evolution of the Large Firm as a Political Actor in the European Union", *Journal of European Public Policy*, Vol. 4 No. 1 (March 1997).
39. M. G. Cowles, "The Changing Architect of Big Business", in J. Greenwood and M. Aspinwall (eds.), *Collective Action in the European Union*, London: Routledge, 1998; M. G. Cowles, "The EU Committee of AmCham: The Powerful Voice of American Firms in Brussels", *Journal of European Public Policy*, Vol. 3, No. 3 (September 1996).
40. R. J. Bennett, "The Impact of European Economic Integration and Business Associations: The UK Case", *West European Politics*, Vol. 20, No. 3 (July 1997).
41. V. Schmidt, "Loosening the Ties that Bind: The Impact of European Integration on French Government and its Relationship to Business", *Journal of Common Market Studies*, Vol. 34, No. 2 (June 1996).
42. S. Hix, *The Political System of the European Union*, 1st edition, London: Macmillan, 1999, p. 206.
43. Coen, "The Evolution of the Large Firm".
44. D. Coen, "The European Business Interest and the Nation State: Large Firm Lobbying in the European Union and Member States", *Journal of Public Policy*, Vol. 18, No. 1 (January 1998), p. 85.
45. Ibid., p. 96.
46. Cowles, "The EU Committee of AmCham".
47. Ibid., pp. 352–4.
48. B. Balanyá, A Doherty, O Hoedeman, A. Ma'anit and E. Wesselius, *Europe Inc.: Regional and Global Restructuring and the Rise of Corporate Power*, London: Pluto, 2000, p. 19.
49. Ibid., p. 20.
50. B. Van Apeldoorn, *Transnational Capitalism and the Struggle over European Integration*, London: Routledge, 2002.
51. In the UK, for example, businesses found that "adapting to the lobbying opportunities of the EU came as second nature," due to the "long tradition of competing for government

attention" (Coen, "The European Business Interest", p. 97). Similar conclusions can be drawn from the work of Bennett who examines how direct lobbying in Brussels is a route taken by UK business as a result of integration (Bennett, "The Impact of European Economic Integration"). In contrast to the UK, in France, Germany and Italy "it took longer to recognize that national channels (where business previously enjoyed a privileged position) were diminishing in importance" (Coen, "The European Business Interest", pp. 97–8.) Yet, even in these latter countries, integration has loosened ties that previously bound: as Schmidt's work demonstrates, integration has rendered the French government incapable of unilaterally formulating policies, and French business now turns to Europe for policy making because of its increasing importance (Schmidt, "Loosening the ties that bind").

52. I. Bartle, "Transnational Interests in the European Union: Globalization and Changing Organization in Telecommunications and Electricity", *Journal of Common Market Studies*, Vol. 37, No. 3 (September 1999).
53. Hix, *The Political System of the European Union*, 1st edition, pp. 204–7.
54. Coen, "The Evolution of the Large Firm", p. 106; in J. Greenwood and M. Aspinwall (eds.), *Collective Action in the European Union*, London: Routledge, 1998, p. 23.
55. Hix, *The Political System of the EU*, p. 206.
56. G. Schneider and L. E. Cederman, "The Change of Tide in Political Cooperation", *International Organization*, Vol. 48, No. 4 (Autumn 1994).
57. J. Golub, "State Power and Institutional Influence in European Integration", *Journal of Common Market Studies*, Vol. 34, No. 3 (September 1996).
58. K. Alter, "The EU's Legal System and Domestic Policy", *International Organization*, Vol. 54, No. 3 (Summer 2000).
59. For a contrary view see I. Michalowitz, *EU Lobbying: Principles, Agents and Targets*, LIT: Verlan Munster, 2004.
60. W. Wessels, "The Growth and Differentiation of Multi-Level Networks", in H. Wallace and A. R. Young (eds.), *Participation and Policy-Making in the EU*, Oxford: Clarendon, 1997.
61. Greenwood, *Interest Representation in the EU*.
62. Coen, "The Evolution of the Large Firm", pp. 99–101.
63. www.etuc.org/r/5, accessed February 2006.
64. As taken from www.etuc.org.
65. Such as Hix, *The Political System of the EU*, 2nd edition, pp. 216–17.
66. G. Falkner, "European Works Councils and the Maastricht Social Agreement", *Journal of European Public Policy*, Vol. 3, No. 2 (June 1996).
67. R. S. Chari, "The EU 'Dimensions' in Economic Policy-Making at the Domestic Level: Some Lessons from Labour Market Reform In Spain", *South European Society and Politics*, Vol. 6. No. 1 (Summer 2001).
68. As taken from www.copa-cogeca.be/en/copa_objectives.asp.
69. L. Dobson and A. Weale, "Governance and Legitimacy", in Bomberg and Stubb, *The EU: How does it Work*? p. 164.
70. Taken from http://www.ecre.org/about/mission_statement.shtml.
71. Taken from www.ilga.info/About%20ILGA/A_overview.htm , page 1.
72. These reports include the Squarcialupi Report of 1984 and the Roth Report of 1994.
73. www.ilga.info/About%20ILGA/A_overview.htm, p. 3.
74. Taken from www.eeb.org/activities/general.htm.
75. A. Héretier, 1994, "Leaders and Laggards in European Policy-Making: Clean Air Policy Changes in Britain and Germany", in F. van Waarden and B.Unger (eds.), *Convergence or Diversity? Internationalization and International Policy Response*, Aldershot: Avebury, 1994.
76. R. Webster, 1998, "Environmental Collective Action", in Greenwood and Aspinwall, *Collective Action*.

3. Understanding EU policy making: major theories and new insights

1. R. Alford and R. Friedland, *Powers of Theory: Capitalism, the State and Democracy*, Cambridge: Cambridge University Press, 1985.
2. P. B. Evans, D. Rueshemeyer, and T. Skocpol (eds.), *Bring the State back in*, Cambridge: Cambridge University Press, 1985.

3. A. Moravcsik, "Negotiating the Single European Act: National Interests and Conventional Statecraft in the European Community", *International Organization*, Vol. 45, No. 1 (Winter 1991); and Moravcsik, "Preferences and Power in the European Community: A Liberal Intergovernmentalist Approach", *Journal of Common Market Studies*, Vol. 31, No. 4 (December 1993).

4. R. Dahl, *Who Governs*, London: Yale University Press, 1961.

5. P. Schmitter and G.Lembruch, *Trends Towards Corporatist Intermediation*, London: Sage 1979.

6. Evans *et al*, *Bring the State back in*; J. March and J. Olsen, *Rediscovering Institutions*, New York: Free Press, 1989.

7. J. Colomer, *Political Institutions: Democracy and Social Choice*, Oxford: Oxford University Press, 2003.

8. A. Stone Sweet, W. Sandholtz and N. Fligstein, *The Institutionalization of Europe*. Oxford: Oxford University Press, 2001, p. 6.

9. J. Peterson and M. Shackleton, *The Institutions of the European Union*, Oxford: Oxford University Press, 2002, p. 7.

10. P.A. Hall and R. C. R. Taylor, "Political Science and the Three New Institutionalisms", MPIFG Discussion Paper, 96/6 (June 1996).

11. S. Steinmo, *Structuring Politics: Historical Institutionalism in Comparative Analysis*, New York: Cambridge University Press, 1992; S. Bulmer, "Institutions and Policy Change in the European Communities", *Public Administration*, Vol. 72, No. 3 (1994).

12. N. Fligstein, *Markets, Politics and Globalization*, Uppsala: Uppsala University Press, 1997.

13. G. Tsebelis and G. Garrett, "Legislative Politics in the European Union", *European Union Politics*, Vol. 1, No. 1 (February 2000).

14. Hall and Taylor, "Political Science", pp. 937–42.

15. Fligstein, *The Institutionalization of Europe*.

16. Hall and Taylor, op cit., 946–50.

17. For example, institutions such as electoral formulae, determine payoffs and the efficiency or otherwise of certain strategies.

18. Hall and Taylor, "Political Science", pp. 942–6.

19. E. Haas, *The Uniting of Europe: Political, Economic and Social Forces*, Stanford: Stanford University Press, 1958.

20. J. G. Ruggie, *Multilateralism Matters: The Theory and Praxis of an Institutional Form*, New York: Columbia University Press, 1993, p. 259.

21. A. Stone Sweet and W. Sandholtz, *European Integration and Supranational Governance*, Oxford: Oxford University Press, 1998.

22. Ibid., p. 162.

23. As discussed by D. Puchala, "Institutionalism, Intergovernmentalism and European Integration", *Journal of Common Market Studies*, Vol. 37, No. 2 (June 1999).

24. K. Armstrong and S. Bulmer, *The Governance of the Single European Market*, Manchester: Manchester University Press, 1998, p. 255.

25. Stone Sweet *et al*, *The Institutionalization of Europe*, p. 7.

26. Armstrong and Bulmer, *Governance*, p. 255.

27. Puchala, "Institutionalism".

28. Stone Sweet *et al*, *Institutionalization*.

29. Moravcsik, "Negotiating the Single European Act", and A. Moravcsik, *The Choice for Europe: Social Purpose and State Power from Messina to Maastricht*, London: UCL Press, 1998.

30. Moravcsik, *The Choice for Europe*.

31. A. Verdun, "Why EMU Happened?", in P.M Crowley (ed.), *Before and Beyond EMU*, London: Routledge, 2002, p. 27.

32. Moravcsik, "Negotiating the Single European Act".

33. For a full overview of the works of Stanley Hoffmann, please see S. Hoffman, *European Sisyphus: Essays on Europe, 1964–1994*, Boulder: Westview, 1995.

34. Stone Sweet *et al*, *Institutionalization*, p. 14.

35. J. G. March and J. P. Olsen, *Rediscovering Institutions: The Organizational Basis of Politics*, New York: Free Press, 1996; Bulmer, "Institutions".

36. S. Hix, *The Political System of the EU*, 2nd edition, London: Palgrave, 2005.

37. J. Greenwood, J. R. Grote and K. Ronit (eds.), *Organized Interests and the European Community*, London: Sage, 1992.
38. G. Falkner, "European Works Councils and the Maastricht Social Agreement: Towards a New Policy Style?" *Journal of European Public Policy*, Vol. 3, No. 2 (June 1996).
39. A. Lijphart, *Democracies*, New Haven : Yale University Press, 1984.
40. Dahl, *Who Governs*.
41. P. Schmitter, "Still the Century of Corporatism", *Review of Politics*, Vol. 36, No. 1 (January 1974).
42. P. Dunleavy and B. O'Leary, *Theories of the State*, Chicago: Ivan R. Dee, 2001.
43. J. K. Galbraith, *American Capitalism: The Concept of Countervailing Power*, London: Hamilton, 1957.
44. P. Dunleavy and B. O'Leary, *Theories of the State*, p. 274.
45. C. Lindblom, *Politics and Markets*, New York: Basic Books, 1977.
46. P. Schmitter, "Interest Intermediation and Regime Governability in Contemporary Western Europe and North America", in S. Berger (ed.), *Organizing Interests in Western Europe: Pluralism, Corporatism and the Transformation of Politics*, Cambridge: Cambridge University Press, 1981, p. 295.
47. C. Crouch and A. Menon, "Organized Interests and the State", in M. Rhodes, P. Heywood and V. Wright (eds.), *Developments in West European Politics*, New York: St Martin's, 1997, p. 153.
48. Ibid.
49. Ibid.
50. F. W. Scharpf, *Crisis and Choice in European Social Democracy*, Ithaca, NY: Cornell University Press, 1991.
51. P. Diaz, *Towards a Civil Society*, Cambridge: Cambridge University Press, 1993.
52. N. Hardiman, "From Conflict to Coordination: Economic Governance and Political Innovation in Ireland", *West European Politics*, Vol. 25, No. 4 (Oct. 2002).
53. Ibid.
54. Ibid.
55. G. Taylor, "Labour Market Rigidities, Institutional Impediments and Managerial Constraints: Some Reflections on the Recent Experience of Macro-Political Bargaining in Ireland", *The Economic and Social Review*, Vol. 27, No. 3 (April 1996).
56. G. Taylor, "Hailing With an Invisible Hand: A "Cosy" Political Dispute Amid the Rise of Neo-Liberal Politics in Modern Ireland", *Government and Opposition*, Vol. 37, No. 4 (Autumn 2002).
57. P. Heywood, "Power Diffusion or Concentration? In Search of the Spanish Policy Process", *West European Politics*, Vol. 21, No. 4 (October 1998).
58. Hardimann, "From Conflict to Coordination".
59. H. Laswell, *Politics: Who Gets What When and How*, New York: Peter Smith, 1990 (1936) p. 13.
60. G. Mosca, *The Ruling Class*, New York: Greenwood, 1980.
61. R. Michels, *Political Parties: A Sociological Study of the Oligarchical Tendencies of Modern Democracy*, New Brunswick: Transaction Publishers, 1998.
62. J. Schumpeter, *Capitalism, Socialism and Democracy*, New York: Harper, 1950.
63. C. Wright Mills, *The Power Elite*, Oxford: Oxford University Press, 1956.
64. The discussion of the DEC perspective in this book has been heavily influenced by ideas raised by, and discussions with, one of the foremost contemporary political philosophers we have ever known, Dr. J. L. (Eddie) Hyland of Trinity College Dublin. We are grateful for his insights in developing this perspective. For those interested in seeing Eddie's classical interpretation of democratic theory, please see J. L. Hyland, *Democratic Theory: The Philosophical Foundations*, Manchester: Manchester University Press.
65. Marxism is also distinguishable from pluralism on several grounds. For example, unlike pluralists, Marxists would argue that access to the policy-making process is not equal for all potential private interests. Nor, Marxists would argue, can the idea that capital has a political advantage over other groups be seen simply as an anomaly that occurred over time because the pluralist system has become "deformed" or "corrupted", as argued by neo-pluralists. Marxists argue that capital will always have an irreversibly privileged position over other potential interest groups.
66. R. Miliband, *The State in Capitalist Society*, London: Weidenfeld and Nicolson, 1969.

67. N. Poulantzas, "The Capitalist State: A Reply to Miliband and Laclau." *New Left Review*, Vol. 95 (January 1976).
68. Miliband came to accept the validity of some of Poulantzas' criticisms. He agreed that political élites, whatever their own affiliation, were constrained in the policies they could realistically pursue by the fact that the political system was dependent on the adequate functioning of the economic system. Given that the economic system is capitalist by definition, this results in a high priority being afforded to capital interests. This is not necessarily incompatible with the direct attempt to shape policy by representative of capitalist interests.
69. Puchala, "Institutionalism".

4. Single market policy: creating a strong neo-liberal market in the global economy

1. Patricia Hewitt, UK Minister for Trade and Industry, as quoted in European Commission, *The Internal Market: 10 Years without Frontiers*, Luxembourg: Office for Official Publications of the European Communities, 2002, p. 1.
2. http://europa.eu.int/comm/dgs/internal_market/mission_en.htm.
3. S. George and I. Bache, *Politics in the European Union*, Oxford: Oxford University Press, 2001, p. 325.
4. Ibid., p. 326.
5. Ibid., p. 327.
6. For a discussion of EU developments throughout the 1970s, please see J. Gillingham, *European Integration 1950–2003*, Cambridge: Cambridge University Press, 2003, pp. 81–144.
7. As discussed in the next section, the 1992 Programme formed part of the Single European Act that was accepted in 1986.
8. George and Bache, *Politics*, p. 329.
9. For a thorough discussion of regulating public procurement please see K. Armstrong and S. Bulmer, *The Governance of the Single European Market*, Manchester: Manchester University Press, 1998, pp. 117–43.
10. It is important to note here that the single market programme does not discuss the "harmonization of EU social and welfare policies" per se. That is, there are clearly differences between the member states in the Community with regard to social and welfare benefits that are received, with some states having a large social security-net (e.g. Sweden and Finland), and others a relatively smaller one (e.g. the UK and Ireland). Dynamics with regard to development of a "EU Social policy" are discussed in more detail in Chapter 8.
11. The procedures not only extended qualified majority voting in the Council of Ministers on issues related to technical (not physical or fiscal) barriers, but also created the cooperation procedure for the EP.
12. M. Calingaert, "Creating a European Market", in L. Cram, D. Dinan, and N. Nugent (eds.), *Developments in the European Union*, Basingstoke and London: Macmillan, 1999, p. 157.
13. Guiseppe Gargani, Chairman of the EP Committee on Legal Affairs and the Internal Market, quoted in European Commission, *The Internal Market: 10 Years without Frontiers*, p. 1.
14. European Commission, *The Internal Market: 10 Years without Frontiers*, p. 10.
15. Intra-EU trade is calculated as the average of imports and exports within the EU-15. Ideally, the value of imports and exports within the EU would be equal. However, they will generally diverge year to year as they are measured using different data sources (Eurostat, for example, will use data based on a plethora of nationally based statistical office estimates). The components of the two measurements – imports and exports within the EU 15 – are thus adjusted here and an average of both is taken as an indicator of the total product of intra EU trade.
16. Data taken from The European Union Trade Policy – May 2005, (accessed on DG Trade website, June 17, 2005, page 5), available on http://europa.eu.int/comm/trade/gentools/downloads_en.htm. It is interesting to note that in terms of public opinion, 56 per cent of European citizens see benefits for industry as new markets are opened up in the world economy, as taken from http://europea.eu.int/comm/trade/issues/newround/pr171103_en.htm (accessed on May 7, 2005).
17. Many see the increase in exports from China as being a consequence of the low value of the yuan throughout the 1990s and the first five years of the 2000s. In late July 2005,

however, the Chinese government revalued the yuan. While some states (most particularly the United States) welcomed the revaluation because the weak yuan had been in part responsible for domestic industrial decline, some economists stated at the time that its revaluation would have a limited short-term (beneficial) effect on Western economies. Please see *El Pais*, 22 July, pp. 52–3.

18. All data on goods that are imported and exported presented in this paragraph are based on Eurostat data.

19. The index is calculated using the average value of imports and exports divided by GDP, multiplied by 100.

20. For more information, see: http://europa.eu.int/solvit/site/statistics/index_en.htm.

21. J. Anderson, "The State of the (European) Union : From Singular Events to General Theories", *World Politics*, Vol. 47, No. 3 (April 1995), p. 444.

22. This conceptualization of the debate in the literature is based on ideas raised by D. Cameron, "The 1992 Initiative: Causes and Consequences", in A.M Sbragia (ed.), *Euro-Politics: Institutions and Policy-making in the 'New' European Community*, Washington: The Brookings Institute, 1992, pp. 25–6.

23. W. Sandholtz and J. Zysman, "1992: Recasting the European Bargain", *World Politics*, Vol. 42, No. 1 (October 1989), p. 86.

24. A. Moravcsik, "Negotiating the Single European Act", in R. Keohane and S. Hoffman (eds.), *The New European Community: Decision making and Institutional Change*, Boulder: Westview, 1991, pp. 41–84.

25. K. Alter and S. Meunier, "Judicial Politics in the European Community: European Integration and the Pathbreaking Cassis de Dijon Decision", *Comparative Political Studies*, Vol. 26, No. 4 (January 1994), pp. 535–561.

26. Ibid., pp. 538–539.

27. Ibid., p. 539.

28. Ibid., p.535.

29. As described by Cameron, "The 1992 Initiative", p 51.

30. Alter and Meunier, "Judicial Politics", p. 542.

31. Ibid., p.555.

32. M. G. Cowles, "Setting the Agenda for a New Europe: The ERT and EC", *Journal of Common Market Studies*, Vol. 33, No. 4 (December 1995), p. 514.

33. Commission of the European Communities, *La consolidation du Marché Interieur*, COM (84) 1305, Document Interne OJ 739-30.5.1984.

34. Cowles, "Setting the agenda", p. 514.

35. J. Gillingham, *European Integration 1950–2003*, Cambridge: Cambridge University Press, 2003, pp. 157–8.

36. H. Schmitt von Sydow, "The basic strategies of the Commission's's White Paper", in R. Bieber *et al* (eds.), *1992: One European Market*, Baden-Baden: Nomos, 1988, pp. 79–106.

37. Cameron, "The 1992 Initiative", p. 36.

38. George and Bache, *Politics*, p. 330.

39. Cameron, "The 1992 Initiative", p. 37.

40. D. Allen, "European Union, the SEA and the 1992 Programme", in D. Swann (ed.), *The Single European Market and Beyond: A Study of the Wider Implications of the SEA*, London: Routledge, 1992, p. 33.

41. H. Wallace, "The British Presidency of the European Communitys Council of Ministers", *International Affairs*, Vol. 62 (1986), p. 590.

42. European Commission White Paper, *Completing the Internal Market*, Brussels: COM (85) 310 final.

43. Cowles, "Setting the Agenda".

44. Ibid., p. 503.

45. B. Balanyá *et al*, *Europe Inc. Regional and Global Restructuring and the Rise of Corporate Power*, London: Pluto, 2000, pp. 20–1. When the ERT was founded in 1983 it had close ties with Commissioner Davignon (Industry) and Commissioner Francois Xavier Ortoli (Finance). Interestingly, after both Commissioners left their posts, they took corporate jobs in the Belgian holding company Societe Generale de Belgique and the French oil company Total. As CEOs of these companies, they would later become ERT members themselves.

46. Cowles, "Setting the Agenda", p. 514.
47. This was done by way of the Cecchini Report (1988). This report represented an analysis of the benefits of the single integrated market as hypothesized by leading European economists.
48. This is similar to ideas raised by P. Bouwen, "Corporate Lobbying in the EU: The Logic of Access", *Journal of European Public Policy*, Vol. 9 No. 3 (June 2002).
49. The establishment of the ERT represented important new fora that sought to collectively represent capital interests at the EU. By organizing and presenting a unified vision of Europe, these organizations developed legitimacy in the public sphere and thus were considered "politically safe" policy partners by the EC institutions.
50. R. Rose, "Policy Networks in Globalisation: From Local to Cosmopolitan Networking", *NIRA Review*, Vol. 7, No. 1 (Winter 2000), p. 7.
51. As discussed in Chapter 2, several pieces have been influenced by this school of thought attempting to understand business's influence on EU policy making given the new centre of European governance.
52. At this time, the Council also agreed to set up an IGC to consider decision-making reforms to the Community.
53. Moravcsik, "Negotiating the Single European Act", pp. 45–8; and Moravcsik, *The Choice for Europe*, London: UCL Press, 1998.
54. Moravcsik, "Negotiating the Single European Act"; and Moravcsik, "Preferences and Power in the European Community: A Liberal Intergovernmentalist Approach", *Journal of Common Market Studies*, Vol. 31, No. 4 (December 1993).
55. Moravcsik, *The Choice for Europe*, pp. 316–17. This reflects how Moravcsik's position was somewhat modified in his later work, where it seems to indicate the importance of elements of supranational governance. It is also interesting to note that Hoffmann (1989), a leading intergovernmentalist of the 1960s, even talked about the importance of Jacque Delors in formulation of the 1992 Programme, showing that even the most hardened intergovernmentalists realized the limitation of their perspective in explaining single market reform.
56. R.S. Chari, "Spanish Socialists, Privatising the Right Way?" *West European Politics*, Vol. 21, No. 4 (October 1998).

5. Competition policy: ensuring a competitive European market

1. European Commission, *24th Report on Competition Policy*, Luxembourg: Office for Official Publications of the European Communities, 1994.
2. F. McGowan, "Competition Policy", in H. Wallace and W. Wallace, *Policy-Making in the EU*, 4th edition, Oxford: Oxford University Press, 2000, p. 131.
3. R. S. Chari and F. Cavatorta, "Economic Actors' Political Activity on 'Overlap Issues': Privatisation and EU State Aid Control", *West European Politics*, Vol. 25, No. 4 (October 2002).
4. T. Prosser and M. Moran, "Conclusions: From national Uniqueness to Supranational Constitution", in M. Moran and T. Prosser (eds.), *Privatisation and Regulatory Change in Europe*, Buckingham: Open University Press, 1994, p. 152.
5. M. P. Smith, "Autonomy by the Rules: The European Commission and the Development of State Aid Policy", *Journal of Common Market Studies*, Vol. 36, No. 1 (March 1998).
6. R. S. Chari, "Spanish Socialists, Privatising the Right Way?", in P. Heywood (ed.), Politics and Policy in Democratic Spain, London: Frank Cass Publishers, 1999, pp. 163–79.
7. Data based on figures presented by McGowan, "Competition Policy", p. 132 and data from Competition Policy Reports of the Commission.
8. R. S. Chari, *State Aids in the Airline Sector: A Comparative Analysis of Iberia and Aer Lingus*, Dublin: The Policy Institute, 2004.
9. European Commission, *Competition Policy in Europe and the Citizen*, Luxembourg: Office for Official Publications of the European Communities, 2000, p. 23.
10. R. S. Chari and F. Cavatorta, "Economic Actors' Political Activity on 'Overlap Issues': Privatisation and EU State Aid Control", West European Politics, Vol. 25, No. 4 (October 2002).
11. McGowan, "Competition Policy", p. 133.
12. Ibid.

13. Commission, *Competition Policy in Europe*, 2000, p. 26.
14. *Official Journal of the European Communities*, L 76 18/03/1997, pp. 19–29.
15. *Official Journal of the European Communities*, L 208 18/08/2000, pp. 36–46.
16. Commission, *Competition Policy in Europe*, p. 12.
17. Ibid., p. 16.
18. I. S. Forrester and C. Norall, *The Laicization of Community Law: Self-Help and the Rule of Reason: How Competition Law Is and Could Be Applied*, 21 Common Mkt. L. Rev. 11, 22 (1984).
19 Commission Decision of 24.03.2004 Case Comp/C-3/37.782 Microsoft. Accessed on http://europa.eu.int/comm/competition/antitrust/cases/decisions/37792/en.pdf.
20. Ibid., p. 12.
21. Ibid., p. 296.
22. Ibid., p. 296.
23. Ibid., pp. 296–7.
24. Report by Reuters entitled " Microsoft Won't appeal EU sanctions", January 24, 2004, http://money.cnn.com/2005/01/24/news/international/microsoft_eu.reut/
25. Commission, *Competition Policy in Europe*, p. 21.
26. W. K. Viscusi, J. M. Vernon and J. E. Harrington, Jr. *Economics of Regulation and Antitrust*, Cambridge: MIT Press, 1995, pp. 195–215.
27. European Commission, *XXVIIth Report on Competition Policy 1998*, Luxembourg: Office for Official Publications of the European Communities, 1999, p. 50. The first two criteria represent the original thresholds as set in Article 1.2 of the MCR in 1990. The last two were added in 1997 and expanded the MCR's jurisdiction to those transactions with a reasonably large turnover in at least three member states.
28. E. Shea and R.S. Chari, *Policy Formulation, Implementation and Feedback in EU Merger Control*, forthcoming working paper for the Institute for International Integration Studies, Trinity College Dublin.
29. Ibid.
30. T. Frazer, *Monopoly Competition and the Law: The Regulation of Business Activity in Britain, Europe and America*, London: Harvester Wheatsheaf, 1992.
31. E. Shea, *European Merger Control Policy: Private Interests, Policy Communities and Entrepreneurship*, Ph.D. Thesis, Trinity College Dublin, 2005.
32. Ibid., p. 57.
33. BAT and RJ Renolds v. Commission and Philp Morris Cases 143 and 156/84, 4 CMLR 24 (1987).
34. Shea, *EU Merger Control Regulation*, p. 58.
35. B. Eberlein, "To Regulate or not to Regulate Electricity: Explaining the German Sonderweg in the EU Context", *Journal of Network Industries*, Vol. 2 (2001).
36. G. Garrett and D. Mitchell, "Globalization, government spending and taxation in the OECD", *European Journal of Political Research*, Vol. 39, No. 2 (2001). The two main constraining effects are "(a) increasing competition in international goods and services markets and (b) the ability of the holders of capital to move money around the world in search of higher rates of return".
37. Shea and Chari, *Policy Formulation*, p. 9.
38. J. Peterson and E. Bomberg, *Decision-Making in the European Union*, London: Macmillan, 1999.
39. D. Coen, "The European Business Interest and the Nation State: Large Firm Lobbying in the European Union and Member States", *Journal of Public Policy*, Vol. 18, No. 1 (January 1998).
40. European Commission, *The Commission's Approach Towards Special Interest Groups: General Overview* (http://europa.eu.int/comm/secretariat_general.sgc/lobbies/approche/apercu_en.htm).
41. Shea and Chari, *Policy Formulation*, p. 9.
42. Other DGs that were involved in the negotiation process and which all supported the idea of merger control in order to create a truly single integrated market included Economic and Financial Affairs, Industry, Transport, and Internal Markets and Financial Services (see K. A. Armstrong and J. S. Bulmer, *The Governance of the Single European Market*, Manchester: St Martin's, 1999.
43. Shea, *EU Merger Control Regulation*, pp. 62–76.

44. Ibid., pp. 62–4. It should also be noted that the Council added what are referred to as the German and Dutch clauses to the MCR. In the former, the Commission can refer a merger back to national authorities, and in the latter two or more member states may refer a decision to the Commission, even if the merger falls below the thresholds.
45. European Roundtable of Industrialists (ERT), "Internal Memorandum on Merger Regulation", Brussels, 1988.
46. Article 2.1 states that:

> Concentrations within the scope of this Regulation shall be appraised in accordance with the following provisions with a view to establishing whether or not they are compatible with the common market. In making this appraisal, the Commission shall take into account: (a) the need to preserve and develop effective competition within the common market in view of, among other things, the structure of all the markets concerned and the actual or potential competition from undertakings located either within or without the Community;
> (b) the market position of the undertakings concerned and their economic and financial power, the opportunities available to suppliers and users, their access to supplies or markets, any legal or other barriers to entry, supply and demand trends for the relevant goods and services, the interests of the intermediate and ultimate consumers, and the development of technical and economic progress provided that it is to consumers' advantage and does not form an obstacle to competition.

One may argue that the "the development of technical and economic progress" may represent an exception to the "competition only" criteria. For a discussion on this see J. S. Venit, "The Evaluation of Concentrations Under Regulation 4064/89: the Nature of the Beast", presented at the Fordham Corporate Law Institute: International Mergers and Joint Ventures, New York, 1990, p. 523.

47. European Commission, DG IV, European Competition Policy and the Public, 2001.
48. M. Cini and L. McGowan, *Competition Policy in the EU*, London: Macmillan, 1998, p. 125.
49. Shea, *EU Merger Control Regulation*, p. 73.
50. Ibid., p. 76.
51. In the issues of the types of joint ventures to be considered under the MCR and the worldwide turnover threshold, both the Commission and capital had to compromise with the Council. In both instances these concessions were deemed necessary to convince the members of the Council (particularly the UK and Germany) to vote in the affirmative. Nevertheless, the 1997 amendments to the MCR effectively re-instated the thresholds sought by both capital and the Commission in the earlier draft.
52. Shea and Chari, *Policy Formulation*, p. 12.
53. European Commission, *XXVIIth Report on Competition Policy 1997*, Luxembourg: Office for Official Publications of the European Communities, 1998, p. 49.

6. **Economic and Monetary Union: the making of the money tree**

1. T. Padoa-Schioppa, "The Genesis of the EMU: a Retrospective View", *European University Institute-RSCAS Working Papers*, No. 96/40, 1996, p. 2.
2. Ibid., p. 3.
3. Ibid., p. 2.
4. P. De Grauwe, *The Economics of Monetary Integration*, Oxford: Oxford University Press, 1997.
5. Taken from http://europa.eu.int/scadplus/leg/en/lvb/l25014.htm.
6. R. S. Chari, "The EU 'Dimensions' in Economic Policy-Making at the Domestic Level: Some Lessons from Labour Market Reform In Spain", *South European Society and Politics*, Vol. 6, No. 1 (Summer 2001).
7. The *Economist*, October 14, 1995 and December 9, 1995.
8. This did not come without criticisms that some of the criteria were not met by all states, notably Italy. In other words, a "flexible interpretation" was taken on the criteria, especially those with respect to the deficit and debt. As agreed in the Maastricht Treaty, the deficit must have "declined substantially" and the debt "sufficiently diminished" towards the specific value.

9. 1997 was the year whose data is of significance: it was on the basis of this year's data that the Council decided (in 1998) which states would be eligible for EMU entry.
10. Chari, "The EU 'Dimensions'".
11. In 2003, the value was 5.78 and in 2004 the value was 6.90. Source: Eurostat.
12. For analysis of privatization of both loss-making and revenue generating public enterprises see R. S. Chari and F. Cavatorta, "Economic Actors' Political Activity on 'Overlap Issues': Privatisation and EU State Aid Control", *West European Politics*, Vol. 25, No. 4 (October 2002), and R. S. Chari, *State Aids in the Airline Sector: A Comparative Analysis of Iberia and Aer Lingus*, Dublin: The Policy Institute, 2004.
13. See note 8, this chapter.
14. Please see the report from the BBC at http://news.bbc.co.uk/2/hi/business/3211596.stm.
15. Ibid.
16. Ibid.
17. European Commission Directorate General for Economic and Financial Affairs, *European Economy: The EMU After 5 Years*, Special Report No. 1, 2004, p. 174. Please note that a PDF file of the 260 page report is available online at www.europa.eu.int/comm/economy_finance.
18. Ibid., 175.
19. HBOS Treasury Services is a 100 per cent subsidiary of the bank of Scotland, the fourth-largest banking group in the UK with assets of £400 billion.
20. Data gathered from ECB, *Review of the International Role of the Euro*, January 2005.
21. Ibid., pp. 179–80.
22. A. Verdun, "Why EMU Happened?", in P. M Crowley (ed.), *Before and Beyond EMU*, London: Routledge, 2002.
23. A. Verdun, "The Role of the Delors Committee in the Creation of EMU: An Epistemic Community?" *European University Institute RSC Working Paper*, No. 98/44, 1998.
24. Padoa-Schioppa, "The Genesis of the EMU".
25. K. Dyson, *Elusive Union: The Process of Economic and Monetary Union in Europe*, London: Longman, 1994; and K. Dyson and K. Featherstone, *The Road to Maastricht: Negotiating Economic and Monetary Union*, Oxford: Oxford University Press, 1999.
26. A. Moravcsik, *The Choice for Europe*, London, UCL Press, 1998.
27. Although Verdun looks exclusively at European integration theories (and not those such as the dominant economic class and corporatist perspective from the comparative politics literature), the idea that a plurality of perspectives are necessary in order to understand EMU formulation is also developed by her in a piece entitled, "Merging Neo-functionalism and Intergovernmentalism: Lessons from EMU", in A. Verdun (ed.), *The Euro: European Integration Theory and Economic and Monetary Union*, Oxford: Rowman and Littlefield, 2000.
28. Padoa-Shioppa, "The Genesis of the EMU", p. 1.
29. Ibid., pp. 1-2.
30. G. Ross, *Jacques Delors and European Integration*, Oxford: Oxford University Press, 1995.
31. Verdun, "The Role of the Delors Committee", p. 8.
32. D. R. Cameron, "Transnational relations and the development of European Economic and Monetary Union", in T. Risse-Kappen (ed.), *Bringing Transnational Relations Back In: Non-State Actors, Domestic Structures and International Institutions*, Cambridge: Cambridge University Press, 1995.
33. B. Connolly, *The Rotten Heart of Europe: The Dirty War for Europe's Money*, London: Faber and Faber, 1995, p. 78.
34. Verdun, "The Role of the Delors Commission", p. 8.
35. For the strength and importance of Pöhl in the Delors Committee, see Connolly, *The Rotten Heart of Europe*, p. 79.
36. Verdun, "The Role of the Delors Commission", p. 9. For comments on price stability and why it is good, see the ECB report of 2004, entitled *The Monetary Policy of the ECB*, 2004, p. 42, which is available on-line at the ECB's website at www.ecb.int.
37. For a critical evaluation on the role of the ECB, please see J. Forder, "The ECB and the Decline of European Democracy", in J. Ljungberg (ed.), *The Price of the Euro*, London: Palgrave, 2004.
38. On various aspects of the three stage process, see Connolly, *The Rotten Heart of Europe*, pp. 120–1; Verdun, "The Role of the Delors Commission", p. 10; *Financial Times*, April 18,

1989, p. 24; and S. George and I. Bache, *Politics in the European Union*, Oxford: Oxford University Press, 2001, p. 348.

39. Delors Report, *Report on Economic and Monetary Union in the European Community*, Luxembourg, Office for Official Publications of the European Communities, 1989.
40. Verdun, "The Role of the Delors Commission", p. 9.
41. Dyson and Featherstone, *The Road to Maastricht*, p. 691.
42. Clearly, a main issue for Thatcher was also transferring power to Brussels and the potential loss of sovereignty. When the Delors' report was tabled, she stated:

> we hoped that paragraphs would be inserted (in the Report) which would make it clear that EMU was in no way necessary for the completion of the Single Market and which would enlarge upon the full implications of EMU for the transfer of power and authority from national institutions to a central bureaucracy.
> (M. Thatcher, *The Downing Street Years*, London: Harper Collins, 1993, p. 708)

For a fuller discussion of the British position to the Delors' Report and views on EMU in general, please see Dyson and Featherstone, *The Road to Maastricht*, pp. 534–600, as well as A. Szász, *The Road to European Monetary Union*, London: Macmillan, 1999, pp. 120–9.
43. Dyson, *Elusive Union*, p. 308.
44. Dyson and Featherstone, *The Road to Maastricht*, p. 744.
45. Moravcsik, A. *The Choice for Europe: Social Purpose and State Power from Messina to Maastricht*, London: UCL Press, 1998.
46. Dyson, *Elusive Union*, 750.
47. Connolly, *The Rotten Heart of Europe*, p. 117.
48. On the nature of national negotiating teams: Dyson and Featherstone (*The Road to Maastricht*, p. 755) argue that "the EMU negotiating teams in different national capitals were broadly similar. They were comprised of finance ministry, foreign ministry, chancellery and central bank officials." They also note (on page 756) the importance of Ecofin (Council of Economic and Finance Ministers) in the negotiation process by stating that:

> ECOFIN acted to locate as many of the negotiations venues. ... One of the key informal rules guiding the EMU negotiations was that an agreement hammered out in these venues and ECOFIN was infinitely better than an agreement left to the European Council and the rest of the Council of Ministers structure.

49. Interestingly, reports indicate that even though the final decision with regard to whether Stage III would officially start in 1997 or 1999 was to be confirmed by the Heads of State in 1995, by early 1994 Mitterrand, Kohl and Gonzalez had concluded that 1999 would be a more realistic date. For further information on this see *El Pais*, May 31, 1994.
50. Dyson and Featherstone, *The Road to Maastricht*, p. 747.
51. Ibid., p. 738.
52. G. Garrett, "The Politics of Maastricht", *Economics and Politics*, Vol. 5, No. 2 (July 1993).
53. Dyson and Featherstone, *The Road to Maastricht*, p. 751.
54. Garrett, "The Politics of Maastricht", p. 105.
55. Dyson and Featherstone, *The Road to Maastricht*, p. 771.
56. Verdun, "Why EMU Happened?", p. 27.
57. B. Balanyá, A Doherty, O Hoedeman, A. Ma'anit and E. Wesselius, *Europe Inc.: Regional and Global Restructuring and the Rise of Corporate Power*, London: Pluto, 2000, p. 56.
58. B. Van Apeldoorn, *Transnational Capitalism and the Struggle over European Integration*, London: Routledge, 2002, p. 156.
59. B. Balanyá *et al*, *Europe Inc.*, p. 49.
60. Ibid., p. 50.
61. Ernst and Young Management Consultants (ed.), *A Strategy for the ECU, Report prepared for the Association for the Monetary Union of Europe*, London: Kogan Page, 1990.
62. B. Balanyá *et al*, *Europe Inc.*, p. 23.
63. European Roundtable of Industrialists (ERT), *Reshaping Europe*, Brussels, 1991. Although numbers and letters are added to this quote for the sake of clarity, the text itself is taken directly from page 46 of this report.

64. B. Balanyá *et al*, *Europe Inc.*, p. 23 and 51; see also A. Bieler, "European Integration and Eastern Enlargement: The Widening and Deepening of Neo-liberal Restructuring in Europe", *Queen's Papers on Europeanisation*, No. 8, 2003, pp. 6–7 for similar comments.

65. Also, B. Balanyá *et al*, *Europe Inc.*, p. 23, notes that before the introduction of the currency was confirmed at the Madrid Summit in December 1995, Keith Richardson of the ERT stated: "We wrote a formal letter to all heads of government saying: 'when you meet at the Madrid Summit, will you please decide once and for all that monetary union will start on the day agreed in Maastricht and with the criteria agreed at Maastricht.' We wrote to them, we asked them to do that. And they did. They put out an announcement in Madrid and said exactly that: 'we will do it.'"

   With regard to national business organizations, Verdun's data, based on interviews conducted in 1991 and repeated in 1992, highlight how business associations "emphasized the need for a single currency in Europe for economic efficiency and to strengthen the role of Europe and the European single currency in the world economy" (Verdun, "Why EMU Happened?", p. 21). Although Verdun falls short of fully demonstrating how such national business organizations directly participated in the process, she does contend that "national and European employers' associations ... have actively promoted the European objective at both the national and European level" (p. 27). She particularly notes that national employers' associations in France (Conseil National du Patronat Francais, CNPF) and Germany (Bundesverband der Deutschen Industrie, BDI) were very positive about the EMU, in a similar fashion to the Spanish Employers' Association, CEOE. She states, "the CNPF did publish joint statements with its German counterpart in support of EMU" (p. 22.) as seen in BDI–CNPF, *Gemeinsames Arbeitspapier zur Wirtschafts- und Wahrungsunion der Europaischen Gemeinsschaft*, Cologne and Paris, Oct 2, 1990.

7. The Common Agricultural Policy: redistributive policy in favour of whom?

1. E. Rieger, "Agriculture Policy Constrained Reforms", in W. Wallace, H. Wallace and M. Pollack (eds.), *Policy-Making in the European Union*, 5th edition, Oxford: Oxford University Press, 2005, p. 180.
2. Simon Hix, *The Political System of the EU*, 2nd edition, London: Palgrave, 2005, p. 282.
3. E. Rieger, "Agriculture Policy Constrained Reforms", p. 162.
4. Ibid., p. 170.
5. E. Rieger, "The Common Agricultural Policy: Politics Against Markets", in H. Wallace and W. Wallace (eds.), *Policy-Making in the European Union*, 4th edition, 2000, pp. 179–210, 187.
6. Rieger, "Agriculture Policy", p. 166.
7. Ibid., p. 180.
8. L. N. Lindberg and S. A. Scheingold, *Europe's Would-Be Polity: Patterns of Change in the European Community*, Englewood Cliffs: N.J.: Prentice-Hall, 1970, p. 41.
9. Rieger, "The Common Agricultural Policy", p. 184.
10. Rieger, "Agriculture Policy", p. 171.
11. E. Fouilleux, "The Common Agricultural Policy", in M. Cini (ed.), *European Union Politics*, Oxford: Oxford University Press, 2003, pp. 246–63, 255; W. D. Coleman and Stefan Tangermann, "The 1992 CAP Reform, the Uruguay Round and the Commission: Conceptualizing Linked Policy Games", *Journal of Common Market Studies*, Vol. 37, No. 3 (September 1999).
12. W. Moyer and T. Josling, *Agriculture Policy Reform: Politics and Process in the EU and US in the 1990s*, Aldershot: Ashgate, 2003, pp. 98–100.
13. Ibid., p. 98.
14. Ibid.
15. Fouilleux, "The Common Agricultural Policy", p. 254.
16. S. George and I. Bache, *Politics in the European Union*, Oxford: Oxford University Press, 2001, p. 316.
17. Moyer and Josling, *Agriculture Policy Reform*.
18. Fouilleux, "The Common Agricultural Policy", p. 251. Unsurprisingly, the literature has also noted that the EP has played a limited, although increasingly important, role within the CAP: although it has no control over CAP expenditure, it has been offered (non-binding) consultation in some areas. See Rieger, "The Common Agricultural Policy", p. 185.

19. Rieger, "The Common Agricultural Policy"; Fouilleux, "The Common Agricultural Policy".
20. Moyer and Josling, *Agriculture Policy Reform*, p. 101.
21. Ibid., p. 101.
22. W. Grant, *The Common Agricultural Policy*, London: Macmillan, 1997, pp. 167–8.
23. Ibid. In the following discussion of "large farmers", or agri-businesses, we define them as those farmers who have larger amounts of land than smaller and medium-sized farmers and can therefore minimize the costs of production and increase their profits, due to their relatively higher resource base.
24. Rieger, "Agriculture Policy", pp. 172–3.
25. Fouilleux, "The Common Agricultural Policy", p. 257.
26. W. Grant, "The Limits of Common Agricultural Policy Reform and the Option of Dena-tionalisation", *Journal of European Public Policy*, Vol. 2, No. 1 (1995); C. Daugbjerg, "Reforming the CAP: Policy Networks and Broader Institutional Structures", *Journal of Common Market Studies*, Vol. 37, No. 3 (September 1999); A. Kay, "Path Dependency and the CAP", *Journal of European Public Policy*, Vol. 10, No. 3 (June 2003).
27. COPA stands for "Confederation of Professional Agricultural Organization", COGECA for "General Committee of Agricultural Cooperation".
28. For a more detailed discussion please see Chapter 2.
29. W. Legg, (1993/4). "Direct Payments for Farmers?", *OECD Observer*, No. 185 (1993/4), pp. 26–8.
30. C. Daugbjerg, "Reforming the CAP", p. 419.
31. Ibid. p. 417.
32. A. Kay, "Towards a Theory of the Reform of the Common Agricultural Policy", *European Integration Online Papers*, Vol. 4, No. 9 (2000), p. 5.
33. O. W. Gray, *Pressure Groups and Their Influence on Agricultural Policy and its Reform in the European Community*, Ph.D. thesis, University of Bath, 1989, p. 222.
34. A. Kay, *The Reform of Common Agricultural Policy: The case of the MacSharry reforms*, Wallingford: CAB International, 1998.
35. Kay, "Path Dependency and the CAP", p. 410. See also M. J. Smith, *Pressure, Power and Society*, Chicago: University of Chicago Press, 1993, regarding policy communities and state institutions' autonomy.
36. Kay, "Towards a Theory", p. 9.
37. Kay, "Path Dependency and the CAP", p. 410.
38. Grant, "The Limits of Common Agricultural Policy Reform", p. 11.
39. Rieger, "Agriculture Policy Constrained Reforms", p. 162.
40. Rieger, "The Common Agricultural Policy", p. 189.
41. Daugbjerg, "Policy Feedback and Paradigm Shift in EU Agricultural Policy: The Effects of the MacSharry Reform on Future Reform", *Journal of European Public Policy*, Vol. 10, No. 3 (June 2003).
42. R. W. Ackrill, "CAP Reform 1999: A Crisis in the Making?" *Journal of Common Market Studies*, Vol. 38, No. 2 (June 2000), p. 346.
43. European Commission, Directorate-General for Agriculture, *The Agricultural Committees: Tools for the Common Agricultural Policy*, Luxembourg, 1999.
44. *Agra Focus*, March 1998, p. 1.
45. *Agra Focus*, November 1996.
46. *Agra Focus*, November 1996.
47. *Agra Focus*, August 1997.
48. *Agra Focus*, December 1997.
49. Rieger, "Agriculture Policy Constrained Reforms", p. 166.
50. Oxfam, "Spotlight on Subsidies", *Oxfam Briefing Paper*, No. 55 (2004), p. 1.
51. Ibid., p. 1.
52. Ibid., p. 1. Another way of phrasing this is "the more you have, the more you get", as Oxfam states on p. 11 of the same report.
53. Ibid., p. 8.
54. Ibid., p. 2. Oxfam note on page 3 that of the eight farms in Lincolnshire that received an average subsidy of £338,000 pounds, the owners include none other than: the Duke of Westminster (the UK's richest man), the Duke of Marlborough, Sire Adrian Swire (who

heads the group than own Cathay Pacific), and Lord de Ramsey (the former head of the UK Environmental Agency). It is also significant to note that developments in the cereals sector are also found in the sugar sector where large landholders have disproportionately gained more subsidies.

55. Ibid., p. 25.
56. Ibid., p. 25.
57. *Agra Focus*, November 1997, p. 4.
58. Fouilleux, "The Common Agricultural Policy", p. 256.
59. M. Brew, *Measuring the Economic Returns of Food Research and Development in Ireland*, M. Litt, Department of Economics, Trinity College Dublin 2004, Section 2.4.3.
60. European Commission, *Mid-term Review of the Common Agricultural Policy*, COM (2002) 394 final Brussels: European Commission.
61. In June 2002 Fischler presented the "mid-term review" which officially is not yet the reform package. The official reform plan was only presented in January 2003, but includes the points and reform plans put forward in the "mid-term review". As such we consider the June 2002 review to have been the start of the reform process.
62. Rieger, "Agriculture Policy", p. 178.
63. The *Economist*, "The Devil in the Details", June 26, 2003.
64. Future negotiations will be much more difficult as farmers account for 14 per cent of the workforce in new member states while in the EU-15 the proportion is many times smaller.
65. The *Economist*, "Cap It All: The European Union's farm Reforms Need to Go a Lot Further and Faster", June 26, 2003.
66. The *Economist*, "More Fudge Than Breakthrough", June 26, 2003.
67. Ibid.
68. Fouilleux, "The Common Agricultural Policy".
69. The *Economist*, "The Devil in the Details", June 26, 2003.
70. The *Economist*, "Cleansing the Augean Stables: Europe Must Not Put Off Reforming the Common Agricultural Policy", July 11, 2002.
71. *Food & Drink*, "Chirac Attacks CAP Reform", September 2, 2002.
72. The *Economist*, "Sowing Trouble", October 29, 2002.
73. RTE News, Walsh Rejects Fischler's Proposal on CAP Reform", January 27, 2003.
74. BBC News, "Europe Unveils Farm Reform Plans", January 23, 2003.
75. COPA and CODEGA'S first reaction to the Commission's legislative proposal for a mid-term reform of the CAP, April 11, 2003.
76. BBC News, "Europe Unveils Farm Reform Plans".
77. P. J. Epstein, "Beyond Policy Community: French Agriculture and the GATT", *Journal of European Public Policy*, Vol. 4, No. 3 (September 1997).

8. Social policy: demonstrating European incapability and differences

1. R. Gomà, "The Social Dimension of the European Union: A New Type of Welfare System?", *Journal of European Public Policy*, Vol. 3, No. 2 (June 1996); G. Falkner, "The EU's Social Dimension", in M. Cini (ed.), *European Union Politics*, Oxford: Oxford University Press, 2003, pp. 264–77.
2. C. Arnold, "The Politics Behind the Social Protocol of the Maastricht Treaty: Does the Maastricht Treaty Have a Strong Social Dimension?", Working Paper, Department of Political Science, University of Massachusetts, Amherst, 1999.
3. S. Hix, *The Political System of the European Union*, 2nd edition, London: Palgrave, 2005.
4. Arnold, "The Politics behind the Social Protocol", p. 8.
5. G. Falkner, *EU Social Policy in the 1990s: Towards a Corporatist Policy Community*, London, New York: Routledge, 1998.
6. J. Addison and S. Siebert, "The Social Charter of the European Community: Evolution and Controversies", *Industrial and Labor Relations Review*, Vol. 44, No. 4 (1991).
7. As S. Leibfried and P. Pierson put it, "economic action is embedded within dense networks of social and political institutions" (S. Leibfried and P. Pierson, "Social Policy: Left to the Judges and the Markets?", in H. Wallace and W. Wallace (eds.), *Policy Making in the European Union*, Oxford: Oxford University Press, 2000, p. 268).

8. V. Eichener, "Effective European Problem Solving: Lessons from the Regulation of Occupational Safety and Environmental Protection", *Journal of European Public Policy*, Vol. 4, No. 4 (December 1997).
9. G. Falkner, "How Intergovernmental are Intergovernmental Conferences? An Example from the Maastricht Treaty Reform", *Journal of European Public Policy*, Vol. 9, No. 1 (February 2002).
10. Later on the Commission turned the Social Charter into the "Social Action Programme".
11. EC Social Charter, points 7 and 8.
12. S. Hix, *The Political System of the EU*, 1st edition, London: Macmillan, 1999, p. 227.
13. P. Lange, "The Politics of the Social Dimension", in A. Sbragia (ed.), *EuroPolitics: Institutions and Policymaking in the 'New' European Community*, Washington D. C.: Brookings Institution, 1992, pp. 225–56.
14. The Social Protocol was annexed to the Maastricht treaty. Thus, the British were not affected by the social provisions.
15. Hix, *The Political System of the European Union*; Arnold, "The Politics behind the Social Protocol".
16. P. Lange, "Maastricht and the Social Protocol: Why Did They Do It?", *Politics and Society*, Vol. 21, No. 1 (March 1993).
17. G. Falkner, "Kontinuität und/oder Wandel? Zahlen und Fakten zur EU-Sozialpolitik", *Working Paper, Political Science Series*, No. 100, Vienna, Institute for Advanced Studies, 2004, p. 17 http://www.ihs.ac.at/index.php3?id=450.
18. Ibid., pp. 26–8.
19. Ibid., p. 38.
20. Ibid., p. 32–5.
21. As an example Falkner points out the recommendation for the reduction of working hours released in 1978, which however was not implemented in practice. Only the directive on working hours that was passed in 1994 was actually able to harmonize national laws on working hours. Ibid., p. 32–5.
22. Ibid., p. 39.
23. Eichener, "Effective European Problem Solving"; C. Joerges and J. Neyer, "Vom intergouvernementalen Verhandeln zur deliberativen Politik. Gründe und Chance für eine Konstitutionalisierung der europäischen Komitologie", *Politische Vierteljahresschrift*, Vol. 29, pp. 207–33 (1998).
24. L. Cram, "The European Commission as a Multi-Organization: Social Policy and IT Policy in the EU", *Journal of European Public Policy*, Vol. 1, No. 2 (Autumn 1994).
25. G. Ross, "Das 'Soziale Europa' des Jacques Delors: Verschachtelung als politische Strategie", in S. Leibfried and P. Pierson, *Standort Europa: Sozialpolitik zwischen Nationalstaat und Europäischer Integration*, Frankfurt a. Main: Suhrkamp, 1998, p. 341.
26. As Lange states, the Commission's Directorate dealing with the Social Charter were referred to by a business representative as "closet social democrats" (Lange, "The Politics of the Social Dimension", p. 254).
27. F. W. Scharpf, "Introduction: The Problem-Solving Capacity of Multi-Level Governance", *Journal of European Public Policy*, Vol. 4, No. 4 (December 1997).
28. G. Falkner, "EG-Sozialcharta: Feierlich erklärt ist nicht gewonnen", *Österreichische Zeitschrift für Politikwissenschaft*, Vol. 20, No. 1 (1991), p. 291.
29. Ross, "Das 'Soziale Europa' des Jacques Delors".
30. Member states rather envisaged a upwards spiral for poorer countries.
31. This might also be the reason why the policy area "security and health protection in the working environment" has nominally the most directives and the fewest non-binding measures (Falkner, "Kontinuität und/oder Wandel?"). Non-binding measures would not have "forced" nation states to adapt but rather would have left open the possibility of utilizing the lower standards to achieve an advantage in competition.
32. In 1987 the Belgian Presidency published a memorandum which contained the idea of a "social foundation" to be included in a Single Market Programme. Moreover, ECOSOC moved in its Beretta Report of 1987 to introduce a directive focussing on social rights (the Beretta Report was adopted against the votes of the employers" representatives). However, both actors had close contacts with the Commission, and thus their initiatives

NOTES

cannot be regarded as independent of the Commission's ideas (C. Wörgötter, "Enhancing EU Social Integration through social right politics: process matters", Paper presented at the 2nd Pan-European Conference on EU Politics, Bologna, June 24–6, 2004.).

33. Falkner, "EG-Sozialcharta".
34. Formally, the Commission had to present the draft.
35. C. Wörgötter, "Enhancing EU Social Integration".
36. The UK and Denmark opposed or ignored the Belgian Memorandum 1989 whereas the other member states were in favour of it.
37. And of course also national trade unions (Lange, "The Politics of the Social Dimension").
38. Except for reservations that were held regarding the new legal instrument of the Charter.
39. This attitude is believed to be also the reason for the UNICE approval of the social dialogue.
40. Hix, *The Political System of the European Union*, 2nd edition.
41. Falkner, "EG-Sozialcharta; Wörgötter, "Enhancing EU Social Integration".
42. Wörgötter, "Enhancing EU Social Integration".
43. Wörgötter, "Das Konventsmodell: Auflösung des Zielkonfliktes zwischen demokratischer Legitimität und Effizienz?", *Österreichische Zeitschrift für Politikwissenschaft*, Vol. 4 (2005). Falkner also argues that this is not surprising, as the other EC institutions did not support the basic rights declaration as initially hoped by the EP (Falkner, "EG-Sozialcharta", p. 290). Thus, as they could not even convince the EC level it is not surprising that they were not able to go further, and for example convince the diverse national levels.
44. F. Mitterrand, *Agence Europe*, December 10, 1989, Agence international pour la presse, News Bulletin on European Affairs (daily), Brussels/Luxembourg.
45. Hence, no legal action can be referred to the ECJ.
46. And even from this agreement the UK chose an opt-out.
47. Ross "Das "Soziale Europa" des Jacques Delors".
48. P. Teague and J. Grahl, *Industrial Relations and European Integration*. London: Lawrence & Wishart, 1991.
49. For example Falkner argues that the Social Charter had no impact due to the negative attitude of the British, who vetoed every initiative (Falkner, "How Intergovernmental are Intergovernmental Conferences?").
50. G. Falkner, "The Maastricht Social Protocol: Theory and Practice", *Sussex European Institute Working Papers*, No. 15, Sussex European Institute, 1995, p. 1.
51. O. Schulz, *Maastricht und die Grundlagen einer Europäischen Sozialpolitik*, Köln: Heymans, 1996. See also the argument put forward on the distortion of competition in cases where diverging social standards apply in the different member states in Scharpf, "Introduction: The Problem-Solving Capacity of Multi-Level Governance".
52. Lange, "Maastricht and the Social Protocol", p. 10.
53. This was made possible by the Belgian memorandum that claimed the invitation of social partners. Thus the Commission – hiding behind a national proposal – had the opportunity to frame the negotiation process on the basis of its own notions.
54. L. Cram, "Calling the Tune Without Paying the Piper? Social Policy Regulation: the Role of the Commission in European Union Social Policy", *Policy and Politics*, Vol. 21, No. 1 (March 1993); Cram, "The European Commission as a Multi-Organization"; L. Cram, *Policy-Making in the EU: Conceptual Lenses and the Integration Process*, London: Routledge, 1997.; G. Falkner,. "European Works Councils and the Maastricht Social Agreement: Towards a New Policy Style?" *Journal of European Public Policy*, Vol. 3, No. 2 (June 1996).
55. Schulz, *Maastricht und die Grundlagen*; B. Bercusson,. "Maastricht: A Fundamental Change in European Labour Law", *Industrial Relations Journal*, Vol. 23, No. 3 (Autumn 1992); S. George and I. Bache, *Politics in the European Union*, Oxford: Oxford University Press, 2001.
56. J. E. Dølvik, "ETUC and Europeanisation of trade unionism in the 1990s" *ARENA Report 1*, Oslo, 1997.
57. Falkner, "How Intergovernmental are Intergovernmental Conferences?", p. 100.
58. Arnold, "The Politics Behind the Social Protocol".
59. Not having the approval of the single member organization was putting the whole social partnership greatly at risk.
60. Arnold, "The Politics Behind the Social Protocol", p. 16.

61. Falkner, "How Intergovernmental are Intergovernmental Conferences?".
62. Lange, "The Politics of the Social Dimension", p. 249.
63. Ibid., p. 249.
64. For unanimous decisions see Article 3: social security and social protection of workers, financial contributions for promotion of employment and job creation, etc.
65. Gomà, "The social dimension of the European Union", p. 224.
66. Scharpf, "Introduction: The Problem-Solving Capacity of Multi-Level Governance".
67. Lange, "Maastricht and the Social Protocol".
68. Falkner, "How Intergovernmental are Intergovernmental Conferences?", p. 107; emphasis added.
69. Lange, "The Politics of the Social Dimension", p. 255.
70. Ibid., p. 255.
71. Within the Council only QMV is required, so not all positions have to be considered. It would be sufficient to satisfy a majority within the Council.
72. Adding the national position agreements might be far from the best outcome. The Commission was also quite aware that it might not be enough to include only the social partners at the European level, but that it had also to include the different national ones. Even though it was quite difficult to do that during the Social Protocol negotiations, in later directives the Commission often included requirements that foresaw that national social partners have to be heard and included.
73. Lange, op cit., "Maastricht and the Social Protocol", p. 13–14.
74. Ibid, p. 29.
75. The EU does not have a welfare bureaucracy as such, nor can it dispose of direct taxes or other contributions. Please see Leibfried and Pierson, op cit., 2000.
76. W. Streek, "Neo-Voluntarism: A New European Social Policy Regime?", *European Law Journal*, Vol. 1, No. 1 (1995).
77. Leibfried and Pierson, "Social Policy", p. 270.

9. Policies of freedom, security and justice: a limited role for the EU

1. As stated by the European Commission, the Directorate General for Justice, Freedom and Security has as its mandate to "ensure that the whole European Union is an area of freedom, security and justice." With this in mind, this book refers to such policies as "freedom, security and justice policies" even though the reader will notice that the actual DG in Brussels is of a slightly different name. Please see: http://europa.eu.int/comm/dgs/justice_home/index_en.htm.
2. This is related to ideas raised by A. Luedtke who has argued that although "the EU has gained some control over immigration policy ... [it] has faced strong opposition from reluctant national politicians." Please see A. Luedtke, "European Integration, Public Opinion and Immigration Policy", *European Union Politics*, Vol. 6, No. 1 (2005), p. 83.
3. As discussed by the European Commission at http://euopa.eu.int/comm/justice_home/fsj/immigration accessed in August 2005.
4. As stated on the Justice and Home Affairs website from which this data was taken, "the calculation of this rate is based on the difference between population change and natural increase, including corrections due to population censuses, register counts, etc. which cannot be classified as births, deaths or migrations. The calculations include all citizens (national and non nationals). The rates are not directly calculated from measured migration flows." For further information, please see: http://europa.eu.int/comm./justice_home/doc_centre/asylum/statistical/docs/mig_rates_en.pdf accessed in August 2005.
5. As discussed by authors such as W. Cornelius, P. Martin and J. Hillified (eds.) *Controlling Immigration: A Global Perspective*, Stanford: Stanford University Press, 1994.
6. C. Joppke, "European Immigration Policies at the Crossroads", in P. Heywood, E. Jones and M. Rhodes (eds.), *Developments in West European Politics*, London: Palgrave, 2002.
7. Council Directive 2003/86/EC of 22 September 2003 on the Right to Family Unification, found in the *Official Journal*, L251/13 October 3, 2003, Article 1.
8. Please see Council Directive 2003/109/EC of 25 November 2003 concerning the status of third-country nationals who are long term residents. *Official Journal*, L 16/44, 23.1.2004.

9. http://europa.eu.int/comm./justice_home/fsj/asylum/printer/fsj_asylum_intro_ en.htm. accessed in August 2005.

10. Source: Eurostat data found on Justice and Home Affairs website located at http://europa. eu.int/comm./justice_home/doc_centre/asylum/statistical/docs accessed August 2005.

11. DG Justice, Freedom and Security, EURODAC: The Fingerprint Data Base to Assist the Asylum Procedure, August 2004 (found on http://europa.eu.int/comm./justice_home) accessed in August 2005.

12. This is based on analysis of information found on: http://europa.eu.int/comm./ justice_home/doc_centre/citizenship ; accessed in August 2005.

13. This freedom of movement within the Community, however, is not necessarily guaranteed for citizens of the ten new accession states: the EU-15 can apply their own national regulations on admittance of those from the ten countries that joined in 2004. For more details, please see E. Jileva, "Visa and Free Movement of Labour: The Uneven Imposition of the EU Acquis on Accession States", *Journal of Ethnic and Migration Studies*, Vol. 28, No. 4 (2002).

14. For example, see the Irish Council for Civil Liberties, ICCL Briefing on Proposal for a Referendum on Citizenship (Dublin, May 2004).

15. The only case of an EU citizen being allowed to vote in another EU jurisdiction during national elections is in Ireland, where citizens with a UK passport are allowed to vote in Irish national elections. EU citizens from member states other than the UK, however, do not have this privilege.

16. Council Directive 2003/86/EC on the Right to Family Unification, Article 1. Within this paragraph, the Articles referred to are from taken from this Directive 2003/86/EC.

17. COM (1999), 638 Final, accessed in November 2005, which can be found on http:// europa.eu.int/eur-lex/lex/LexUriServ/site/en/com/1999/com1999_ 0638en01.pdf.

18. COM (1999), 638 Final, point 6.6, page 8.

19. COM (1999), 638 Final, point 7.2, page 9.

20. COM (1999), 638 Final, Article 1. Within this paragraph, the Articles referred to are taken from COM (1999), 638 Final.

21. COM (2000), 624 Final, which is an amended proposal of COM (1999) and which can be found on http://europa.eu.int/eur-lex/en/com/pdf/2000/en_500PC0624.pdf.

22. COM (2002) 225 Final, which can be found on http://europa.eu.int/eur-lex/en/com/pdf/2002/com2002_0225en01.pdf.

23. As discussed in COM (1999), 638 Final, Article 5.1.a.

24. Council Directive 2003/86/EC Article 4.1.

25. As discussed in COM (1999), 638 Final, Article 7.2.

26. Council Directive 2003/86/EC Article 5.3.

27. As discussed in COM (1999), 638 Final, Article 8.1.

28. Council Directive 2003/86/EC, Article 6.2.

29. As discussed in COM (1999), 638 Final, 9.1.c.

30. Council Directive 2003/86/EC Article 7.1.c.

31. As discussed in COM (1999), 638 Final, Article 11.1.

32. From Article 13.1, which appears in the final version of Council Directive 2003/86/EC.

33. As discussed in COM (1999), 638 Final, Article 12.1.

34. As seen in Article 14.2 of Council Directive 2003/86/EC.

35. As discussed in COM (1999), 638 Final, Article 14.1.

36. Council Directive 2003/86/EC, Article 16.1.a.

37. Council Directive 2003/86/EC, Article 16.1.c.

38. ECRE Information Note on the Council Directive 2003/86/EC of 22 September 2003 on the right to family reunification, found on www.ecre.org/statements/frdirective.shtml/; accessed in August 2005, p. 3.

39. ECRE Information Note on the Council Directive 2003/86/EC of 22 September 2003 on the right to family reunification, found on www.ecre.org/statements/frdirective.shtml/; accessed in August 2005, p. 7.

40. Conference of European Churches, *Position on the Amended EU Commission Proposal for a Council Directive on the Right to Family Reunification*, found on www.cec-kek.org/ English/ccmefamreu-print.htm accessed in August 2005, p. 4.

41. Ibid., p. 3.

42. ECRE Information Note on the Council Directive 2003/86/EC of September 22, 2003 on the right to family reunification, found on www.ecre.org/statements/frdirective.shtml/; accessed in August 2005. Nor was this additional condition found in the original Commission proposal, COM (1999), 638 Final Article 3.1.a.
43. Ibid.
44. Conference of European Churches, Position on the Amended EU Commission, p. 2.
45. ILGA-Europe, *Position Paper on the Amended Proposal for a Council Directive in the Right to Family Unification*, IE doc.4/2002, September 2002 found on www.ilga-europe.org.
46. Ibid.

10. External policies: divided we stand, united we fall

1. M. Smith, "The Framing of European Foreign and Security Policy: Towards a Post-modern Policy Framework?", *Journal of European Public Policy*, Vol. 10, No. 4 (August 2003), p. 599.
2. Ibid., p. 599.
3. D. Allen, R. Rummel and W. Wessels (eds), *European Political Cooperation*, London: Butterworth, 1982.
4. S. Hoffmann, "Obstinate or Obsolete? The Fate of the Nation State and the Case of Western Europe" *Daedalus*, Vol. 95, No. 3 (Summer 1966).
5. Smith, "The Framing of European Foreign and Security Policy", 2003, p. 561.
6. As found on DG External Relations webpage: http://europea.eu.int/comm./external_relations/cfsp/intro, accessed December 2005.
7. R. H. Ginsburg, "The EU's Common and Foreign and Security Policy: An Outsider's Retrospective on the First Year", *ECSA Newsletter*, Pittsburgh: European Community Studies Association, 1994, p. 13.
8. Smith, "The Framing of European Foreign and Security Policy", 2003.
9. N. Chomsky, *The New Military Humanism: Lessons from Kosovo*, London: Pluto, 1999.
10. Smith, "The Framing of European Foreign and Security Policy", p. 562.
11. Taken from http://europea.eu.int/comm/trade/gentools/faqs_en.htm (accessed May 5, 2005.)
12. S. George and Ian Bache, *Politics in the European Union*, Oxford: Oxford University Press, 2001, p. 393.
13. According to recent data, 58 per cent of all EU citizens are positive about the Commission negotiating trade agreements on behalf of the Council. http://europea.eu.int/comm/trade/issues/newround/pr171103_en.htm (accessed on May 7, 2005).
14. http://europea.eu.int/comm/trade/gentools/faqs_en.htm; see also Commission, *Making Globalization Work for Everyone: The EU and World Trade*, Luxembourg: Office for Official Publications of the European Communities, 2003, pp. 8–10.
15 The European Union Trade Policy, February 2005, found on DG Trade website, May 7, 2005, p. 39.
16. The European Union Trade Policy, February 2005, found on DG Trade website, May 7, 2005, p. 39.
17. European Commission, *The European Union, Latin America and the Caribbean: A Strategic Partnership*, Luxembourg: Office for Official Publications of the European Communities, 2004.
18. European Commission, *A New Approach in the Relations between the EU and ACP Countries*, Luxembourg: Office for Official Publications of the European Communities, 2002, pp. 3–4.
19. With this in mind, Manners has identified five core "norms" within the corpus of EU treaties, foreign policy declarations, policies and practices: peace, liberty, democracy, rule of law and human rights. Such core norms are said to underpin the EU's *acquis communautaire* and *acquis poltique*, which were most particularly seen during the accession process to the EU of the latest entrants from central and eastern Europe where the "Copenhagen Criteria" outlining economic, political and social criteria needed to be fulfilled (K. Gilland and R. Chari, "European Integration: Enlargement Now and Then", *Irish Studies in International Affairs*, Vol. 12, 2001).
   In addition, Manners posits four additional but more contested "minor norms" (social progress, anti-discrimination, sustainable development and good governance) as being significant inputs to the construction of EU foreign policy. These are not simply

declaratory positions but are considered to be the constitutive foundations of EU foreign policy. In this context, it is only natural that the EU is regarded as a leading actor when promoting and exporting democracy. Its own history is about the expansion of democracy through legitimate constitutional means, something that sets it apart from other international actors. According to such a view, it was inevitable that the EU would attempt to export democratic governance to other regions of the globe, and one of the early "targets" has been the Mediterranean basin. Through the Barcelona process, the EU sought to export its own model without posturing while achieving change through dialogue. As Hollis points out "the focus is on dialogue and the EU undertakes to assist with indigenously-generated reform programmes". Please see: I. Manners, "Normative Power Europe: A Contradiction in Terms", http://www.ukc.ac.uk/politics/englishschool/manners00.doc, 2001 (accessed February 2003), and R. Hollis, "Europe and the Middle East", in L. Fawcett (ed.), *International Relations of the Middle East*, Oxford: Oxford University Press, 2005, p. 321.

20. The countries include Morocco, Albania, Cyprus, Algeria, Egypt, Gibraltar, Croatia, Israel, Jordan, Lebanon, Libya, Malta, Macedonia, Slovenia, Syria, Tunisia, Serbia and Montenegro.

21. With regard to aid from the EU to Morocco, the evidence also demonstrates how this has increased since the start of the Barcelona process. Overall, "under the MEDA programme Morocco has so far received a total of €1,180.5 million in commitment appropriations: €656 million under MEDA I (1995–9) and €524.5 million under MEDA II (2000 – 2003)". In addition, the European Investment Bank loaned Morocco, "during the period 1995–2002, €1,220 million, intended among others for construction and upgrading of highways and rural roads, improvements to sewerage and water management systems, rehabilitation of the railway network and the development of the banking sector" (http://www.europa.eu.int/comm/europeaid/projects/med/bilateral/morocco_en.htm, accessed on March 27th 2005).

22. European Commission, *Euro-Med Partnership: Morocco. National Indicative programme 2005-2006*, June 2004, p. 1.

23. It is also interesting to note that the recent local elections have been marred by government interference in the process, whereby the Party for Development and Justice (an Islamic legal formation) was "told" to refrain from fielding too many candidates because the government did not want to see them win too many city councils.

24. "Le Maroc, de nouveau épinglé", *Le Journal Hebdomadaire*, March 5–11, 2005, p. 8.

25. To this end, Amnesty International has stated:

> the sharp rise in reported cases of torture or ill-treatment in the context of 'counter-terrorism' measures in Morocco/Western Sahara since 2002 has been well documented. Reports on the subject have been published in recent months by Amnesty International [itself] and other international human rights organizations, as well as by Moroccan human rights groups, including the Moroccan Human Rights Association (Association marocaine des droits humains, AMDH), and the Moroccan Human Rights Organization (Organization marocaine des droits humains, OMDH). Human rights lawyers and victim support groups such as the Forum for Truth and Justice (Forum pour la vérité et la justice, FVJ), have spoken out about the violations.
>
> (http://web.amnesty.org/library/Index/ENGMDE290042004?open&of=ENG-MAR, accessed March 29, 2005)

26. This idea is based on élite interviews carried out with former high-level Commission officials in Dublin in March 2005.

27. The ideas for the second explanation are taken from an interview with an EU senior official, Dublin, March 2005.

28. In philosophical terms, perhaps many would argue that an abuse of human rights is an abuse of human rights and the reaction to it should be the same irrespective of the scale of such abuses. When it comes to democracy, some scholars, such as Schlumberger, claim that ranking countries according to degrees of democracy weakens the very notion of democracy: a state is ultimately either a democracy or it is not. Please see O. Schlumberger, "The Arab Middle East and the Question of Democratization: Some Critical Remarks", *Democratization*, Vol. 7, No. 4, (2000), pp. 104–32.

29. See what can be considered the association's and Yassine's political manifesto at http://www.yassine.net//lettres/memorandum.htm. Accessed on July 22, 2003.
30. Z. Daoud, "L'Alternance à l'Epreuve des Faits", *Le Monde Diplomatque*, No. 541 (1999), p. 29.
31. Personal Interview with leading member of the European parliament, Brussels, June 2001.
32. R. S. Chari, "The March 2000 Spanish Election: A 'Critical Election'?" *West European Politics*, Vol. 23, No. 3 (July 2000).
33. Ideas were also raised in interview with Spanish Officials, June 2005.
34. H. Smith, *European Union Foreign Policy: What It Is and What It Does*, London: Pluto, 2003.
35. T.Y. Ismael and J. S. Ismael, *The Iraq Predicament: People in the Quagmire of Politics*, London: Pluto, 2004.
36. J. J. Terry, *US Foreign Policy in the Middle East: The Role of Lobbies and Special Interest Groups*, London: Pluto, 2005.
37. A. Dorfman, *Exorcising Terror: The Incredible Unending Trial of General Augusto Pinochet*, London: Pluto, 2003.
38. For a discussion on America's illegal actions on the world stage, see M. Mandel, *How America Gets Away With Murder: Illegal Wars, Collateral Damage and Crimes Against Humanity*, London: Pluto, 2004.
39. T. Y. Ismael and W. Haddad, *Iraq: The Human Cost of History*, London: Pluto, 2003.
40. A. Anrove (ed.), *Iraq Under Siege: The Deadly Impact of Sanctions and War*, London: Pluto, 2003.
41. S. Kritzinger, "Public Opinion in the Iraq Crisis: Explaining Developments in the UK, France, Italy and Germany", *European Political Science*, Vol. 3, No. 1 (Autumn 2003).
42. SWG survey, February 2003.
43. BBC survey, February 13, 2003.
44. S. Kritzinger, "Public Opinion in the Iraq Crisis".
45. For a discussion of the "conservativism" that guides Blair's Labour Party, please see T. Honderich, *Conservativism: Burke, Nozick, Bush and Blair*, London: Pluto, 2005.
46. R. S. Chari, "The 2004 Spanish Election: Terrorism as a Catalyst for Change?" *West European Politics*, Vol. 27, No. 5 (November 2004).
47. Channel 4 poll, February 22, 2003.
48. BBC-online, "Polls Find Europeans Oppose Iraq War", February 11, 2003.
49. R. S. Chari and F. Cavatorta, "The Iraq War: Killing Dreams of a Unified EU?" *European Political Science*, Vol. 3, No. 1 (Autumn 2003).
50. C. Hill, "The Capability–Expectation Gap, or Conceptualising Europe's International Role", *Journal of Common Market Studies*, Vol. 31, No. 3 (1993).
51. S. Hoffmann, "Towards a Common European Foreign and Security Policy", *Journal of Common Market Studies*, Vol. 38, No. 2 (June 2000).
52. Chari and Cavatorta, "The Iraq War", pp. 25–26.
53. P. Heywood, "Desperately Seeking Influence: Spain and the War in Iraq", *European Political Science*, Vol. 3, No. 1 (Autumn 2003).
54. S. B. Hobolt and R. Klemmensen, "Follow the leader? Divergent positions on Iraq in Denmark and Ireland", *European Political Science*, Vol. 3, No. 1 (Autumn 2003).
55. Speech to the European Parliament delivered in Strasbourg, March 12, 2003.
56. Chari and Cavatorta, "The Iraq War", p. 27.

11. Conclusions: understanding the present, changing the future

1. It was also argued that even those states which did not eventually join the EMU – such as the UK and Sweden – also witnessed declining inflation and interest rates as well as deficits and debts. We argued that this reflected these states potential intentions to prime their economies for EMU entry one day.
2. As discussed in Chapter 10, no formal policy position was adopted by the EU towards the Iraq crisis. As such, the chapter does not explain the formulation of a policy per se. Rather, it is intended to explain why the EU was unable to speak with a united voice during one of the most serious international crises of the decade. It was felt that better understanding of this dynamic helps illustrate which actors are important when decisions are made in the issue area.

Bibliography

Ackrill, R. W. "CAP Reform 1999: A Crisis in the Making?" *Journal of Common Market Studies*, Vol. 38, No. 2 (June 2000).

Addison, J. and S. Siebert, "The Social Charter of the European Community: Evolution and Controversies", *Industrial and Labor Relations Review*, Vol. 44, No. 4, 1991.

Alford R. and R. Friedland, *Powers of Theory: Capitalism, the State and Democracy*, Cambridge: Cambridge University Press, 1985.

Allen, D. "European Union, the SEA and the 1992 Programme", in D. Swann (ed.), *The Single European Market and Beyond: A Study of the Wider Implications of the SEA*, London: Routledge, 1992.

Allen, D., R. Rummel and W. Wessels (eds), *European Political Cooperation*, London: Butterworth, 1982.

Alter K. and S. Meunier, "Judicial Politics in the European Community: European Integration and the Pathbreaking Cassis de Dijon Decision", *Comparative Political Studies*, Vol. 26, No. 4 (January 1994).

Alter, K. "The EU's Legal System and Domestic Policy", *International Organisation*, Vol. 54, No. 3 (Summer 2000).

Anderson, J. "The State of the (European) Union : From Singular Events to General Theories", *World Politics*, Vol. 47, No. 3 (April 1995).

Anrove, A. (ed.), *Iraq Under Siege: The Deadly Impact of sanctions and war*, London: Pluto, 2003.

Armstrong K. A. and J. S. Bulmer, *The Governance of the Single European Market*, Manchester: St. Martin's Press, 1999.

Arnold, C. "The Politics behind the Social Protocol of the Maastricht Treaty: Does the Maastricht Treaty Have a Strong Social Dimension?" Working Paper, Department of Political Science. University of Massachusetts, Amherst, 1999.

Balanyá, B., A. Doherty, O. Hoedeman, A. Ma'anit and E. Wesselius, *Europe Inc: Regional and Global Restructuring and the Rise of Corporate Power*, London: Pluto Press, 2000.

Bartle, I. "Transnational Interests in the European Union: Globalization and Changing Organization in Telecommunications and Electricity", *Journal of Common Market Studies*, Vol. 37, No. 3 (September 1999).

Bennett, R. J. "The Impact of European Economic Integration and Business Associations: The UK Case", *West European Politics*, Vol. 20, No. 3 (July 1997).

Bercusson, B. "Maastricht: a fundamental change in European labour law", *Industrial Relations Journal*, Vol. 23, No. 3 (Autumn 1992).

Berger, S. (ed.), *Organizing Interests in Western Europe: Pluralism, Corporatism and the Transformation of Politics*, Cambridge: Cambridge University Press, 1981.

Bomberg E. and A. Stubb (eds), *The EU: How Does it work?* Oxford: Oxford University Press, 2003.

Bomberg, E., L. Cram and D. Martin, "The EU's Institutions", in E. Bomberg and A. Stubb (eds), *The EU: How Does it work?* Oxford: Oxford University Press, 2003.

Bouwen, P. "Corporate lobbying in the EU: the logic of access", *Journal of European Public Policy*, Vol. 9, No. 3 (June 2002).

Bulmer, S. "Institutions and Policy Change in the European Communities", *Public Administration*, Vol. 72, No. 3 (1994).

Calingaert, M. "Creating a European Market", in L. Cram, D. Dinan, and N. Nugent (eds), *Developments in the European Union*, Basingstoke and London: Macmillan, 1999

Cameron, D. "The 1992 Initiative: Causes and Consequences", in A. M Sbragia (ed.), *Euro-Politics: Institutions and Policy-making in the "New" European Community*, Washington: The Brookings Institute, 1992.

Cameron, D. R. "Transnational relations and the development of European Economic and Monetary Union", in T. Risse-Kappen (ed.), *Bringing Transnational Relations Back In: Non-State Actors, Domestic Structures and International Institutions*, Cambridge: Cambridge University Press, 1995.

Chari, R. S. "Spanish Socialists, Privatising the Right Way?", *West European Politics*, Vol 21, No.4 (October 1998).

Chari, R. S. "The March 2000 Spanish Election: A 'Critical Election'?" *West European Politics*, Vol. 23, No. 3, (July 2000).

Chari, R. S. "The EU 'Dimensions' in Economic Policy-Making at the Domestic Level: Some Lessons from Labour Market Reform In Spain", *South European Society and Politics*, Vol. 6. No.1 (Summer 2001).

Chari, R. S. *State Aids in the Airline Sector: A Comparative Analysis of Iberia and Aer Lingus*, Dublin: The Policy Institute, 2004.

Chari, R. S. "The 2004 Spanish Election: Terrorism as a Catalyst for Change?" *West European Politics*, Vol. 27, No. 5 (November 2004).

Chari, R. S. and F. Cavatorta, "Economic Actors' Political Activity on 'Overlap Issues': Privatisation and EU State Aid Control", *West European Politics*, Vol. 25, No.4 (October 2002).

Chari, R. S. and F. Cavatorta, "The Iraq War: Killing Dreams of a Unified EU?" *European Political Science*, Vol. 3, No. 1 (Fall 2003).

Chomsky, N., *The New Military Humanism: Lessons from Kosovo*, London: Pluto, 1999.

Christiansen T. and S. Piattoni (eds), *Informal Governance in the EU*, London: Edward Elgar, 2004.

Cini, M. (ed.), *European Union Politics*, Oxford: Oxford University Press, 2003.

Cini, M.and L.McGowan, *Competition Policy in the EU*, London: Macmillan, 1998.

Coen, D. "The European Business Interest and the Nation State: Large Firm Lobbying in the European Union and Member States", *Journal of Public Policy*, Vol. 18, Part 1 (January 1998).

Coen, D. 1997, "The Evolution of the Large Firm as a Political Actor in the European Union", *Journal of European Public Policy*, Vol. 4 No. 1 (March 1997).

Coleman, W. D. and Stefan Tangermann, "The 1992 CAP Reform, the Uruguay Round and the Commission: Conceptualizing Linked Policy Games", *Journal of Common Market Studies*, Vol. 37, No. 3 (September 1999).

Colomer, J. *Political Institutions: Democracy and Social Choice*, Oxford: Oxford University Press, 2003.

Connolly, B. *The Rotten Heart of Europe: The Dirty War for Europe's Money*, London: Faber and Faber, 1995.

Cornelius, W., P. Martin and J. Hillified (eds), *Controlling Immigration: A Global Perspective*, Stanford: Stanford University Press, 1994.

Cowles, M. G. "Setting the agenda for a new Europe: the ERT and EC", *Journal of Common Market Studies*, Vol. 33, No. 4 (December 1995).

Cowles, M. G. "The Changing Architect of Big Business", in J. Greenwood and M. Aspinwall (eds), *Collective Action in the European Union*, London: Routledge, 1998.

Cowles, M. G. "The EU Committee of AmCham: the powerful voice of American Firms in Brussels", *Journal of European Public Policy*. Vol. 3, No 3 (September 1996).

Cram, L. "Calling the Tune Without Paying the Piper? Social Policy Regulation: the Role of the Commission in European Union Social Policy", *Policy and Politics* Vol. 21, No. 1 (March 1993).

Cram, L. "The European Commission as a Multi-Organization: Social Policy and IT Policy in the EU", *Journal of European Public Policy*, Vol. 1, No. 2 (Autumn 1994).

Cram, L. *Policy-Making in the EU: Conceptual Lenses and the Integration Process*, London: Routledge, 1997.

Crouch, C. and A. Menon, "Organized Interests and the State", in M. Rhodes, P. Heywood and V. Wright (eds), *Developments in West European Politics*, New York: St. Martin's Press, 1997.

Crowley, P.M. (ed.), *Before and Beyond EMU*, London: Routledge, 2002.

Dahl, R. *Who Governs*, London: Yale University Press, 1961.

Daoud, Z. "L'Alternance à l'Epreuve des Faits", *Le Monde Diplomatque*, No. 541 (1999).

Daugbjerg, C. "Policy Feedback and Paradigm Shift in EU Agricultural Policy: The Effects of the MacSharry Reform on Future Reform", *Journal of European Public Policy*, Vol. 10, No. 3 (June 2003).

Daugbjerg, C. "Reforming the CAP: Policy Networks and Broader Institutional Structures", *Journal of Common Market Studies*, Vol. 37, No. 3 (September 1999).

De Grauwe, P. *The Economics of Monetary Integration*, Oxford: Oxford University Press, 1997.

Diaz, P. *Towards a Civil Society*, Cambridge: Cambridge University Press, 1993.

Dobson L. and A. Weale, "Governance and Legitimacy", in E. Bomberg and A. Stubb (eds), *The EU: How Does it work?* Oxford: Oxford University Press, 2003.

Dorfman, A. *Exorcising Terror: The Incredible Unending Trial of General Augusto Pinochet*, London: Pluto, 2003.

Drake, H. "France on trial? The challenge of change and the French Presidency of the European Union, July-December 2000", *Modern and Contemporary France*, Vol. 9, No. 4 (Nov. 2001)

Dunleavy, P. and B. O'Leary, *Theories of the State*, Chicago: Ivan R. Dee, 2001.

Dyson, K. and K. Featherstone, *The Road to Maastricht: Negotiating Economic and Monetary Union*, Oxford: Oxford University Press, 1999.

Dyson, K. *Elusive Union: The Process of Economic and Monetary Union in Europe*, London: Longman, 1994.

Eberlein, B. "To Regulate or Not to Regulate Electricity: Explaining the German Sonderweg in the EU Context", *Journal of Network Industries*, Vol. 2 (2001).

Edwards G., and G. Wiessala (eds), *The European Union: Annual Review of the EU 2000–2001*, Oxford: Blackwell, 2001.

Edwards G., and G. Wiessala, "Conscientious Resolve: The Portuguese Presidency of 2000", in G. Edwards and G. Wiessala (eds), *The European Union: Annual Review of the EU 2000–2001*, Oxford: Blackwell, 2001.

Eichener, V. "Effective European Problem Solving: Lessons from the Regulation of Occupational Safety and Environmental Protection", *Journal of European Public Policy*, Vol. 4, No. 4 (December 1997).

Elgie, R., *Political Leadership in Liberal Democracies*, London: Macmillan, 1995.

Epstein, P. J. "Beyond Policy Community: French Agriculture and the GATT", *Journal of European Public Policy*, Vol. 4, No. 3 (September 1997).

European Commission Directorate General for Economic and Financial Affairs, *European Economy: The EMU After Five Years*, Special Report No. 1, 2004.

European Commission White Paper, *Completing the Internal Market*, Brussels: COM (85) 310 final.

European Commission, *24th Report on Competition Policy*, Luxembourg: Office for Official Publications of the European Communities, 1994.

European Commission, *Amended proposal for a Council Directive on the Right to Family Reunification*, COM (2000), 624 Final, which can be found on http://europa.eu.int/eur-lex/en/com/pdf/2000/en_500PC0624.pdf

European Commission, *Competition Policy in Europe and the Citizen*, Luxembourg: Office for Official Publications of the European Communities, 2000.

European Commission, DG IV, *European Competition Policy and the Public*, 2001.

European Commission, Directorate-General for Agriculture, *The Agricultural Committees, Tools for the Common Agricultural Policy*, Luxembourg, 1999.

European Commission, *La consolidation du Marché Interieur*, COM (84) 1305, Document Interne OJ 739-30.5.1984.

European Commission, *Mid-term Review of the Common Agricultural Policy*, COM (2002) 394 final. Brussels: European Commission.

European Commission, *Proposal for a Council Directive on the Right to Family Reunification*, COM (1999), 638 Final, accessed in November 2005 and which can be found on http://europa.eu.int/eur-lex/lex/LexUriServ/site/en/com/1999/com1999_0638en01.pdf.

European Commission, *The Commission's Approach Towards Special Interest Groups: General Overview* (http://europa.eu.int/comm/secretariat_general.sgc/lobbies/approche/apercu_en.htm).

European Commission, *The Internal Market: Ten Years without Frontiers*, Luxembourg: Office for Official Publications of the European Communities, 2002.

European Commission, *XXVIIIth Report on Competition Policy 1998*, Luxembourg: Office for Official Publications of the European Communities, 1999.

European Commission, *XXVIIth Report on Competition Policy 1997*, Luxembourg: Office for Official Publications of the European Communities, 1998.

Evans, P. B., D. Rueshemeyer, and T. Skocpol (eds), *Bring the State Back In*, Cambridge: Cambridge University Press, 1985.

Falkner, G. "European Works Councils and the Maastricht Social Agreement: Towards a New Policy Style?", *Journal of European Public Policy*, Vol. 3, No. 2 (June 1996).

Falkner, G. "EG-Sozialcharta: Feierlich erklärt ist nicht gewonnen", *Österreichische Zeitschrift für Politikwissenschaft*, Vol. 20, No. 1 (1991).

Falkner, G. "How Intergovernmental are Intergovernmental Conferences? An Example from the Maastricht Treaty Reform", *Journal of European Public Policy*, Vol. 9, No. 1 (February 2002).

Falkner, G. "Kontinuität und/oder Wandel? Zahlen und Fakten zur EU-Sozialpolitik", Working Paper, Political Science Series. No. 100, Vienna, Institute for Advanced Studies, 2004 <http://www.ihs.ac.at/index.php3?id=450>.

Falkner, G. "The EU's Social Dimension", in M. Cini (ed.), *European Union Politics*, Oxford: Oxford University Press, 2003.

Falkner, G. "The Maastricht Social Protocol: Theory and Practice" Sussex European Institute Working Papers. No. 15. Sussex European Institute, 1995.

Falkner, G. *EU Social Policy in the 1990s: Towards a Corporatist Policy Community*, London, New York: Routledge, 1998.

Fligstein, N. *Markets, Politics and Globalization*, Uppsala: Uppsala University Press, 1997.

Forder, J. "The ECB and the Decline of European Democracy", in J. Ljungberg (ed.), *The Price of the Euro*, London: Palgrave, 2004.

Fouilleux, E. "The Common Agricultural Policy", in M. Cini (ed.), *European Union Politics*, Oxford: Oxford University Press, 2003.

Frazer, T. *Monopoly Competition and the Law: The Regulation of Business Activity in Britain, Europe and America*, London: Harvester Wheatsheaf, 1992.

Galbraith, J. K. *American Capitalism: The Concept of Countervailing Power*, London: Hamilton, 1957.

Gallagher, M. "Electoral Systems and Voting Behaviour in 1997", in M. Rhodes, P. Heywood and V. Wright (eds), *Developments in West European Politics*, London: Macmillan, 1997.

Garrett G. and D. Mitchell, "Globalization, Government Spending and Taxation in the OECD", *European Journal of Political Research*, Vol. 39, No. 2 (2001).

Garrett, G. "The Politics of Maastricht", *Economics and Politics*, Vol. 5, No. 2 (July 1993).

George S. and I. Bache, *Politics in the European Union*, Oxford: Oxford University Press, 2001.

Gillingham, J. *European Integration 1950–2003*, Cambridge: Cambridge University Press, 2003.

Ginsburg, R. H. "The EU's Common and Foreign and Security Policy: An Outsider's Retrospective on the first Year", *ECSA Newsletter*, Pittsburgh: European Community Studies Association, 1994.

Golub, J. "State Power and Institutional Influence in European Integration", *Journal of Common Market Studies*, Vol. 34, No. 3 (September 1996).

Gomà, R. "The Social Dimension of the European Union: A New Type of Welfare System?", *Journal of European Public Policy*, Vol. 3, No. 2 (June 1996).

Grant, W. "The Limits of Common Agricultural Policy Reform and the Option of Denationalisation", *Journal of European Public Policy*, Vol. 2, No. 1 (1995).

Grant, W. *The Common Agricultural Policy*, London: Macmillan, 1997.

Gray, O. W. *Pressure Groups and their Influence on Agricultural Policy and its Reform in the European Community*, Ph.D. thesis, University of Bath, 1989.

Greenwood J. and M. Aspinwall (eds), *Collective Action in the European Union*, London: Routledge 1998.

Greenwood, J. *Interest Representation in the EU*, London: Palgrave, 2003.

Greenwood, J., J. R. Grote and K. Ronit (eds), *Organized Interests and the European Community*, London: Sage 1992.

Haas, E. *The Uniting of Europe: Political, Economic and Social Forces*, Stanford: Stanford University Press, 1958.

Hall, P.A. and R. C. R. Taylor, "Political Science and the Three New Institutionalisms", MPIFG Discussion Paper, 96/6 (June 1996).

Hardiman, N. "From Conflict to Coordination: Economic Governance and Political Innovation in Ireland", *West European Politics*, Vol. 25, No. 4 (October 2002)

Héretier, A. 1994, "Leaders and Laggards in European Policy-Making: Clean Air Policy Changes in Britain and Germany", in F. van Waarden and B.Unger (eds), *Convergence or Diversity? Internationalization and International Policy Response*, Aldershot: Avebury, 1994.

Heywood, P. "Desperately Seeking Influence: Spain and the War in Iraq", *European Political Science*, Vol. 3, No. 1 (Autumn 2003).

Heywood, P. "Power Diffusion or Concentration? In Search of the Spanish Policy Process", *West European Politics*, Vol. 21, No. 4 (October 1998).

Heywood, P. and V. Wright, "Executives, Bureaucracies and Decision Making", in M. Rhodes, P. Heywood and V. Wright (eds), *Developments in West European Politics*, London: Macmillan, 1997.

Hill, C. "The Capability–Expectation Gap, or Conceptualising Europe's International Role", *Journal of Common Market Studies*, Vol. 31, No. 3 (1993).

Hix, S. "Constitutional Agenda Setting through Discretion in Rule Interpretations: Why the European Parliament Won at Amsterdam", *British Journal of Political Science*, Vol. 32, No. 2 (April 2002).

Hix, S. "Legislative Behaviour and Party Competition in the European Parliament: An Application of Nominate to the EU", *Journal of Common Market Studies*, Vol. 39, No. 4 (November 2001).

Hix, S. *The Political System of the European Union*, 1st edn, London: Macmillan, 1999.

Hix, S. *The Political System of the European Union*, 2nd edn, London: Palgrave, 2005.

Hobolt, S. B. and R. Klemmensen, "Follow the leader? Divergent Positions on Iraq in Denmark and Ireland", *European Political Science*, Vol. 3, No. 1 (Fall 2003).

Hoffman, S. *European Sisyphus: Essays on Europe, 1964–1994*, Boulder: Westview Press, 1995

Hoffmann, S. "Obstinate or Obsolete? The Fate of the Nation State and the Case of Western Europe" *Daedalus*, Vol. 95, No. 3 (Summer 1966).

Hoffmann, S. "Towards a Common European Foreign and Security Policy", *Journal of Common Market Studies*, Vol. 38, No. 2 (June 2000).

Hollis, R. "Europe and the Middle East", in L. Fawcett (ed.), *International Relations of the Middle East*, Oxford: Oxford University Press, 2005.

Honderich, T. *Conservativism: Burke, Nozick, Bush and Blair*, London: Pluto, 2005.

Horeth, M. "Neither Breathtaking nor Path-Breaking: The Europe Commission's White Paper on Governance", *Journal of International Relations and Development*, Vol. 5, No. 1 (March 2002).

(http://europa.eu.int/eur-lex/en/com/pdf/2002/com2002_0225en01.pdf)

Hyland, J. L, *Democratic Theory: The Philosophical Foundations*, Manchester: Manchester University Press, 1995.

Ismael, T. Y. and J. S. Ismael, *The Iraq Predicament: People in the Quagmire of Politics*, London: Pluto, 2004.

Ismael, T. Y. and W. Haddad, *Iraq: The Human Cost of History*, London: Pluto Press, 2003.

Jileva, E. "Visa and Free Movement of Labour: The Uneven Imposition of the EU Acquis on Accession States", *Journal of Ethnic and Migration Studies*, Vol. 28., No. 4 (2002).

Joerges, C. and J. Neyer, "Vom intergouvernementalen Verhandeln zur deliberativen Politik. Gründe und Chance für eine Konstitutionalisierung der europäischen Komitologie", *Politische Vierteljahresschrift*, Vol. 29, pp. 207-233 (1998).

Joppke, C. "European Immigration Policies at the Crossroads", in P. Heywood, E. Jones and M. Rhodes (eds), *Developments in West European Politics*, London: Palgrave 2002.

Kay, A. "Path dependency and the CAP", *Journal of European Public Policy*, Vol. 10, No. 3 (June 2003).

Kay, A. "Towards a Theory of the Reform of the Common Agricultural Policy", *European Integration Online Papers*, Vol. 4, No. 9 (2000).

Kay, A. *The Reform of Common Agricultural Policy: The Case of the MacSharry Reforms*, Wallingford: CAB International, 1998.

Keohane R. and S. Hoffman (eds), *The New European Community: Decisionmaking and Institutional Change*, Boulder: Westview Press, 1991.

Kritzinger, S. "Public Opinion in the Iraq Crisis: Explaining Developments in the UK, France, Italy and Germany", *European Political Science*, Vol. 3, No. 1 (Autumn 2003).

Lamy, P. "L'administration exterieure de la Comission europeenne et les defies de la mondialisation", *Revue francaise d'administration publique*, No. 95 (July–Sept 2000).

Lange, P. "Maastricht and the Social Protocol: Why Did They Do It?", *Politics and Society*, Vol. 21, No. 1 (March 1993).

Lange, P. "The Politics of the Social Dimension", in A. Sbragia (ed.), *EuroPolitics: Institutions and Policymaking in the "New" European Community*, Washington D. C.: Brookings Institution, 1992.

Laswell, H. *Politics: Who Gets What When and How*, New York: Peter Smith, 1990 (1936).

Leibfried S. and P. Pierson, "Social Policy: Left to the Judges and the Markets?", in H. Wallace and W. Wallace (eds), *Policy Making in the European Union*, Oxford: Oxford University Press, 2000.

Leibfried, S. and P. Pierson, *Standort Europa: Sozialpolitik zwischen Nationalstaat und Europäischer Integration*, Frankfurt am. Main: Suhrkamp, 1998.

Lijphart, A. *Democracies*, New Haven : Yale University, 1984.

Lindberg, L. N. and S. A. Scheingold, *Europe's Would-Be Polity: Patterns of Change in the European Community*, Englewood Cliffs, N.J.: Prentice-Hall, Inc., 1970.

Lindblom, C. *Politics and Markets*, New York: Basic Books, 1977

Ljungberg, J. (ed.), *The Price of the Euro*, London: Palgrave, 2004.

Lowi, T. J. and B. Ginsberg, *American Government: Freedom and Power*, New York: Norton & Company, 1991

Luedtke, A. "European Integration, Public Opinion and Immigration Policy", *European Union Politics*, Vol. 6, No. 1 (2005).

Macchi, A. "Il semester di presidenza belga dell'Unione Europa", *Civilta Cattolica*, No. 3639 (2 February, 2002)

MacMullen, A. "Political Responsibility for the Administration of Europe: The Commission's Resignation March 1999", *Parliamentary Affairs*, Vol. 52, No. 4 (October 1999).

Mandel, M. *How America Gets Away With Murder: Illegal Wars, Collateral Damage and Crimes Against Humanity*, London: Pluto: 2004.

Manners, I. "Normative Power Europe: A Contradiction in Terms", http://www.ukc.ac.uk/politics/englishschool/manners00.doc, 2001.

March J. and J. Olsen, *Rediscovering Institutions*, New York: Free Press, 1989.

March, J. G. and J. P. Olsen, *Rediscovering Institutions: The Organisational Basis of Politics*, New York: Free Press, 1996.

Mazey S. and J. Richardson (eds), *Lobbying in the European Community*, Oxford: Oxford University Press, 1993.

McGowan, F. "Competition Policy", in H. Wallace and W. Wallace, *Policy-Making in the EU*, 4th edn, Oxford: Oxford University Press, 2000.

Metcalf, L. "Reforming the (European) Commission: Will Organizational Efficiency Produce Effective Governance?", *Journal of Common Market Studies*, Vol. 38, No. 5 (Dec 2000).

Michalowitz, I. *EU Lobbying: Principles, Agents and Targets*, LIT: Verlan Munster, 2004.

Michels, R. *Political Parties: A Sociological Study of the Oligarchical Tendencies of Modern Democracy*, New Brunswick: Transaction Publishers, 1998.

Miliband, R. *The State in Capitalist Society*, London: Weidenfeld and Nicolson, 1969.

Moravcsik, A. "Negotiating the Single European Act: National Interests and Conventional Statecraft in the European Community", *International Organization*, Vol. 45, No.1 (Winter 1991)

Moravcsik, A. "Negotiating the Single European Act", in R. Keohane and S. Hoffman (eds), *The New European Community: Decisionmaking and Institutional Change*, Boulder: Westview Press, 1991.

Moravcsik, A. "Preferences and Power in the European Community: A Liberal Intergovernmentalist Approach", *Journal of Common Market Studies*, Vol. 31, No. 4 (December 1993).

Moravcsik, A. *The Choice for Europe: Social Purpose and State Power from Messina to Maastricht*, London: UCL Press, 1998.

Mosca, G. *The Ruling Class*, New York: Greenwood Press, 1980.

Moyer, W. and T. Josling, *Agriculture Policy Reform: Politics and Process in the EU and US in the 1990s*, Aldershot: Ashgate, 2003.

Nugent N. and S. Saurugger, "Organizational Structuring: The Case of the European Commission and its External Policy Responsibilities", *Journal of European Public Policy*, Vol. 9, No. 3 (June 2002).

Ortega, A. "A mitad de la presidencia Espanola", *Política Exterior*, No. 87 (May-June 2002).

Padoa-Schioppa, T. "The Genesis of the EMU: A Retrospective View", European University Institute-RSCAS Working Papers, No. 96/40, 1996.

Pedlar R. H. and M. P. C. M. Van Schendelen (eds), *Lobbying the European Union: Companies, Trade Associations and Interest Groups*, Aldershot: Dartmouth, 1994.

Pennings, P. "The Dimensionality of EU Policy Space: The European Elections of 1999", *European Union Politics*, Vol. 3, No. 1 (March 2002).

Peterson J. and E. Bomberg, *Decision-Making in the European Union*, London: Macmillan, 1999.

Peterson J. and M. Shackleton, *The Institutions of the European Union*, Oxford: Oxford University Press, 2002.

Peterson, J., "Decision-Making in the EU: Towards a Framework for Analysis", *Journal of European Public Policy*, Vol. 2, No. 1 (1995).

Poulantzas, N. "The Capitalist State: A Reply to Miliband and Laclau." *New Left Review*, Vol. 95 (January 1976).

Prosser, T. and M. Moran, "Conclusions: From national Uniqueness to Supranational Constitution", in M. Moran and T. Prosser (ed.), *Privatisation and Regulatory Change in Europe*, Buckingham: Open University Press, 1994.

Puchala, D. "Institutionalism, Intergovernmentalism and European Integration", *Journal of Common Market Studies*, Vol. 37, No. 2 (June 1999).

Rhodes, M., P. Heywood and V. Wright (eds), *Developments in West European Politics*, New York: St. Martin's Press, 1997.

Richardson, J. (ed.), *European Union Power and Policy-Making*, London: Routledge, 2001.

Rieger, E. "Agriculture Policy Constrained Reforms", in W. Wallace, H. Wallace and M. Pollack (eds), *Policy-Making in the European Union*, 5th edn, Oxford: Oxford University Press, 2005.

Rieger, E. "The Common Agricultural Policy: Politics Against Markets", in H. Wallace and W. Wallace (eds), *Policy-Making in the European Union*, 4th edn, 2000.

Risse-Kappen, T. (ed.), *Bringing Transnational Relations Back In. Non-State Actors, Domestic Structures and International Institutions*, Cambridge: Cambridge University Press, 1995.

Rose, R., "Policy Networks in Globalisation: From Local to Cosmopolitan Networking", *NIRA Review*, Vol. 7, No. 1 (Winter 2000).

Ross, G. "Das 'Soziale Europa' des Jacques Delors: Verschachtelung als politische Strategie", in S. Leibfried and P. Pierson, *Standort Europa: Sozialpolitik zwischen Nationalstaat und Europäischer Integration*, Frankfurt on Main: Suhrkamp, 1998.

Ross, G. *Jacques Delors and European Integration*, Oxford: Oxford University Press, 1995

Royo, S. "'A New Century of Corporatism?' Corporatism in Spain and Portugal", *West European Politics*, Vol. 25, No. 3 (July 2002).

Ruggie, J. G. *Multilateralism Matters: The Theory and Praxis of an Institutional Form*, New York: Columbia University Press, 1993.

Sandholtz W. and J. Zysman, "1992: Recasting the European Bargain", *World Politics*, Vol. 42, No. 1 (October 1989).

Sandholtz, W. and A. Stone Sweet (eds), *European Integration and Supranational Governance*, Oxford: Oxford University Press, 1998.

Scharpf, F. W. "Introduction: The Problem-Solving Capacity of Multi-Level Governance", *Journal of European Public Policy*, Vol. 4, No. 4 (December 1997).

Scharpf, F. W. *Crisis and Choice in European Social Democracy*, Ithaca, NY: Cornell University Press, 1991.

Schlumberger, O. "The Arab Middle East and the Question of Democratization: Some Critical Remarks", *Democratization*, Vol. 7, No. 4, (2000).

Schmidt, V. "Loosening the Ties that Bind: The Impact of European Integration on French Government and its Relationship to Business", *Journal of Common Market Studies*, Vol. 34, No. 2 (June 1996).

Schmitt von Sydow, H. "The basic strategies of the Commission's White Paper", in R. Bieber *et al* (eds), *1992: One European Market*, Baden-Baden: Nomos, 1988.

Schmitter P. and G.Lembruch, *Trends Towards Corporatist Intermediation*, London: Sage 1979.

Schmitter, P. "Still the Century of Corporatism", *Review of Politics*, Vol. 36 No. 1 (January 1974).

Schmitter, P. 1981. "Interest Intermediation and Regime Governability in Contemporary Western Europe and North America", in S. Berger (ed.), *Organizing Interests in Western Europe: Pluralism, Corporatism and the Transformation of Politics*, Cambridge: Cambridge University Press, 1981.

Schneider G. and L. E. Cederman, "The Change of Tide in Political Cooperation", *International Organisation*, Vol. 48, No. 4 (Autumn 1994).

Schulz, O. *Maastricht und die Grundlagen einer Europäischen Sozialpolitik*, Köln: Heymans, 1996.

Schumpeter, J. *Capitalism, Socialism and Democracy*, New York: Harper and Brothers, 1950.

Shea, E. *European Merger Control Policy: Private Interests, Policy Communities and Entrepreneurship*, Ph.D. Thesis, Trinity College Dublin, 2005.

Shea E. and R. S. Chari, *Policy Formulation, Implementation and Feedback in EU Merger Control*, forthcoming working paper for the Institute for International Integration Studies, Trinity College Dublin.

Siebert W. S. and J. T. Addison, "Internal Labour Markets: Causes and Consequences", *Oxford Review of Economic Policy*, Vol. 7, No. 1 (1991).

Smith, H. *European Union Foreign Policy: What It Is and What It Does*, London: Pluto, 2003.

Smith, M. "The framing of European Foreign and Security Policy: Towards a Post-Modern policy framework?", *Journal of European Public Policy*, Vol. 10, No. 4 (August 2003).

Smith, M. J. *Pressure, Power and Society*, Chicago: University of Chicago Press, 1993.

Smith, M. P. "Autonomy by the Rules: The European Commission and the Development of State Aid Policy", *Journal of Common Market Studies*, Vol. 36, No. 1 (March 1998).

Steinmo, S. *Structuring Politics: Historical Institutionalism in Comparative Analysis*, New York: Cambridge University Press, 1992.

Stevens, A. "La Chute de la Commission Santer" *Revue francaise d'administration publique*, No. 95 (July-Sept 2000).

Stone Sweet, A. and W. Sandholtz, *European Integration and Supranational Governance*, Oxford: Oxford University Press, 1998.

Stone Sweet, A., W. Sandholtz and N. Fligstein. *The Institutionalization of Europe*. Oxford: Oxford University Press, 2001.

Stone Sweet, A. "Constitutional Courts and Parliamentary Democracy", *West European Politics*, Vol. 25, No.1 (2002).

Streek, W. "Neo-Voluntarism: A New European Social Policy Regime?", *European Law Journal*, Vol. 1, No. 1 (1995).

Swann, D. (ed.), *The Single European Market and Beyond: A Study of the Wider Implications of the SEA*, London: Routledge, 1992.

Szász, A. *The Road to European Monetary Union*, London: Macmillan, 1999.

Taylor G. "Hailing With an Invisible Hand: A 'Cosy' Political Dispute Amid the Rise of Neo-Liberal Politics in Modern Ireland", *Government and Opposition*. Vol. 37 No. 4 (Autumn 2002).

Taylor, G. "Labour Market Rigidities, Institutional Impediments and Managerial Constraints: Some Reflections on the Recent Experience of Macro-Political Bargaining in Ireland", *The Economic and Social Review*, Vol. 27, No. 3 (April 1996).

Teague, P. and Grahl, J. *Industrial Relations and European Integration*, London: Lawrence & Wishart, 1992.

Teague, P. and J. Grahl, "The European Community Social Charter and Labour Market Regulation", *Journal of Public Policy*, Vol. 11, No. 2 (Fall 1991).

Terry, J. J. *US Foreign Policy in the Middle East: The Role of Lobbies and Special Interest Groups*, London: Pluto, 2005.

Tihonen, S. "Continuita e cambiamento nell'amministrazione della commissione euopea", *Amministrare*, Vol. 31, No. 2 (August 2001).

Tsebelis G. and G. Garrett, "Legislative Politics in the European Union", *European Union Politics*, Vol. 1, No. 1 (February 2000).

Van Apeldoorn, B. *Transnational Capitalism and the Struggle over European Integration*, London: Routledge, 2002

Venit, J. S. "The Evaluation of Concentrations Under Regulation 4064/89: the Nature of the Beast", presented at the Fordham Corporate Law Institute: International Mergers and Joint Ventures, New York, 1990.

Verdun, A. "Why EMU Happened?", in P.M Crowley (ed.), *Before and Beyond EMU*, London: Routledge, 2002.

Verdun, A. (ed.), *The Euro: European Integration Theory and Economic and Monetary Union*, Oxford: Rowman and Littlefield, 2000.

Verdun, A. "The Role of the Delors Committee in the Creation of EMU: An Epistemic Community?" European University Institute RSC Working Paper, No. 98/44, 1998.

Verdun, A., *Gemeinsames Arbeitspapier zur Wirtschafts-und Wahrungsunion der Europaischen Gemeinsschaft, BDI-CNPF*, Cologne and Paris, Oct 2, 1990.

Viscusi, W. K., J. M. Vernon and J. E. Harrington, Jr. *Economics of Regulation and Antitrust*, Cambridge: MIT Press, 1995.

Vos, E. "Les Agences et la reforme de l'administration europeenne", *Revue francaise d'administration publique*, No. 95 (July-Sept. 2000)

Wallace H. and A.R. Young (eds), *Participation and Policy-Making in the EU*, Oxford: Clarendon, 1997.

Wallace H. and W. Wallace, *Policy Making in the EU*, 4th edn, Oxford: Oxford University Press, 2000.

Wallace, H. "The British Presidency of the European Community's Council of Ministers", *International Affairs*, Vol. 62 (1986).

Wallace, H., W. Wallace and M. A. Pollack, *Policy-Making in the EU*, 5th edn, Oxford: Oxford University Press, 2005

Watson R. and M. Shackleton, "Organized Interests and Lobbying in the EU", in E. Bomberg and A. Stubb, *The EU: How Does it work?* Oxford: Oxford University Press, 2003.

Webster, R. 1998, "Environmental Collective Action", in J. Greenwood and M. Aspinwall (eds), *Collective Action in the European Union*, London: Routledge, 1998..

Wessels, W. "The Growth and Differentiation of Multi-Level Networks", in H. Wallace and A.R. Young (eds), *Participation and Policy-Making in the EU*, Oxford: Clarendon, 1997.

Wiessala, G. "European Union in a Changing World: *Trompe l'Oeil* or Revolution? Reform of the European Commission on the Eve of 2000", *World Affairs*, Vol. 3, No. 4 (October-December 1999).

Wörgötter, C. "Das Konventsmodell: Auflösung des Zielkonfliktes zwischen demokratischer Legitimität und Effizienz?", *Österreichische Zeitschrift für Politikwissenschaft*, Vol. 4, (December 2005).

Wörgötter, C. *EU-Chartas sozialer Grundrechte*, Ph.D. Thesis, University of Vienna (2005)

Wright Mills, C. *The Power Elite*, Oxford: Oxford University Press, 1956.

Index